Welsh Environments in

Writing Wale

CW00457814

CREW

CREW series of Critical and Scholarly Studies
General Editor: Professor M. Wynn Thomas (CREW, Swansea University)

This *CREW* series is dedicated to Emyr Humphreys, a major figure in the literary culture of modern Wales, a founding patron of the *Centre for Research into the English Literature and Language of Wales*, and, along with Gillian Clarke and Seamus Heaney, one of *CREW*'s Honorary Associates. Grateful thanks are extended to Richard Dynevor for making this series possible.

Other titles in the series
Stephen Knight, *A Hundred Years of Fiction* (978-0-7083-1846-1)
Barbara Prys-Williams, *Twentieth-century Autobiography* (978-0-7083-1891-1)
Kirsti Bohata, *Postcolonialism Revisited* (978-0-7083-1892-8)
Linden Peach, *Contemporary Irish and Welsh Women's Fiction* (978-0-7083-1998-7)
Chris Wiggington, *Modernism from the Margins* (978-0-7083-1927-7)
Sarah Prescott, *Eighteenth-century Writing from Wales* (978-0-7083-2053-2)

Welsh Environments in Contemporary Poetry

Writing Wales in English

MATTHEW JARVIS

UNIVERSITY OF WALES PRESS
CARDIFF
2008

British Library Cataloguing-in-Publication Data
A catalogue record for this book is available from the British Library.

ISBN   978-0-7083-2152-2

THE *A*SSOCIATION FOR
*W*ELSH *W*RITING IN *E*NGLISH
*C*YMDEITHAS *L*ÊN *S*AESNEG *C*YMRU

Recommended text

The publishers wish to acknowledge the financial support of the Higher Education Funding Council for Wales in the publication of this book.

Printed in Wales by Dinefwr Press, Llandybïe

*To Kate, Danny, and Ethan
and in memory of Anthony Dyson*

CONTENTS

General Editor's Preface

The aim of this series is to produce a body of scholarly and critical work that reflects the richness and variety of the English-language literature of modern Wales. Drawing upon the expertise both of established specialists and of younger scholars, it will seek to take advantage of the concepts, models and discourses current in the best contemporary studies to promote a better understanding of the literature's significance, viewed not only as an expression of Welsh culture but also as an instance of modern literatures in English worldwide. In addition, it will seek to make available the scholarly materials (such as bibliographies) necessary for this kind of advanced, informed study.

M. Wynn Thomas
Director, *CREW* (*Centre for Research into the English Language and Literature of Wales*)
Swansea University

ACKNOWLEDGEMENTS

Whatever the solitary name on its front cover may suggest, a book with a single author is never a solo project. My thanks are due to a wide variety of people who have supported the work that has produced this volume. Most specifically, I am deeply grateful for the friendship and editorial insight of Wynn Thomas, who has scrutinized my manuscript at every stage with unwavering precision and kindness. Without his enthusiasm for this project, it simply would not have happened. Sarah Lewis at the University of Wales Press has also been exemplary in her assistance, having shepherded the book on its way from proposal to submission. Beyond the book itself, I also owe significant thanks to Francesca Rhydderch, Robert Minhinnick and Tony Brown, all of whom, as editors of (respectively) *New Welsh Review*, *Poetry Wales* and *Welsh Writing in English*, have for some years encouraged and published my writing on the anglophone poetry of Wales. Alongside them, I am constantly grateful for the kind support I have received from long-suffering friends – especially Peter Barry, Jasmine Donahaye, Alice Entwistle, Martin Padget, Francesca Rhydderch, Luke Thurston and Damian Walford Davies. Indeed, to Damian I owe particular thanks for discussing with me my very first ideas about the book and for his suggestion to pitch it to UWP's CREW series. In terms of beginnings, I must also note a special debt to Grahame Davies for an e-mail conversation about earth, air, water and fire – all in a Welsh context – which helped to develop my thoughts in particularly useful ways just before I started writing the bulk of the volume. I am, furthermore, significantly indebted to the University of Wales, Lampeter, whose decision to appoint me, in September 2007, to undertake full-time research in the

Department of English as the Anthony Dyson Fellow in Poetry has so greatly assisted this book's completion. Finally, of course, love and gratitude are due in great measure to my parents, who not only introduced me to Wales when I was young – on very fondly remembered family holidays – but who have also furnished me with otherwise-forgotten details about those childhood visits here. To all these people, then – and to those many others with whom I have talked about the ideas covered here and about literature in Wales in general – *Welsh Environments in Contemporary Poetry* is offered back as a reflection of their various and ongoing generosity. Whatever problems the volume may have are, of course, entirely my own responsibility.

   For granting permission to use quotations in this book, I am grateful to the following: Ruth Bidgood and Seren for the poetry of Ruth Bidgood; Carcanet Press for the poetry of Gillian Clarke; Ian Davidson for the poetry of Ian Davidson; Christine Evans and Seren for the poetry of Christine Evans; Bryn Griffiths for the poetry of Bryn Griffiths; Mike Jenkins, Gwasg Carreg Gwalch, Planet and Seren for the poetry of Mike Jenkins; Robert Minhinnick, Carcanet Press and Seren for the poetry of Robert Minhinnick; the estate of R. S. Thomas for the poetry of R. S. Thomas (© Kunjana Thomas 2001) – 'A Peasant', 'Ire' and 'Country Church (Manafon)' from R. S. Thomas, *The Stones of the Field* (Carmarthen: Druid Press, 1946); 'The Minister' from R. S. Thomas, *Song at the Year's Turning: Poems 1942–1954* (London: Rupert Hart-Davis, 1955); 'Afforestation' from R. S. Thomas, *The Bread of Truth* (London: Rupert Hart-Davis, 1963); 'The Moor' and 'The Face' from R. S. Thomas, *Pietà* (London: Rupert Hart-Davis, 1966); 'Reservoirs' and 'Tenancies' from R. S. Thomas, *Not That He Brought Flowers* (London: Rupert Hart-Davis, 1968); Jean Henderson for the poetry of John Tripp; the University of Minnesota Press for the work of Yi-Fu Tuan; and Meic Stephens for the poetry of Harri Webb. For permission to cite or quote from personal correspondence, I am grateful to Ruth Bidgood, Gillian Clarke, Ian Davidson, Mike Jenkins and Robert Minhinnick. Earlier versions of Chapters 8 and 9 of this book appeared (respectively) in volumes 11 and 10 of *Welsh Writing in English: A Yearbook of Critical Essays*; I am grateful to the editor, Tony Brown, for his permission to reprint here. Chapters 4 and 5 contain some elements of my essay 'Repositioning Wales: poetry after the Second Flowering', in Daniel Williams (ed.), *Slanderous Tongues: Essays on Welsh Poetry in English 1975–2005* (Bridgend, Seren, forthcoming); I am grateful to Seren for permission to reuse relevant material here.

It was the birth of my son Danny in July 2004 that let me escape formal employment the following summer to become, for a couple of years, a full-time father and part-time writer. I am quite unable to repay him for the chance he gave me to rediscover what really mattered to me, both personally and as a literary critic. And to my wife, Kate, who has kept faith with my slow, disorderly, flawed journey, there are never sufficient words of thanks for all her kindness.

Llanbadarn Fawr
January 2008

I

Starting with Trees

1

Conifers

As a boy, I used to go with my family to north-west Wales for our yearly holidays. We would make our slow way from the English midlands in a white Morris Marina that was well past its sell-by date. Seeing the Rhinogs rise up sternly to the west of the A470 would signal our arrival, and it is a view that still fills me with a surge of excitement when I see it. Those Welsh holidays were highlights of my early years. They were an escape to a place I felt was entirely different from the one where I passed my day-to-day life. I couldn't quite believe it when, after a fatefully inclement July in 1988, my parents said that they were fed up with the Welsh weather and that we would be visiting somewhere else from then on. We had been holidaying in Wales since June 1979, when I was not quite 8 years old, so when those yearly pilgrimages stopped it felt like the final passing of childhood. But while our Welsh escapes lasted, I was always particularly drawn to the Coed y Brenin forest, just a few miles to the north of Dolgellau. Whenever I could, I would drag my sometimes-reluctant family down as many of its way-marked woodland paths as possible, making a particular point of seeking out the steep ones if such a route could be engineered. What was the attraction? For one thing, I think I assumed that the forest around me was thoroughly ancient. Isn't that what forests *were*? Especially in Wales, which somehow seemed to my boyhood self so much *older* than England. I think I would have been startled to learn that Coed y Brenin was not even sixty years old when I started visiting it.[1] But perhaps more important was the fact that this coniferous place felt so entirely un-English – certainly by comparison with the 1980s suburban landscape that I knew in Derby. In fact, along with the view of that part of the Rhinogs where the Roman Steps make their way between Moel Ysgyfarnogod and Rhinog Fawr, it is fair enough to say that the conifers of Coed y Brenin were pretty much Wales for me when I was 9 or 10 years old.[2]

So I imagine I would have been thoroughly perplexed if anyone at the time had shown me R. S. Thomas's poem 'Afforestation' which, published around fifteen years before my Welsh holidays began,[3] figures the conifers of Wales in a way so different from that of my own boyhood perceptions. At the very start of the poem, for example, the trees are aggressive, 'Colonising the old / Haunts of men'. What I had thought of as embodying Wales, in other words, were for Thomas nothing less than a colonizing attack on its communities – a takeover by an alien force. In the words of Kirsti Bohata, the trees of 'Afforestation' are explicitly 'colonial instrument[s] designed to usurp traditional Welsh life'.[4] Indeed, their oppressive presence is emphasized by the way in which, at night, the poem sees them as menacing, threatening, 'Standing in black crowds / Under the stars', whilst by day they block out the sun (they are 'in the sun's way'). Moreover, unlike the grass or the sheep that feed upon the grass, the trees are without value:

> The grass feeds the sheep;
> The sheep give the wool
> For warm clothing, but these – ?

The final questioning blank here suggests Thomas's absolute inability to see anything good coming from the conifers. Instead, the poem goes on to connect them with the 'Thin houses for dupes' and 'Pages of pale trash' which characterize the 'cheap times / Against which they grow'. The new conifers visited upon Thomas's Wales are thus seen as growing up against the background of an impoverished era, which their existence both defines and helps to produce.[5] This is, as the poem puts it, a 'world that has gone sour / With spruce'. But I think it is the poem's finish that would have most perplexed my younger self, happily roaming those paths amongst Coed y Brenin's Sitka spruce. Thomas's solution to the coniferous invasion is simple: 'Cut them down', says the poem. Why? Because they are unable to:

> take the weight
> Of any of the strong bodies
> For which the wind sighs.

For Thomas, this newly forested landscape is weak in a way that manifestly constitutes a moral judgement, as the conifers' flimsiness is set in emphatic negative against the 'strong bodies' for which the speaker hears the wind sighing. This is not the innocent landscape of a boy's holiday wanderings. Rather, Thomas's Welsh environment is a crucially cultural and political event to which the poem is a deeply felt and deeply critical response.[6]

2

A Digression on Writing and Environment

Such poetic renditions of the Welsh environment are what concern me in this book. Specifically, I am interested in how a selection of recent English-language poets writing from Wales – Gillian Clarke, Ruth Bidgood, Robert Minhinnick, Mike Jenkins, Christine Evans and Ian Davidson – each constructs the idea of Welsh space and place, and to what purpose. Their immediate forebears – the poets of the 1960s revival of Welsh poetry in English and R. S. Thomas as senior figure at the start of the 1970s – also concern me in Part I. In effect, I am trying to answer this question: what are the landscapes that these poets have made for Wales? Or alternatively: what Wales do the hills, valleys, towns, farms, industry, pollution or weather of these poets create? Or again: on what terms and to what apparent ends do these poets offer up their Welsh environments?

Discussion of literature in terms of its engagement with the environment has become a significant trend in recent years, particularly in the USA, where ecocriticism – 'the omnibus term by which the new polyform literature and environment studies movement has come to be labeled'[1] – is a notable presence on the critical scene.[2] Whether my work in this volume constitutes ecocriticism is, however, open to question. As Greg Garrard explains, 'Ecocritics generally tie their cultural analyses explicitly to a "green" moral and political agenda.'[3] By contrast, my agenda here is far more to do with Welsh cultural identity than it is to do with 'green' politics: the ultimate concern of this book is the rhetorical construction of Welsh environments – not literature and environmental crisis, nor literary manifestations of 'green' politics, nor again literature analysed in the light of ecological science. What I am writing here is, in short, far less green-focused than it is Welsh-focused. Which is not to say that questions to do with environmental problems and particular sorts of green consciousness do not play a part in the analysis which follows; for example, my discussion of Mike Jenkins is, in part, concerned with the environmental degradation caused by pollution, whilst my analysis of Robert Minhinnick engages with issues to do with human/nature dualism. However, such considerations are always ultimately in the service of my primary aim: to provide an analysis of the idea of Welsh space and place, as that idea is manifest in the visions of recent English-language poetry from Wales. As such, it might be best to describe what I am trying to achieve in this study as a work of literary geography.

My approach is thus distinct from that taken by Jonathan Bate – Britain's highest-profile proponent of ecocritical literary analysis and author of two important volumes, *Romantic Ecology: Wordsworth and the Environmental Tradition* (1991) and *The Song of the Earth* (2000). The preface to *The Song of the Earth* explains the latter book's purpose:

> This is a book about why poetry continues to matter as we enter a new millennium that will be ruled by technology. It is a book about modern Western man's alienation from nature. It is about the capacity of the writer to restore us to the earth which is our home.[4]

Bate's idea, in short, is to offer up literature – and poetry in particular – as a means to environmental salvation, returning what the book presents as a humanity alienated from the earth to an awareness of the non-human world, a respect for 'A planet that is fragile, a planet of which we are a part but which we do not possess' (p. 282).[5] Thus, in the book's concluding analysis, Bate asks 'What are poets for in our brave new millennium?' and offers the following answer to his own question:

> Could it be to remind the next few generations that it is we who have the power to determine whether the earth will sing or be silent? As earth's own poetry, symbolized for Keats in the grasshopper and the cricket, is drowned ever deeper – not merely by bulldozers in the forest, but more insidiously by the ubiquitous susurrus of cyberspace – so there will be an ever greater need to retain a place in culture, in the work of human imagining, for the song that names the earth. (p. 282)

I have absolutely no argument with Bate's sense of a need for 'the next few generations' – clearly including our own – to become increasingly aware of our responsibility towards planetary environmental health. Indeed, it was just such a sense of ethical responsibility which spurred on my initial thoughts about the status of space, place, environment and landscape in poetry. But there are manifest problems with this passage – including the sense that poetry should be tied to a particular programme (even one as important as writing 'the song that names the earth'),[6] and the rhetorical attempt to align a linguistic art form with non-human sounds by calling the latter 'earth's own poetry' in an apparent effort to claim poetry as the primary cultural mode in which the earth can be remembered. However, such issues to one side, this passage also makes clear the distinction in approach between the current book and that of the ecocriticism in *The Song of the Earth*: if Bate is interested in poetry insofar as it provides a 'song that names the earth', I am here interested in poetry insofar as it names Wales – Wales, that is, in all of its environmental diversity.

Having said which, however, I must acknowledge that this book manifestly shares a number of preoccupations with ecocriticism, and draws various perspectives from its now considerable literature as well as from that of the more broadly defined green humanities. It would be critically mean-spirited and fundamentally disingenuous to deny such debts and affiliations,[7] and these connections will become apparent as the book progresses. More important to acknowledge in this initial discussion, however, is that such debts also underlie ways of understanding a number of key ideas used throughout this study – ideas such as *environment*, *nature* ('perhaps the most complex word in the [English] language', according to Raymond Williams),[8] *landscape*. But prior to all of these – to which I shall return in a moment – is Simon Schama's sense, put forward in his magisterial *Landscape and Memory*, that any human attempt to approach even the most natural of environments as in some way free from human culture is defeated before it even starts. Schama writes this:

> The founding fathers of modern environmentalism, Henry David Thoreau and John Muir, promised that 'in wildness is the preservation of the world.' The presumption was that the wilderness was out there, somewhere, in the western heart of America, awaiting discovery, and that it would be the antidote for the poisons of industrial society. But of course the healing wilderness was as much the product of culture's craving and culture's framing as any other imagined garden.[9]

To support this idea, Schama goes on to discuss 'the first and most famous American Eden: Yosemite', suggesting that however much it may have been developed and despoiled – he cites parking 'almost as big as the park' and 'bears rooting among the McDonald's cartons' – Yosemite remains, in the imagination, 'the way Albert Bierstadt painted it or Carleton Watkins and Ansel Adams photographed it: with no trace of human presence'. The cultural framings, in other words, have given us the wilderness (which is not to say, of course, that they have actually created the land itself):[10]

> The wilderness, after all, does not locate itself, does not name itself. It was an act of Congress in 1864 that established Yosemite Valley as a place of sacred significance for the nation, during the war which marked the moment of Fall in the American Garden. Nor could the wilderness venerate itself. It needed hallowing visitations from New England preachers like Thomas Starr King, photographers like Leander Weed, Eadwaerd Muybridge, and Carleton Watkins, painters in oil like Bierstadt and Thomas Moran, and painters in prose like John Muir to represent it as the holy park of the West; the site of a new birth; a redemption for the national agony; an American re-creation.[11]

To put it another way, the nature that is on view through the operation of human discourse is never natural – by which I mean that it is always cultural.[12] Indeed, the very idea of 'landscape' should suggest precisely this. As Schama explains, the word entered the English language 'as a Dutch import at the end of the sixteenth century', with '*landschap*, like its Germanic root, *Landschaft*, signif[ying] a unit of human occupa-tion'. In other words, the idea of landscape was inextricably tied up with what Schama calls 'human design and use' from its very beginning. Thus Schama observes that 'it is our shaping perception that makes the difference between raw matter and landscape'.[13] Patently, this applies to built environments too. Admittedly, roads, houses, tower blocks are all human cultural products in a way that the 'geology and vegetation' (p. 12) Schama discusses as 'raw matter' are not. But when such cultural products are spoken or written about (or painted, or photographed) they are culturally produced again, framed, re-created, manifest as landscape. Thus, just as the production of American wilderness was an act of culture (as Schama explains, the longing for a place in which to heal the 'national agony' of the Civil War), so here I understand poetic productions of Welsh landscape as acts of culture in precisely the same way – as the products of human desire, commitment, conflict, fear, memorial.

Of course, this is not to deny that such cultural makings of 'the palpable world' can have real-world (by which I mean extra-textual)

effects.[14] As Lawrence Buell suggests, 'acts of environmental imagina-
tion' can, for example, 'make [the physical world] feel more or less
precious or endangered or disposable', when 'a moderately attentive
reader read[s] about a cherished, abused, or endangered place'.[15] The
upshot is that, for Buell, literary imaginings of the environment may
thus 'affect one's caring for the physical world' – although (and this is
elided in Buell's writing at this point) there is an important gap between
a change in an individual's imaginative construction of the physical
world's fragility and an alteration in his or her behaviour towards that
world. Literary 'acts of environmental imagination' may affect the
former (the imaginative construction); they can have no direct impact
on the latter (the behaviour). Which is basically to say that a poem
cannot wrestle its reader to the ground to stop him or her driving a car
when walking would do just as well. And so much should be obvious.
But, as Buell's comments suggest, a poem's capacity to function as an
element within a reader's conceptual (re)ordering of the world cannot
be denied. Thus, within the context of my own study, I certainly do
acknowledge that, in reading about Wales as a 'cherished ... place',
particular constructions of its topographies may well impact on our
real-world (extra-textual) understanding of Wales as an idea. Whether
such imaginative changes work to alter our actual behaviour towards
Wales as its citizens is another matter entirely – and not a literary one.

Furthermore, by arguing that landscape is, as I have put it, an act of
culture, I do not wish to suggest that discursive constructions of the
physical world essentially have nothing to do with the 'raw matter' that
is out there. In other words, this is in no way to deny the capacity of
literature to be a linguistic response to the 'extra-discursive reality' of,
for example, a specific mountain or forest.[16] It is simply to acknowledge
that, as soon as the mountain or forest in question is written about, the
'geology and vegetation' themselves are not what is in the text.[17]
However, nor do I want to fall back on the idea that what *is* in the text
should be understood in terms of representation – that sense of reflec-
tion which will always and anyway fall short, in terms of simple
insufficiency of descriptive power, given the vast complexity of the
physical world itself.[18] Rather, as a discursive response to the physical
world, the text constitutes an active engagement with that world in the
sense that the linguistic act offers a *judgement* upon the world, a judge-
ment on how that world (or, at least, the part of it under consideration)
should be seen, understood or conceptually approached. Rather than
being reduced to a process of mimicry – which will always, of necessity,

be entirely partial – each act of writing the environment is, at its core, an argument about how the world should be seen: it is nothing less than an invitation to understand, to approach the world in a particular way (though whether or not a reader will accept that invitation is, as my previous paragraph acknowledges, always moot).

As such, when I read about a particular landscape in a work of literature, my recognition of it effectively requires my own construction of the place in question to mesh in some way with the linguistic judgement of it offered up by (my reading of) the text. If it does not, a significant problem is created – as is suggested by the critique of R. S. Thomas advanced by the poet Leslie Norris in a letter to *Poetry Wales*:

> Thomas's world is a restricted one, but consistent and recognisable. It has the considerable merit of being understood at once by people who do not know Wales at all, and it can be treated directly and with perfect simplicity. It is of course, an inner world, an invention; apart from the names of its inhabitants and a generally mountainous terrain, *it is not Wales.*[19]

Here, Norris's construction of Welsh space – apart from the most general recognition of names and 'mountainous terrain' – simply does not match Thomas's. The result is a refusal on Norris's part to acknowledge that Thomas is writing about Wales at all. In short, what Norris's argument puts at stake here is the very *legitimacy* of Thomas's literary vision of Welsh place: it has, he suggests, no truth before the world.[20] 'There is nothing wrong with that', Norris concludes, 'except that [Thomas's Wales] seems to be accepted as a faithful portrait of the country'. Or, to put it another way (and to return to a previous point), Norris is concerned about Thomas's act of environmental imagination – and it is, he suggests, almost entirely imaginary (i.e. made up) – because it has real-world consequences (the general acceptance of Thomas's idea of Wales). Or, to say it differently again, acts of *environmental* imagination are – always and inescapably and simultaneously – acts of *cultural* imagination with great potential power.

Two points remain in this digression on ideas before I can return to poetry. First, the difficulties suggested by that incidence of 'nature' and 'natural' in my earlier proposition that 'the nature that is on view through the operation of human discourse is never natural'. As I have already noted, Raymond Williams famously declared that 'Nature is perhaps the most complex word in the language', explaining that it brings with it immense amounts of ideological freight: it is a word, he explained, 'which carries, over a very long period, many of the major

variations of human thought – often, in any particular use, only implic-
itly'.[21] Defining what one means by 'nature' is manifestly important,
even if the environments I will be discussing are not all 'natural' by any
means – in other words, my concern is with buildings and streets, just as
much as it is with rivers, valleys or the experience of sunlight.[22] Clearly,
however, any attempt to offer some comprehensive definition of nature
lies far beyond the scope of this brief theoretical digression. As such, I
follow the threefold model of understanding put forward by Kate
Soper, who distinguishes between 'the "metaphysical", the "realist" and
the "lay" (or "surface") ideas of nature'.[23] The 'metaphysical' use, Soper
explains, is a typically philosophical distinction, using the word *nature*
to signify:

> the concept of the non-human, even if … the absoluteness of the humanity–
> nature demarcation has been disputed, and our ideas about what falls to
> the side of 'nature' have been continuously revised in the light of changing
> perceptions of what counts as 'human'.

This is, in short, nature as 'that which is opposed to the "human" or the
"cultural"'. The 'realist' use, by contrast, refers to 'the structures,
processes and causal powers that are constantly operative within the
physical world'. These processes, Soper goes on to explain, are 'laws [to
which] we are always subject, even as we harness them to human
purposes' (p. 156), laws which set 'certain limits on what we can do, or
even try to do' and which 'we must observe … on pain either of looking
very foolish (as did Canute) or else perishing in the effort to transcend
them' (p. 159).[24] Finally, the 'lay' or 'surface' mode uses the word *nature*
in the way in which it appears in 'much everyday, literary and theoretical
discourse', to signify 'wildlife, raw materials, the non-urban environ-
ment', the 'nature of immediate experience' (p. 156). This is, Soper
suggests, also the 'nature of … aesthetic appreciation' – in other words,
the nature which we see as a thing of beauty. It is, in short, what we mean
when we talk about 'getting out into nature', if we go for a walk in the
countryside. Thus, for example, when I proposed that the nature which
appears in human discourse is not natural, my first invocation of *nature*
conformed to Soper's 'lay' definition – referring, as it did, to non-urban
environment – whilst my second was an engagement with the 'metaphys-
ical' category (invoking the idea of the 'non-human'). As Jonathan Bate
usefully explains, in a similar moment of terminological groundwork
towards the start of *The Song of the Earth*: within the context of Soper's
typology, the metaphysical sense of *nature* refers to ideas such as '"the

question of man's place in nature" or "nature versus culture/society"'; the 'realist' sense is identifiable in discussion of 'biological and ecological processes'; whilst the 'lay' concept is being invoked when questions are raised about 'the appreciation of "landscapes", the preservation of "wilderness", the valuation of "green spaces"'.[25] However, having said this, Bate sensibly urges his readers to remember that 'it is impossible to hold the three senses fully apart'. Referring to a landscape painter's evocation of nature, for example, may well draw on a sense of those long-standing categories of aesthetic appreciation to which Simon Schama gestures when he talks about 'rolling hills safely grazed by fleecy flocks and cooled by zephyrs moist and sweet' as well as on the notion of the non-human.[26] I thus acknowledge the pertinence of Bate's caveat here, and would suggest that when I use the word 'nature' without further qualification in this study, I am typically referring to a blend between the idea of being amongst those things which we think of as typifying 'green space' – trees, fields, hills, plants, streams – and that which is conceived of as 'other' to the realm of the human. However, when I talk specifically about the non-human, I am more precisely suggesting Soper's concept of nature in its first, 'metaphysical' sense – as that which lies outside the realms of human culture or has not been constructed by it. (I am also invoking 'metaphysical' nature in any discussion of human/nature dualism.) By contrast, reference to 'natural forces' or 'natural processes' is meant to suggest Soper's second, 'realist' category. And, finally, discussions of the rural, the countryside, the non-urban, green spaces, or the forms which are typically associated with such areas – trees, fields, hills, plants, streams, as I put it a moment ago – are primarily engagements with nature in Soper's third ('lay' or 'surface') sense. Of Soper's three categories, it is undoubtedly the first and the third (and their combination) which dominate my discussions of the natural in this study.

All of which leaves the term of the book's title – environment. This is, after all, not a volume which is restricted merely to poetic dealings with non-urban places and their conventionally associated forms. So the necessity of dealing with the term *nature* should not overwhelm the larger aims of the volume: this is not, to put it bluntly, merely a study of 'nature poetry'. Rather, this book is to do with the environment in terms of both the '"natural" and "human-built" dimensions of the palpable world', as Lawrence Buell puts it (nature here, I think, being invoked in precisely that way which blurs ideas of green space with the notion of the non-human).[27] A factory is an environmental phenomenon, in this sense, just as much as mountain or sunlight or the weather.

Having drawn the notion of environment into this duality, however, Buell undercuts it straight away:

> Though I shall ... insist on the distinction [between 'natural' and 'human-built'], one must also blur it by recourse to the more comprehensive term [i.e. 'environment', without qualification]. Human transformations of physical nature have made the two realms increasingly indistinguishable. Perhaps only the last half-century has witnessed what Bill McKibben apocalyptically calls 'the end of nature': a degree of modification so profound that we shall never again encounter a pristine physical environment. But Karl Marx was not far wrong in claiming that by the mid-1800s second nature (nature as re-processed by human labor) had effectively dominated first nature worldwide.[28]

It is with this various sense of environment as 'natural' and environment as 'human-built' but also of environment which blurs this distinction that I shall work throughout this book. Indeed, the latter, blurred notion – the sense of non-natural nature, of a thoroughly cultural green space – was, of course, where I began, with the second nature of Coed y Brenin's conifers and with the cultural violence of those newly planted, colonizing spruce in R. S. Thomas's poem 'Afforestation'.

3

The 1960s Generation and
R. S. Thomas to 1968

The significance to R. S. Thomas's 'Afforestation' of Welsh land and
what is planted on it is merely one instance of an environmental mode
that runs powerfully through Welsh poetry in English in the period
since the 1960s. It is this strand of poetry which concerns me in this
book. The 1960s, of course, were a crucial turning point in Welsh poetic
history, because they saw the rebirth of anglophone poetry in Wales
after its collapse into 'ruins' – to use Tony Conran's term – in the 1950s.[1]
There were only a few 'survivors' from the first great flowering of the
so-called Anglo-Welsh verse of the 1930s and 1940s, and R. S. Thomas
was undoubtedly to prove the most significant of these.[2] Indeed, by the
early 1970s, as Conran goes on to explain, Thomas was the 'new centre
of gravity' for anglophone poetry in Wales:

> For with the death of Vernon Watkins in 1967 the last of Dylan [Thomas]'s
> peers had gone. There was no one to dispute the pre-eminence of the Revd
> R. S. Thomas as the fashioner of the new Anglo-Welsh sensibility, nation-
> alist, seeking a rapprochement with Welsh-speaking Wales, disdainful of
> the London Welsh and all they stood for.[3]

Given this position, Thomas's own substantial engagements with the
Welsh environment meant that his was the senior poetic interpretation
of Welsh space and place at the beginning of the 1970s when the first
of the poets considered in the following chapters of this volume began
to publish their initial collections. It is, then, to Thomas's work up until
that point that I shall return more fully in a moment, in order to finish
setting the stage for what follows after.[4]

But of course, however important he was as a senior figure, Thomas was not one of the new voices that restarted the scene in the 1960s after the general collapse of the previous decade. Indeed, in the winter of 1967–8, a key article by Meic Stephens – founder of *Poetry Wales* and one of the primary energizers of the 1960s resurgence[5] – drew a clear distinction between Thomas and the new generation. Stephens's suggestion, albeit offered with careful respect, was that Thomas's poetry of 'brooding on rural decay' was a potential dead end.[6] By contrast, the new poets (Stephens particularly identifies Raymond Garlick, Harri Webb and John Tripp) were writers of 'Welsh nationhood', primarily concerned with the future – specifically the political future of a liberated Wales – not with worrying over 'things as they are'.[7] All the same, this by no means meant that the 1960s poets themselves were divorced from such matters as Welsh topography and weather: instead, they demonstrated very clearly that environmental awareness which Stephens's phrase about Thomas 'brooding on rural decay' in part suggested, even if this element of their work did not represent the primary direction in which they were taking the recently resurgent scene. That the 1960s poetics of 'Welsh nationhood' were actually rather short-lived is something I have indicated elsewhere.[8] As Tony Conran has explained, English-language poetry in Wales had clearly moved away from future visions of the Welsh state and back to a poetry of 'things as they are' by the late 1970s.[9] Indeed, in figures such as Gillian Clarke and Ruth Bidgood – both considered in this volume – I would suggest that this process was manifestly under way at the very start of the 1970s. However, even while the spirit of the 1960s lasted, there was no sense in which its future visions curtailed poetic engagement with the physical environment of the Welsh past and present.

That the physical environment was an issue which forcefully demanded attention for this generation of poets is suggested by John Tripp in a poem published in his first collection *Diesel to Yesterday* (1966) and then in the important 1969 anthology *The Lilting House*.[10] 'Welcome to Wales' figures the physical state of Wales in various terms: it is a country with 'quite modern' roads; it is characterized by numerous 'places of worship' (which are empty) and 'crumbling pubs' (which, although the poem does not say it, I think we are meant to assume, by contrast with the 'places of worship', are not); its plentiful supply of 'bogus Tudor / expense-account restaurants' suggests that it knows how to trade on fakery and nostalgia; and perhaps most interesting of all, 'You will', says the poem to its tourist addressee, 'feel at home in the petrol fumes'. The physical environment of Wales is, in short, just as polluted as that of England – which, given the reference to Surbiton at the start of the poem, is where the addressee seems to come from. This is, then, the environment of a fairly archetypal Western nation in the twentieth century: road networked (even if only *'quite* [i.e. fairly] modern'; emphasis added), full of places of trade, containing physical references to formerly dominant social structures – and polluted by the internal combustion engine. Interestingly, however, the poem's speaker goes on to suggest that 'Our complaint is apathy, which would not / interest the visitor hungry for landscape'. Landscape is an issue here because the romantic urge of tourists for what Tripp's previous poem in the same anthology calls 'scenery' effectively causes them to ignore what Tripp identifies as a Welsh social malaise. In short, Welsh rural land-scape – and I assume that the reference here is to precisely those sorts of spectacular and mountainous landscapes which I visited as a boy – becomes a way to ignore Welsh people.

Tripp's previous poem in *The Lilting House*, 'The Diesel to Yesterday' – the title poem of his first collection – is one of his most famous. This is a piece that is thoroughly rooted in a sense of geography – specifically, that is, in the sense that the speaker would long to seal the country in, to close its borders. Drawing into Newport on the train, the poem considers 'the entry to my country' and imagines border guards 'keeping out the bacillus / in hammering rain and swirling fog':

> Often I wish it were so, this frontier sealed
>   at Chepstow, against frivolous incursion
> from the tainting eastern zones.

There is something of a disjunction between 'frivolous' and 'tainting' here. Are the visitors from England (the nearest of any possible eastern zone) whom the poet sees 'tumbling into Wales' merely annoying – perhaps fair-weather tourists, clown-like (thus the tumbling?), clogging up the streets; or do they represent something more sinister? In the middle of the poem it is undeniably the latter. Indeed, their actions provide an interesting comment on the polluted state of Welsh space which 'Welcome to Wales' suggested – the sense that its tourist addressee would 'feel at home in the petrol fumes'. In 'The Diesel to Yesterday', then, Tripp observes the tourists and declares:

> They bring only their banknotes
> and a petrol-stenched lust for scenery
> to shut in their kodaks ...

From this perspective, the petrol fumes of 'Welcome to Wales' are homely to visitors because they bring the fumes with them. Moreover, the interest in Welsh scenery is not, it seems, anything to do with an engagement with the country as such, or with its way of life. Rather, the 'lust for scenery' is merely trophy-gathering, with visitors scooping up dramatic images that will help with 'packing out the albums of Jersey / and the anthill beaches of the south'. Indeed, in this sense of Welsh images 'packing out' visitors' photo albums, the Welsh environment sounds like nothing more than photographic filler, merely there to make up space. Welsh environment, in short, is here seen as being doubly abused – polluted and trophy-hunted at the same time. Of course, as the poem concludes, Tripp's anger turns back on himself. 'I ... feel / ignoble in disdain', says the speaker, concluding that the 'bad smell at my nostril' is himself, 'reek[ing] of the museum', yearning for 'the lost day before dignity went, / when all our borders were sealed'. Even at the end, then, in the bleakness of self-criticism, the focus is still environmental: what Tripp's speaker longs for is Wales as a closed space – in which, he implies, its dignity can therefore survive. That such closed borders suggest totalitarian regimes – especially in the 1960s when the Soviet bloc remained intact – is perhaps in part what makes the speaker aware of exuding a 'bad smell'. In short, this sort of environmental dreaming is deeply problematic, and the poem knows it.

Harri Webb's work is similarly bound up with Welsh space and place. Webb's poetry was crucial to the resurgence of anglophone poetic culture in Wales during the 1960s, to the extent that Tony Conran has defined it as one of two dominant strands of work in early editions of *Poetry Wales*.[11] It is, then, indicative of the significance that an environmental awareness held for the 1960s generation that the first poem Webb published in *Poetry Wales* – 'The Boomerang in the Parlour', in the magazine's inaugural issue – articulates its sense of Wales through topographical thinking.[12] Note that I am not talking here about any sort of *environmentalist* position. Admittedly, there are hints of an embryonic green agenda in John Tripp's consciousness of Wales as a place polluted by the petrol fumes generated by tourism. But the sense of a global environmental crisis, in which the entire life-support system of the earth itself is under threat, is not present in such work. Rather, 'The Boomerang in the Parlour' uses topography to think through the condition of Wales – from the 'cramped peninsula' of Gower in the first stanza to the land with 'a desert at its heart' in the final line.

The beginning of the poem is all to do with contrasting one space with another, specifically setting the restrictions of Wales (that 'cramped peninsula') against the openness of the Australian outback, to which the speaker's father (Will Webb) went for some time as a young man. The exchange that Will Webb makes is thus between a Wales that is meagre ('the frugal / Patchwork of fields') and Antipodean release or expansiveness ('prodigal spaces', 'the soaring jarra [*sic*]'). Of course, the use of 'prodigal' here also suggests a certain sense of excess in relation to Australian space – for *prodigality* connotes recklessness as much as lavish availability.[13] But even if this is the case, even if the poem is partially figuring Australia as *too much*, Wales is certainly topographically represented as *too little* – that 'cramped peninsula', those 'frugal' fields. The poem's conclusion, with its assertion that, like Australia, 'This land, too, has a desert at its heart', is thus entirely congruent with its beginning: it is merely an extension of the sense of Wales as a land that is reduced to bare bones: cramped, meagre, desiccated. Of course, at the poem's end, the topography is metaphorical, a figure for a land 'whose past has been forgotten / But for a clutter of legends and nightmares and lies'.[14] However, within the overall context of Webb's work, the desert at the end of 'The Boomerang in the Parlour' connects more broadly with what the title of his 1969 volume of poetry calls *The Green Desert* – a notion that is, for Webb, both literal and symbolic. On the literal side, the green desert is the 'colloquial name given now in Wales to the sparsely inhabited upland area in the Cambrian Mountains between, say, Tregaron and Carno, the last vast emptiness at the heart of Wales'.[15] Symbolically, as Brian Morris indicates, 'it has a double significance':

> The green desert is bleak, forbidding, thinly populated, unproductive save for a few sheep and the massed hordes of conifers planted by the Forestry Commission and a handful of entrepreneurial Englishmen rich enough to be attracted by the tax concessions ... But, at the same time, the desert which is green is a remote, inaccessible place, a forbidden country to those who do not understand its ways and its language, where things grow new, undetected, unexploited, and where a nation can cherish itself, the deepest parts of itself, in a natural and creative silence.[16]

As Meic Stephens points out, the first poem in Webb's output to deal with the green desert was 'Above Tregaron'.[17] In the first half of this poem, the landscape of mid Wales is, in part, rendered as an idyllic arena where 'The sweet breath of cows still hangs in the air / Between rock, bracken and milk-foamed water'. More than this, it is crucially connected to the past; the newly metalled road on which the poem's speaker is travelling is a route that is inimical to cars,[18] but at home with former lives:

> This is a way to come in winter. This is a way
> Of steep gradients, bad corners for cars,
> It is metalled now, but this is a way
> Trodden out by cattle, paced yet by the ghosts
> Of drovers.

Although 'metalled now', the landscape here seems to resist modernization – those 'bad corners for cars' suggesting a certain stubbornness in relation to twentieth-century modes of travel. More important, perhaps, is the way in which the road remains 'paced yet' by drovers (albeit in ghostly form) – symbols of the past and, more specifically, symbols of a mode of transportation before the internal combustion engine. As a result, when cars sound their horns, the valleys answer back, not with echoed horns, but with echoes 'of wise horsemen / Calling across the streams, the slow black herds / Steaming and jostling, the corgi's yelp'. The landscape of mid Wales effectively swallows up the present and responds by replaying the past. Thus, when Webb writes about how lonely the place is, the distance from the chaos of the wider world is temporal as well as physical:

> Away from the road stand the farmhouses,
> The loneliest it is said, even in this land
> Of lonely places, and on the high ground
> Between Irfon and Camddwr you are as far away
> As you will ever be from the world's madness.[19]

This is a place, in other words, in which the past is still tangible. But the poem is not a display of wishful nostalgia, however much it may display an urge towards remoteness of both time and space. For one thing, there is a level of irony involved in the poem's sense of distance 'from the world's madness': to invoke the Irfon river is to recall that it was, as John Davies observes, 'on the bank of the river Irfon' that Llywelyn ap Gruffudd was assassinated in 1282 – an event of such importance that, in Davies's words, 'Henceforth, the fate of the Welsh in every part of their country would be to live under a political system in which they and their characteristics would have only a subordinate role.'[20] More immediately, however, as the speaker considers the land about him, the poem moves into its second half as he declares:

> Look on it for the last time; in a few years
> The pinetrees will have hidden it in their darkness.

Suggesting precisely the sort of reading of Welsh landscape offered in R. S. Thomas's 'Afforestation', aggressive conifers here threaten to darken the land, to hide it – to colonize a place that, for Webb, still echoes forth the precious life of historic Welsh space.[21] Thus, in a moment of sharp self-criticism, Webb suggests that he is, effectively, a tourist – albeit an internal one – bringing a sort of pollution to this remote upland area:

> Flying from madness, maybe we bring it with us,
> Patronising romantics, envying the last survivors
> Of an old way of life, projecting our dreams
> On this conveniently empty scenery, deserted
> By its sons for the hard bright streets we come from.

Not only does the urban-dwelling speaker bring the 'madness' of his world with him – thus potentially bringing change along in his wake – he is also responsible for engaging with the environment, not for its own sake, but for the dreams he can project upon it. Remote Welsh space is, in other words, something to serve a cultural purpose, just as it served a photographic purpose for the trophy-hunting English tourists of John Tripp's 'The Diesel to Yesterday'. Indeed, in his projection of dreams upon it, the speaker of 'Above Tregaron' is effectively colonizing the Welsh environment – just as the conifers are threatening to do.

The environmental vision of Webb's poem is thus emphatically various: upland, remote mid Wales is a place to be treasured as a locus distinct from the chaos of modern life; it is a place, indeed, in which what the poem calls the 'old way' of the Welsh past survives; it is under threat both from what I called earlier 'non-natural nature' (those 'pine-trees' and 'their darkness') and from the alienated romantic visitors who pass through it; it is a blank space on which such visitors can write their dreams; and it is a place which the local population is leaving for urban living. But perhaps the central impression that the poem gives is that the land 'Above Tregaron' is a space which is being *travelled across* – by cars, by drovers, by the tide of conifers, by incoming romantics, by outgoing locals. For all its remoteness, the poem creates the green desert of mid Wales as a place of movement. The only things that Webb seems to see as staying still are its farmhouses ('Away from the road stand the farm-houses', as the poem puts it) – just waiting, it seems, to be smothered by conifers, in a way that would finally destroy those communities already stripped thin by the departure of local people for the towns.

* * *

When Meic Stephens divided the 'new poets' of the 1960s from R. S. Thomas by suggesting that the 'brooding on rural decay and [on] the spineless attitudes of his countrymen' which he said the latter represented was possibly an 'emotional dead-end', he was, in part at least, making a judgement about differing attitudes to Welsh place.[22] For Thomas, the implication ran, rural Wales was not a place to be celebrated in the way that Harri Webb, for example, could see the remote uplands of 'Above Tregaron' as the locus of a kind of lost innocence. Of course, my previous discussion has suggested that the new poets were manifestly not averse to bleak interpretations of Welsh space: just recall Tripp's petrol fumes, his trophy-hunting photographers and Webb's inexorably encroaching conifers. However, it is important to observe the complexity of Thomas's Welsh environments, too, which were far from being merely the locus of decay. It is thus to Thomas's work up to the end of the 1960s that I now turn, in order to complete this brief assessment of the state of play at the point when the first of the poets under discussion in Part II of this volume published their initial collections: Gillian Clarke in 1971 (*Snow on the Mountain*) and Ruth Bidgood in 1972 (*The Given Time*).

Appearing in just the second edition of *Poetry Wales* (autumn 1965), Bryn Griffiths's poem 'A Note for R. S. Thomas' launched an extremely sharp attack on Thomas for those qualities of his Welsh vision which Meic Stephens observed in a rather more restrained fashion. The poem begins as follows:

> Come down, Mr. Thomas, from your austere perch,
> The imposed rigour of thought, your stern pulpit.
> Take back your bleak sermons on us:
> The stone desert in the peasant's mind, decay,
> The dead hearts in the mountain flowers.[23]

Clearly, the environmental ideas here are a mixture: the 'stone desert' is not a topographical reference at all; rather, it suggests a state of mind. The 'mountain flowers', by contrast, *do* suggest a physical landscape – and one that stands in strong contrast to the state of those 'dead hearts' with which the line begins. In effect, in Griffiths's rendition of Thomas's mid Wales, the idea of beautiful landscape (suggested by those 'mountain flowers') is merely in place to emphasize, by contrast, the notion of a very unbeautiful people (those with 'dead hearts' and minds as bleak as a 'stone desert'). Of course, one might also read this final line of the first stanza as not relating to people at all; and if that is the case, then it is the 'mountain flowers' themselves that are, in some way, necrotic; they are dead at the core. In fact, such a reading might be more coherent in terms of the poem as a whole because, by the final lines, Griffiths's idea of Thomas's topographical renditions has become much sharper: the flowers have gone, to be replaced by 'granite uplands'. Thus, Griffiths chides R. S. as follows:

> Beside the granite uplands, the arid plateaus
> Of an old despair, there remain the green valleys,
> The bright chambers of changeless air.

Yes, Griffiths says to the older poet, you can have your 'granite uplands' with the aridity you see in them, that 'old despair'. Such is, he says earlier in the poem, '*one* facet of truth' (emphasis in original) about Wales. But, he argues, don't forget 'the green valleys', with their counterbalancing brightness. Simple as this dichotomy might seem – between bright valleys and arid upland – Griffiths's final lines are not entirely straightforward. Of course, the very act of rendering landscape as pure dichotomy, almost in terms of mythic opposites, indicates very strongly that environment is being produced textually as rhetoric, as argument. But it is also interesting that, in one respect, Griffiths's rendition of the dichotomy works to undercut itself – in the striking parallel between the 'old despair' of the 'granite uplands' and the ascription of changelessness to the valleys. In other words, both topographical formations are less manifestations of the present than they are links to the past, and in this they echo the first part of Harri Webb's 'Above Tregaron'. More important, however, is Griffiths's construction of his valleys as 'bright chambers' – a move which fundamentally domesticates them. The *Oxford English Dictionary* suggests that a chamber is, in perhaps its simplest sense, 'A room (in a house)'. The valleys are thus rendered as inherently habitable, safely enclosed, by contrast with those unbounded 'uplands' and 'plateaus' which Griffiths ascribes to Thomas's topographical imagination. Indeed, the notion of a natural (ex-urban) arena – suggested by the *green* of 'green valleys' – is thus, in a strong parallel with Simon Schama's analysis of the concept of landscape itself, a profoundly humanized space. Griffiths's rejection of Thomas's Welsh landscape vision is not merely to do with anger at what he sees as R. S.'s suggestion of human 'decay' in the hills – the position, in other words, with which the poem overtly begins. Rather, by the end of the piece, it is clear that his rejection of Thomas's poetic is also an attempt to render Welsh space as domesticated, as tamed, and thus to claim it as inherently civilized; he is offended, in other words, by what he sees as Thomas's suggestion of the primitive in Welsh land. His poem thus suggests a profound discomfort with seeing Welsh nature in purely non-human terms, in its final recuperation of such alien otherness into a more comforting domesticity.

Notwithstanding the particulars of his attack, the sort of landscapes which Griffiths ascribes to R. S. Thomas's poetry are fairly recognizable in the latter poet's earlier work. The perennially discussed 'A Peasant' (from Thomas's first collection, *The Stones of the Field*, 1946) is a case in point, offering a vision of 'bald Welsh hills' in its opening lines, complete with 'crude earth' and 'gaunt sky'.[24] Of course, those 'bald Welsh hills' are not actually as bald as all that: we find Iago Prytherch 'Docking mangels', so apparently *something* has been growing here. In other words, Thomas carefully undoes his own landscape rhetoric: the place is seemingly more fertile than the phrase about 'bald ... hills' would initially imply, even if the poem makes clear that the process of agricultural production is so harsh that it feels like hacking at a corpse (Prytherch is seen 'chipping the green skin / From the yellow bones'). Interestingly, the crop itself suggests exactly that sense of continuity or ancientness which Griffiths attributed to both his uplands and his valleys: mangels (mangel-wurzels) are a feed for animals which have been grown by human beings since prehistoric times.[25] However, where Thomas's landscape poetic most clearly moves away from Griffiths's sense of it is in its humanizing of even this harsh environment: the baldness of the hills and the notion of a 'gaunt sky' (complete with cheeks which 'the sun ... cracks' – presumably in a sunny smile – 'perhaps once in a week') suggest together an old face with hair gone and skin tight across the skull. Pictured thus, of course, the physical world is little more than skin and bones. But it is humanized, nonetheless. Indeed, later in the poem, even the idea of Prytherch standing up against a 'siege of rain' is an anthropomorphizing gesture: sieges are military activities undertaken by human beings; to extend them to the non-human world pulls that world into the human sphere. In short, Griffiths's urge to present Welsh land as humanized space is something that R. S. does too: neither poem here is able to see the physical matter of Wales as non-human in any sustained way. Admittedly, Thomas's humanizing gestures might well suggest a figure at death's door, but humanizing gestures they remain: earth's otherness is recuperated into human figuration.

Discussing 'A Peasant', the ecocritic Terry Gifford suggests that its 'images of both man and landscape ... are unremittingly negative'.[26] Indeed, my own reading of landscape rendered as a figure at death's door might imply a similar assessment. But to leave it at that would be to read far too thinly. First, one might point out that the opening description of 'bald Welsh hills' is less simply negative than it is *complex*; in terms of the at-least-partially fertile ecosystem suggested by Prytherch's grim fight with the mangels, it is a rhetorical move, opening the poem with a gesture towards a barrenness which the poem does not actually sustain. It is, then, an opening strike for a particular *idea*. Second, and from a diametrically opposed perspective, there is the very simple point that this is not a world, after all, on which the sun does not shine: occasional its appearances may be, but the sun does break through. And third, what about the poem's third line, describing Prytherch as one 'Who pens a few sheep in a gap of cloud'? This line may well give an indication of emphatically limited agricultural achievement – the sheep are, indeed, 'few'. But the 'gap of cloud' is not inherently negative, as Gifford's analysis must imply that it is. Rather, it can be more fruitfully explained by reference to the thinking of geographer Yi-Fu Tuan about 'inside' and 'outside':

> Interior space as such is a commonplace experience. We have already noted the enduring and universal antithesis between 'inside' and 'outside.' Historically, interior space was dark and narrow. This was true not only of humble dwellings but also of monumental edifices. Egyptian and Greek temples commanded external space with their polish and imposing proportions; their interiors, however, were gloomy, cluttered, and crudely finished.[27]

Thomas's 'gap of cloud' effectively provides an 'inside' in which Prytherch can exist. If the 'bald Welsh hills' suggest a monumental external scale, the narrow space implied by the *gap* in which Prytherch pens his sheep is the limited interior that Tuan ascribes to historical dwellings: inside, Prytherch's world is, in general, physically dark with the sun breaking through only occasionally; even the earth is 'crude' in a way that reflects Tuan's notion of historic interiors being 'crudely finished'. In short, that 'gap of cloud' is not something that can simply be dismissed as a negative vision of nature. Rather, it is a vital function of environmental perception: a way of creating a sort of architectural 'inside' into which Prytherch may be placed. As such it sets itself firmly alongside those 'bright chambers' of the valleys that Bryn Griffiths wanted to offer up as *his* Welsh landscape. The difference between the two poems' perspectives on 'inside' is, then, the difference between two modes of interior design. Having discussed the historical mode of building, with its narrow, dark interiors, Tuan goes on to explain that:

European architectural history has seen many changes of style but, according to the art historian Giedion, among ambitious builders the development of an illuminated and spacious interior was a common ideal from the Roman to the Baroque period.[28]

Griffiths's 'bright chambers' reflect this latter sort of 'inside': he wants his Wales, at least in part, to be understood in just such a history of illuminated beauty. 'A Peasant', by contrast, suggests no such high ambitions.

It would, however, be entirely misleading to suggest that the Welsh environments of Thomas's early poetry are persistently a matter of dark interiors. 'A Peasant', after all, ends on a note of environmental spaciousness, with Prytherch revealed to the gaze of 'the curious stars'. Moreover, the technique that Thomas displays in this poem of recasting exteriors as interiors is just one of his approaches to environmental rendition. So, by contrast, in 'Ire' (again from *The Stones of the Field*), exteriors remain exteriors: the distinction offered is between human-built inside (in the house of the Welsh farmer) and natural outside (the mountain). Yes, the area rendered as 'inside' again suggests Tuan's vision of traditional architectural interiors: it is rough and dark ('the floor unscrubbed / Is no mirror for the preening sun / At the cracked lattice').[29] But such darkness is not unanswered: there is the 'preening sun', peeping at the window. And the world beyond the window is less negative than it is unsympathetic or uncouth, with the poem describing 'the harsh, unmannerly, mountain hay' which the farmer is mowing.

In a passing but illuminating moment of analysis, Yi-Fu Tuan usefully parallels *outside* with the notion of 'exposure',[30] and this is an idea that seems to sit well with Thomas's sense of being outside in Wales – whether that outside is recast as a sort of architectural interior or not. Moreover, such a notion has the useful effect of moving one away from simplistic assessments of Thomas's environmental poetic as merely negative, harsh, or the locus of decay – Terry Gifford's assessment of Thomas's earlier work in terms of 'reluctant pastoral', by which he means a 'wilfully bleak construction of melancholy', being a case in point.[31] For example, the notion of exposure permits the ready coexistence of both the beauty and the potential violence of the external world which breaks upon the eponymous structure of 'Country Church (Manafon)':

> The church stands, built from the river stone,
> Brittle with light, as though a breath could shatter
> Its slender frame, or spill the limpid water,
> Quiet as sunlight, cupped within the bone.

> It stands yet. But though soft flowers break
> In delicate waves round limbs the river fashioned
> With so smooth care, no friendly God has cautioned
> The brimming tides of fescue for its sake.[32]

The non-human environment of rural Wales should not be seen here as either positive or negative. Rather, it is a question of the church in the poem being *exposed* to that which surrounds it – exposed, that is, to the beauty of those 'soft flowers break[ing] / In delicate waves', but also to the implied potential for destruction of human structures that 'The brimming tides of fescue' suggest. (Of course, one should not forget that even 'delicate waves' can wear away stone in time: the beauty of the 'soft flowers' is thus not a gentle pastoral image.)

Wynn Thomas has indicated that such renditions of Welsh space in R. S. Thomas's earliest work are crucially in negotiation with the vision of Wales that is found in what he calls the 'English topographical tradition' – a long-standing artistic and writerly sense of Wales 'as a pastoral refuge, as sanctuary of ancient British values, and therefore as essentially consisting of its mysteriously expressive landscape'.[33] Indeed, Professor Thomas has drawn attention to the parallel between the presentation of the church in 'Country Church (Manafon)' and the appearance of the chapel in the drawing 'Addoldy-y-Bedyddwyr, Glyndyfrdwy' by R. S. Thomas's wife Mildred Eldridge – a drawing which, he suggests, is precisely in the 'English topographical tradition': both buildings stand in the face of a potentially overrunning tide of grass.[34] The same can also be said of the end of 'The Minister' which, again set in the hill-country of mid Wales – like 'A Peasant', 'Ire' and 'Country Church (Manafon)', it dates from Thomas's time in Manafon, Montgomeryshire – sees human endeavour in this particular environment as exposed to a sea of incoming moor grass:

> In the chapel acre there is a grave,
> And grass contending with the stone
> For mastery of the near horizon,
> And on the stone words; but never mind them:
> Their formal praise is a vain gesture
> Against the moor's encroaching tide.[35]

The notion of exposure to natural forces ('the moor's encroaching tide') is the key here. Of course, Thomas's inclusion of the human element in this process – manifest at this point in the gravestone and its engraved words – suggests his location at a critically important distance from the English topographical tradition: Wales has not been rendered 'merely as landscape' and nothing more.[36] But what is crucial is this: the Welsh 'outside' of Thomas's early poetry is one in which humanity is exposed to hill, flower, fescue, rain, soil, birdsong, wind, starlight, moor. Or, to put it another way, to be outside in Thomas's Wales is to be thrown into, alongside, upon, and against elemental forms of earth.[37]

The consequence for a humanity thus exposed is various – because, of course, the poetic point for Thomas is never really the earth itself. Rather, as he puts it in *A Year in Llŷn*, 'the truth is that poetry is not made from fine views, but from words and ideas about the condition of man'.[38] Thus, in 'Tenancies' (from the 1968 volume *Not That He Brought Flowers*), exposure to the environment is exposure to the traumas of the self. Thus, observing the children of tenant farms, Thomas writes:

> They are waiting for someone to die
> Whose name is as bitter as the soil
> They handle. In clear pools
> In the furrows they watch themselves grow old
> To the terrible accompaniment of the song
> Of the blackbird, that promises them love.[39]

Bitter soil on the hands recalls bitter human relationships; the mirror of the pool provides the sight and site of ageing; and the sound of bird-song is the sound of mockery, as it promises that which (so the poem implies) will never be received. Alternatively, in many of the poems to do with the hill farms, humanity confronted by the physical matter of Wales is humanity plunged into struggle. In 'The Face' (from *Pietà*, 1966), to be out on the land, ploughing, is a tussle equivalent to Jacob's wrestling with the unnamed figure in the biblical book of Genesis:[40]

> Sometimes he pauses to look down
> To the grey farmhouse, but no signals
> Cheer him; there is no applause
> For his long wrestling with the angel
> Of no name.[41]

In the context of this biblical reference, the earth throws itself against the farmer in the same way that the rain and wind throw themselves more obviously against Prytherch in 'A Peasant'. And it is to this struggle, with its inevitable hurt – Jacob, of course, goes away from wrestling his assailant with an injury – that both Bryn Griffiths and Meic Stephens were, I think, responding in their critiques of Thomas.

But to be exposed to Thomas's Welsh environments is also to be exposed to beauty – however much that beauty is also run through with

violence and death, as Christopher Morgan has so clearly demon-
strated.[42] Indeed, a failure to respond to such a quality is apparently
what condemns the eponymous character of 'The Minister' to a kind of
fruitlessness; as the narrator puts it, 'He never listened to the hills' /
Music calling to the hushed / Music within'.[43] By contrast, in 'The
Moor' (from *Pietà*), the moorland air breaks upon the poem's receptive
speaker like a sacrament:

> I walked on,
> Simple and poor, while the air crumbled
> And broke on me generously as bread.[44]

Exposure to Welsh upland air here is exposure to the sacred, as that air
is manifest as the broken bread of the Christian Eucharist. Of course,
this is another poem in which outside is rendered as interior: the moor-
land, writes Thomas, is 'like a church to me. / I entered it on soft foot'.
But it is not merely the fact of seeing the moor as a church which is
important in the construction of a kind of sacred space at this point.
Rather it is the *type* of interior created: this is not a dark, narrow place;
rather, it is bright with 'clean colours'. The church of the moor is, in
other words, a construction which evokes what Tuan calls the 'mystical
beauty' identifiable in the tradition of illuminated interiors.[45]

But what of that poem with which my thinking began – what of
'Afforestation', with its tyrannous trees, souring the world and destroying
Welsh communities? Similarly, what of the famous 'Reservoirs' (from
1968's *Not That He Brought Flowers*), with its comparably devastating
waters, like a national 'subconscious', 'troubled far down / With grave-
stones, chapels, villages even'? Indeed, there are aggressive trees in
'Reservoirs' as well:

> There are the hills,
> Too; gardens gone under the scum
> Of the forests; and the smashed faces
> Of the farms with the stone trickle
> Of their tears down the hills' side.[46]

I have suggested that to be outside in the Wales of Thomas's earlier
poetry is to be exposed to elemental forms of earth – to hill, flower,
fescue, rain, soil, birdsong, wind, starlight, moor. Here it is water and
trees. Yes, this is second nature, with water and trees manifest, respec-
tively, behind engineered dams and in the form of plantations. But, in
both of these poems, to exist in the Welsh environment is emphatically
to be exposed to the effects of such water, such wood – to the suffocating

form of new lakes (covering 'gravestones, chapels, villages') and the stone-shattering advance of new forests (tearing down gardens, farms). So, to adapt my suggestion slightly: for Thomas at this point, to be outside in Wales is a matter of exposure to elemental forms of earth – even if those forms are sometimes constructed or engineered. (One must remember that Prytherch's struggle with the mangels is a struggle with second nature; agricultural produce is in no sense a manifestation of untouched land.)

What, then, is the upshot of exposure to such wood and water in 'Reservoirs' and 'Afforestation'? On one level, it is to experience destruction – the destruction of communities and of the material structures on which those communities depended. On another level, it is to be exposed to the politics of environmental disenfranchisement: because this is most importantly a vision of Welsh space under threat from the decisions of political bodies dominated by non-Welsh interests. The flooding of Merioneth's Tryweryn valley in 1965,[47] to create the reservoir of Llyn Celyn that would serve the industries of Liverpool, resulted in the destruction of the Welsh-language community of Capel Celyn. The reservoir drowned 'houses, a school, a post office, a chapel and a cemetery'; '48 people of the 67 who inhabited the valley lost their homes'; even the dead were uprooted, with eight of the bodies in the cemetery being disinterred.[48] Crucially, however, the decision to drown the Tryweryn valley was approved by a Westminster parliament that was dominated by non-Welsh MPs – with only one Welsh MP voting for the measure in its final reading on 31 July 1957. It was, moreover, a decision from which Welsh local authorities were excluded.[49] Similarly, the coniferization of Welsh land which is the historical context for Thomas's 'Afforestation' was driven by the diktat of Westminster policy-makers.[50] As Jim Perrin has observed, 'There springs to my mind the breathtaking announcement concerning conifer plantation by a spokesman for the Attlee administration [of 1945–51]: *We intend to plant 800,000 acres in Wales. We intend to change the face of Wales. We know there will be opposition but we intend to force this thing through.*' 'This *thing*', Perrin observes, 'however monstrous, however inappropriate'.[51] Towards the start of his 2001 volume *Writing for an Endangered World*, Lawrence Buell draws on notions of environmental justice to critique his own earlier work:

> My previous book, *The Environmental Imagination*, centered on an attempt to define 'ecocentric' forms of literary imagining, as instanced especially by nature writing in the Thoreauvian tradition. I continue to believe that

reorientation of human attention and values according to a stronger ethic of care for the nonhuman environment would make the world a better place, for humans as well as for nonhumans. Pressing that argument, however, meant understating the force of such anthropocentric concerns as public health and environmental equity as motivators of environmental imagination and commitment. *To those living in endangered communities, the first environmental priorities will understandably be health, safety, and sustenance, and as guarantors of these the civic priorities of political and economic enfranchisement.*[52]

The key to R. S. Thomas's environmental imagination in 'Reservoirs' and 'Afforestation' is just such a sense of 'endangered communities': Welsh communities drowned, uprooted, cleared from land. Although the end of 'Reservoirs' is bleakly critical of Welsh culture – the English are seen 'elbowing our language / Into the grave that we have dug for it'[53] – a significant part of what fuels these two poems is an anger at the failure of 'political and economic enfranchisement' for those who lived in particular Welsh environments in the middle of the twentieth century, and who were consequently unable to exercise a satisfactory degree of environmental self-determination. As such, one of their primary engagements with Welsh space is the declaration of environmental injustice suffered by Welsh people.

* * *

It is from within the context of this varied poetic of Welsh space – as it stood at the time of the Second Flowering, in the work of both senior and newer figures – that the writing I now go on to consider began to emerge from the early 1970s. The studies which follow are ordered according to the sequence in which each poet published her or his first single-authored volume: Gillian Clarke in 1971 (*Snow on the Mountain*); Ruth Bidgood in 1972 (*The Given Time*); Robert Minhinnick in 1978 (*A Thread in the Maze*); Mike Jenkins in 1979 (*Rat City: Poems from Northern Ireland*); Christine Evans in 1983 (*Looking Inland*); and Ian Davidson in 1989 (*No Passage Landward*).[54] This simple pattern of organization should in no way be taken to imply that I am proposing some equally simple, linear pattern of development between the poets concerned. There is, moreover, no attempt to shoehorn chapters and poets into particular thematic categories: I am certainly not trying to dress up a sequence of thematic studies as examinations of individual poets. However, that is not to say that certain chapters are not more concerned with one sort of idea than another. Thus, for example, my chapter on Christine Evans predominantly deals with the notion of mythical space, whilst that on Mike Jenkins is much concerned with environment as expression of social power. By contrast, in my choice of poets, I have made a deliberate attempt to respond to the geographical breadth of Wales – from the substantially mid or west Welsh visions of Ruth Bidgood and Gillian Clarke, through the focus on south Wales in Mike Jenkins and Robert Minhinnick, to the north Wales of Christine Evans's Bardsey and Ian Davidson's Anglesey. But what binds the whole together is the double-barrelled question that lies behind my analysis of each poet's work: what Welsh environments are created here and to what effect?

II

Welsh Environments in
Contemporary Poetry

4

Gillian Clarke:
Beyond an Environment of the Senses

In her early poem 'At Ystrad Fflur' (from the 1978 collection *The Sundial*),[1] Gillian Clarke renders the environment of mid Wales as colour, shape, sensuous experience. Responding to the landscape around the ruins of the Cistercian abbey of Ystrad-fflur (Strata Florida) near Pontrhydfendigaid in Cardiganshire,[2] the poem's speaker declares the sun 'warm after rain on the red / pelt of the slope', whilst the sun's appearance is 'fragmentary through trees / like torches in the dark'. The nearby Afon Teifi is 'a torc in a brown pool / gleaming for centuries', while its water is given a striking sonic presence in the observation of its 'profound / quietness'. There are 'circled bones'. Changing light shifts the land from 'gold to stone'. The Teifi overruns its banks, with its 'spilt water / whitening low-lying fields'. And, at the poem's end, the speaker observes a 'yellow mustard field' which creates such a strong effect that it is registered emotionally as 'a sheet of flame in the heart': the colour of the land, in other words, is manifest as a sense of heat and light in the body. Clarke's Ystrad-fflur is thus the locus of sensory plurality, as the poem's various appeal to sight, hearing and awareness of temperature makes clear. This is Welsh space, then, as sensation.

The importance of a sensuous response to the environment in Gillian Clarke's work has been observed by various critics. Thus, K. E. Smith refers to the establishment of 'tactile solidities' in her earliest poetry; Wynn Thomas argues that her work displays a 'sensuous immersion in … the ancient particularities' of the west Wales landscape; and Linden Peach notes the sheer importance of a physical response to the land over the breadth of her poetic output ('many of Clarke's poems are actually rooted in demanding, often exhausting, physical work').[3] However, none of this is to imply that what we find in 'At Ystrad Fflur' is merely a 'succession of discrete sensations', as Yi-Fu Tuan puts it, in his discussion of the relationship between 'sensory impacts' and the processes of 'memory and anticipation' which help to order and interpret sensation.[4] Rather, as the description of the Teifi as a torc indicates, landscape is also being ordered according to cultural vision. The river is not merely a gleaming but ultimately non-specific shape; instead its manifestation as a torc suggests a reading of Welsh space which is, in part at least, figured by reference to an archetypal object of ancient Celtic material culture.[5] (Indeed, as a torc *in a pool*, the Teifi is also offered up in terms which recall ancient Celtic ritual – what Miranda Green and Ray Howell call 'the aquatic deposition of prestigious ... objects' in which a 'votive offering of prestige bronze and iron equipment [was made] to the supernatural powers'.[6])

According to Tuan, the observation of patterns in the environment is typical of human perception:

> The mind discerns geometric designs and principles of spatial organization in the environment. For example, Dakota Indians find evidence of circular forms in nature nearly everywhere, from the shape of birds' nests to the course of the stars. In contrast, the Pueblo Indians of the American Southwest tend to see spaces of rectangular geometry.[7]

However, as Tuan later makes clear, such awareness of shapes in the non-human world is unlikely to precede human creation of them in culture: in other words, non-human forms are envisioned in terms of human constructions. Thus he writes:

> Nature is too diffuse, its stimuli too powerful and conflicting, to be directly accessible to the human mind and sensibility. First man creates the circle, whether this be the plan of the tepee or the ring of the war dance, and then he can discern circles and cyclical processes everywhere in nature, in the shape of the bird's nest, the whirl of the wind, and the movement of the stars. (pp. 111–12)

On these terms, by figuring the Teifi as a torc, 'At Ystrad Fflur' offers landscape, in part, as Celtic ornamentation. Admittedly, as a common feature of ancient Celtic material culture, the form of the torc is far from specific to a Welsh context – which is not, on the other hand, to deny the importance of torcs found in Wales.[8] But the use of the torc here *does* represent a movement towards a culturally particular rendition of place, an understanding of Welsh topography in broadly Celtic terms. It is thus, in effect, a subjection of sensory response – here, of sight, in the form of the 'gleaming' river – to cultural memory.

Place in this poem is an amalgam of movement (the speaker crosses a bridge, while the river rushes south and spreads out over the fields), sight (the landscape is a thing of shapes and shifting colours), temperature responsiveness (consciousness of the warm sun) and hearing (the silence of the river's water) – a combination of sensory inputs which are both 'spatializing' (that is, which 'make us aware of a spacious external world inhabited by objects') and 'nondistancing' (qualities such as warmth, which give the spatial world further and enriching character but which are not primary indicators of spaciousness).[9] However, alongside such sensory markers of place, the environment of Clarke's Ystrad-fflur is also cultural and historical. Thus, in addition to dressing the land in a Celtic ornament, Clarke begins the poem by responding to the name of the place – which means 'vale of flowers':

> No way of flowers at this late season.
> Only a river blossoming on stone
> and the mountain ash in fruit.

Although the land may not literally be a 'way of flowers' at this point in the year, it is still flowering – albeit not in terms of plant life – with the 'river blossoming on stone'. The land, in short, is made to display the qualities of its name. Indeed, in the second stanza, it seems that the environment has taken on the characteristics to which it has historically been put by its human inhabitants:

> All rivers are young in these wooded hills
> where the abbey watches and the young Teifi
> counts her rosary on stones.

Under the abbey's watchful eye, the Afon Teifi pursues her devotions, with the land thus understood in terms of its cultural history as the locus of a religious house. Indeed, the speaker's awareness of what has gone on before her in this place is manifest in her observation, in the fifth stanza, that 'They have been here before me' – the ambiguous 'they' at this point being clarified a little by the seventh stanza's sense of 'their circled bones'. 'They' is apparently thus the buried community of Ystrad-fflur – embracing, presumably, the monks themselves, the lay people who were involved with the life of the abbey (as well as the Welsh princes laid to rest at the site)[10] and Dafydd ap Gwilym whose grave, as a note to the poem makes explicit, is at Ystrad-fflur.[11] Alongside environment as sensation, then, this is also environment as linguistic site, cultural use and communal life. Indeed, in the poem's closing lines, Clarke observes how 'desire runs // Like sparks in stubble through the memory / of the place': Ystrad-fflur is, for Clarke, such a memoried place that its ancient desires still burn hot – perhaps an oblique reference to the poetry of Dafydd ap Gwilym, whose own desires are manifest in poems such as 'Morfudd fel yr Haul' ('Morfudd like the Sun'), 'Cyrchu Lleian' ('Wooing the Nuns') and 'Merched Llanbadarn' ('The Girls of Llanbadarn').[12] However, in 1238, Llywelyn ap Iorwerth (Llywelyn Fawr) brought his vassals to Ystrad-fflur to swear loyalty to his heir.[13] Moreover, the abbey also 'played a key role in the compilation and dissemination of *Brut y Tywysogyon*, a laconic, plain-as-a-pikestaff account of the historical development of the Welsh people between 682 and 1282'.[14] So the historic desires of the place are as much to do with power-brokerage and nation-building as they are with Dafydd ap Gwilym's (literary) pursuit of Dyddgu and Morfudd.

It is, finally, worth noting that Clarke's Ystrad-fflur is also a place to be understood in terms of fruitfulness and cyclicality. The opening stanza finds flowers even beyond the season for flowering in the 'river blossoming on stone' that I have already observed, whilst the mountain ash is seen to be 'in fruit'. Later in the poem the Teifi is 'in full flood and rich / with metals'. The bones of the dead 'dissolve in risen corn', arguably claiming fruitfulness even from death. And, in the penultimate stanza, the speaker observes 'the turning trees / where leaf and hour and century fall / seasonally' – a falling from which not death but 'desire runs'. In a striking contrast to R. S. Thomas's rhetorical extension of a *lack* of fertility in his notion of the 'bald Welsh hills' (from 'A Peasant';[15] discussed in Chapter 3 above), Clarke makes flower blossom on rock, corn rise from bone and desire spark from the falling leaves of 'oak and birchwoods'. But perhaps this is no surprise, given Harri Webb's sense of the green desert of mid Wales as a place of potential rebirth: in the remoteness of the area to which this poem is a response, 'At Ystrad Fflur' sees the possibilities of fecundity. In sum, then: if Clarke's Ystrad-fflur is present tense in the immediacy of its sensory impact, and if it is past tense in terms of its framing cultural memories, then it is perpetual and potential in its awareness of seasonality – in the repeating cycles of flower, fruit and fallen leaf.

* * *

What I hope is clear from my analysis of this piece is the variety of fronts on which Gillian Clarke's environmental sensibility has operated from her earliest work. Perhaps most important is this: if the remote mid Wales of Ystrad-fflur is presented as a place of physical sensation, this does not deny a concurrent sense of landscape as culture, as history. Indeed, it is arguably the case that Clarke's striking sensory response to the Welsh environment here is ordered by precisely such acts of memory. Yet, notwithstanding the richness and variety of landscape figuration in this poem, its companion piece in *The Sundial* suggests that there is a problem. 'Dyddgu Replies to Dafydd' is presented as the response of one of the women to whom Dafydd ap Gwilym addressed his love poems.[16] As Wynn Thomas points out, this piece is crucially important for the way in which Clarke claims a female voice out of former silence, as she 'enables the mute object of the praise of Wales's greatest poet to become a speaking subject, and ... thus empowers a woman to speak her own differently erotic love poem'.[17] However, in terms of agency within the environment, the piece offers a far more problematic vision of female empowerment. The poem is a consideration of the relationship between Dyddgu and Dafydd over the course of the year, shifting from its 'bloom[ing] in mild weather', through Dyddgu's sense of 'a coming dark, / your heart changing the subject', to the moment of Dafydd's (temporary?) departure. It is at this point, in the poem's final three stanzas, that Dyddgu proclaims what is manifestly a distinction between the genders in terms of access to Welsh space:

> The feet of young men beat, somewhere far off
>   on the mountain. I would women
>   had roads to tread in winter
>   and other lovers waiting.
>
> A raging rose all summer falls to snow,
>   keeping its continuance in
>   frozen soil. I must be patient
>   for the breaking of the crust.
>
> I must be patient that you will return
>   when the wind whitens the tender
>   underbelly of the March grass
>   thick as pillows under the oaks.

The first of these three stanzas presents what is apparently a fairly simple picture: in her sense that women do not have 'roads to tread in winter' – unlike the 'young men' whose feet she imagines on the mountain – the female speaker perceives for herself and her gender geographical restrictions that her male addressee does not have. Of course, the restrictions are also sexual: Dafydd, by implication unlike Dyddgu, has 'other lovers waiting'. But in terms of the relationship with the material environment, woman is here perceived as being kept away from the land – or, to be more accurate, away from the *geographical breadth* suggested by the mountain paths walked by men. Of course, one might object that the previous nine stanzas of the poem have fairly emphatically placed Dyddgu in the land. This is true. But they have done so in the company of her male lover (she is not, in other words, at large in the world on her own), whilst they have also created the land to which she *does* have access as a crucially *internal* space. Thus, although the poem starts with the idea of the 'open places' where the lovers have met, it is clear that such 'open' (outside or green) spaces are – in an echo of Dafydd ap Gwilym's own poetic – significantly envisioned as buildings (in stanza one, the forest has a 'frescoed … ceiling'; in stanza five, Dyddgu talks about 'our forest room'; and in stanza six, autumn makes the forest into a 'ruin, a roofless minister [*sic*: minster]').[18] The wider and significantly *external* world – signified by the mountain – is, it seems, denied to women. Admittedly, this is not to participate in the 'desacralization of the natural world during the passage from medieval Christianity to the modern industrial age', which Louise Westling usefully links with 'a post-Enlightenment nature defined as a lifeless machine' rather than personified as female:[19] after all, the first part of the poem emphasizes the sacral aspect of the forest in its description both as a place of ceremony and as a minster. But it *is*, perhaps, to see the wider land as a place of primarily male exploration, linking to what Westling sees as the controlling, 'masculinist' (p. 31) attitude of the post-Enlightenment approach to nature.

At the same time, however, the poem offers a strong connection between the female and the non-human: Dyddgu understands herself as a rose, blooming in summer, 'keeping its continuance in / frozen soil' in winter, and waiting for the changing of the seasons for rebirth, 'when the wind whitens the tender / underbelly of the March grass'. Such an association is unsurprising: as Kate Soper indicates, the 'coding of nature as feminine … is deeply entrenched in Western thought, but has also been said by anthropologists to be cross-cultural and well-nigh universal'.[20] Indeed, in 'At Ystrad Fflur', the Teifi is explicitly feminized ('count[ing] her rosary on stones'), whilst Wynn Thomas has argued that, in 'At Ystrad Fflur' as a whole, 'the landscape becomes vividly female in body'.[21] However, in 'Dyddgu Replies to Dafydd', Dyddgu's choice of a rose as self-image does suggest a particularly *cultivated* aspect of the natural world: the rose is an almost archetypal *garden* flower, as well as one that is particularly associated with the human interventions of horti-culture. But as Soper goes on to explain, drawing on the arguments of Sherry Ortner, the conventional, patriarchal association between woman and nature is not a 'simple conflation' of the two; rather, it is more accu-rately understood as an

> alignment of the two that derives from the female role in child-birth and her consequent activities as initial mediator between the natural and the cultural. As those responsible for the nursing and early socialization of chil-dren, women are 'go betweens' who stay closer to nature because of their limited and merely preparatory functions as 'producers' of the cultural.[22]

In Clarke's poem, Dyddgu is thus precisely in the situation of 'go between', in the image of the rose as cultivated flower: she is what might be called natural-but-not-quite. By contrast, the realm of art – in other words, the supremely cultural – is left to Dafydd who, two stanzas before Dyddgu's self-association with the rose, is pictured 'packing [his] songs / in a sack, narrowing [his] / words, as [he] stare[s] at the road'. As Soper explains, again drawing from Ortner, this is typical of the 'limita-tions' that 'Patriarchal relations ... have placed on female participation and access to culture': when something is 'conceived as an "art" form' (Soper's particular example is cooking), 'it typically becomes the province of the male'.[23]

A final twist to all this is also worth noting: in the poem's concluding stanza, seasonal rebirth and the return of the male go hand in hand. In other words, having seen woman initially installed in the land (albeit only so long as the land is understood in terms of interior space) but then excluded from its wider breadth, before being returned to it yet simultaneously restricted to the status of 'in between' the natural and the cultural, it now appears that female association with land is a matter of insufficiency. In the poem's concluding images, the female speaker must wait 'patient[ly] / for the breaking of the crust' – the crust of the 'frozen soil' in which the rose 'keep[s] its continuance'. In short, the female speaker, even though identified at this point with the rose in the earth, must *wait* for fertility to come back – which it does at the point of the returning man. As Page DuBois observes, when discussing developments in ancient Greek culture:

The ideology of the woman's body as fruitful, spontaneously generating earth gives way in time to a cultural appropriation of the body that responds to and rewrites that primary image. Men claim that they must *plough* the earth, create fields, furrow them, and plant seeds if the earth is to bear fruit. They see female bodies as empty ovens that must be filled with grains and made to concoct offspring.[24]

There is nothing quite so explicit as this in Clarke's poem. But the final association between male return and seasonal rebirth certainly indicates that any ideology of what Louise Westling calls the 'independent fertility of the female earth' is absent here.[25] The land's rebirth is linked to the male, not to the female. Or, to put it in another way – and this is key to my whole discussion at this point – the Welsh land in which Dyddgu and Dafydd's relationship is played out is distinctly problematic for women in terms of the extent to which female environmental agency is (or, perhaps more accurately, is *not*) permitted within it.

Moreover, lest one argue that, in 'Dyddgu Replies to Dafydd', Clarke is merely creating what she understands to be a fundamentally historical situation and that her sense of contemporary relationships between woman and land is quite different, the poem 'Scything' (from 1982's *Letter from a Far Country*) again proposes that there are difficulties involved.[26] This is not an *explicitly* Welsh-identified poem, but the sense of getting a place under control suggests Clarke's relationship with her Cardiganshire house, Blaen Cwrt, which she bought in a heavily dilapidated state at the end of the 1960s and to which she moved in 1984.[27] As such, it is fair, I think, to see this poem as responding to the west Wales landscape with which Clarke has particularly identified herself: as she puts it in an interview, when discussing the comparison between Blaen Cwrt and Cardiff (from where she moved), Cardiganshire is 'the Welsh heartland' where she has 'put down even deeper roots' than in south Wales.[28] 'Scything', then, sees the poet-speaker and her son (Dylan) clearing the garden:

> It is blue May. There is work
> to be done. The spring's eye blind
> with algae, the stopped water
> silent. The garden fills
> with nettle and briar.
> Dylan drags branches away.
> I wade forward with my scythe.

However much there may be the sensuousness of immediate colour in the world ('It is blue May'), this is not really a place for aesthetic appreciation. Rather, as the speaker puts it with great simplicity, 'There is work / to be done'. As such, this poem is the inheritor of the Judaeo-Christian sense of ground that will produce weeds and that must be sweated over – a notion to which Louise Westling draws attention in her sense of the 'embattled' relationship with the earth that is visited on humankind by God as a result of Adam and Eve's disobedience in the Garden of Eden.[29] However, beyond the opening stanza, pain in the environment is a particularly female experience. As the poet-speaker advances with her scythe, she discovers a small tragedy:

> There is stickiness on the blade.
> Yolk on my hands. Albumen and blood.
> Fragments of shell are baby-bones,
> the scythe a scalpel, bloodied and guilty
> with crushed feathers, mosses, the cut cords
> of the grass.

The speaker's unwitting destruction of a bird's nest haunts the rest of the day: the female willow warbler drops repeatedly from the 'crown of the hawthorn tree / to the ground' in silent question, while the speaker herself also 'return[s] / to the place', holding the broken eggs, guiltily conscious of their warmth which reminds her of 'how warm birth fluids are'. The distress here is figured as both animal and human – but particularly female in both cases, wrapped around the concept of bearing young.

The challenges of being female in the land that are identifiable in this poem are also clear in the long title piece from the same collection. 'Letter from a Far Country' is a work that is rooted in the landscapes of Carmarthenshire, Pembrokeshire and Cardiganshire, but which blends them to create a kind of agricultural, west Welsh anyplace. Thus, whilst indicating that the poem makes use of three particular locations (Bryn Isaf in Login, Carmarthenshire; Fforest Farm, just west of Newport in Pembrokeshire; and Blaen Cwrt in Cardiganshire),[30] Gillian Clarke has also made clear that she sees herself as having 'br[ought] them together into one fictional geography' – 'physically real', as she puts it, 'if jumbled'.[31] It is apparent from very early on in the poem that the writing of Welsh land is just as complex, in terms of gender relations, as the shifting array of positions in 'Dyddgu Replies to Dafydd': as Linden Peach has shrewdly observed, 'Letter from a Far Country' is 'not reducible to a tract with a well worked-out position'.[32] Thus, as Jane Aaron and Wynn Thomas indicate, there is a negotiation in this poem between a sense of Welsh land as feminine – 'with its hilly curves and crevasses', as they put it – and a restrictive masculinity:[33]

> First see a landscape. Hill country,
> essentially feminine,
> the sea not far off. Bryn Isaf
> down there in the crook of the hill
> under Calfaria's single eye.
> My grandmother might have lived there.
> Any farm. Any chapel.
> Father and minister, on guard,
> close the white gates to hold her.[34]

This is a position that we have seen before, of course: there is a manifest association between the environment and the female, but women are simultaneously kept within a bounded space, restricted from wider access to the land. However, while in 'Dyddgu Replies to Dafydd' there was no clear agent of this restriction, here it is clear: 'Father and minister' – in other words, familial menfolk and religious authority. This is, then, the land as Welsh cultural history, suggesting the oppressions of patriarchal dominance within Wales that are implicit in the notion of 'Land of my fathers' and that have been historically manifest in the power structures of the Welsh chapel culture to which Clarke gestures at this point.[35] Moreover, a couple of stanzas further on, the speaker declares:

> The minstrel boy to the war has gone.
> But the girl stays. To mind things.
> She must keep. And wait. And pass time. (p. 8)

Linden Peach suggests that there is a reference here to menstruation – presumably through the notion of what is *passed*, although he does not make this connection explicit.[36] More important – and far clearer – is the sense of masculine ability to move from place to place, while the female is geographically restrained. As Louise Westling points out, there is a long tradition in Western thought of setting the passive female in contrast to the 'nonfeminine', active male (a tradition that has its environmental manifestation in the sense of the female land needing to be worked upon by the male in order to become fruitful) – and Clarke's poetic gestures towards just such an ideology here.[37] However, the poem also suggests a very different position, by indicating the sheer degree of activity in which women are engaged, and defending its validity against male scepticism. Linden Peach argues that the activities of the poem's opening domestic scene are essentially symbolic of female restriction:

The arrangement of books on the shelves and the neat ordering of clothes in cupboards and drawers signify the larger, hegemonic processes of ordering and classification which legitimise the power of men over women which is in turn reflected later in the poem in the inscription on the stones in the graveyard.[38]

On one level, Peach is clearly right: like the speaker's grandmother, the speaker of the poem also seems to be geographically restricted, caught in the house to serve the absent family's 'loud life'. Indeed, as Jeremy Hooker points out, the poem certainly contains 'images of imprisonment' in relation to the women it depicts.[39] But on another level, Peach misunderstands the poem's sheer pleasure in the activities undertaken and presented as female: as the speaker declares, 'I ... / stand back, take pleasure counting / and listing what I have done' (p. 7). I can detect no ironic undercutting of this statement here. Instead, it appears to be a celebration of activity – albeit within the geographically bounded sphere I have already observed.[40] As a celebration of *activity* the poem thus manifestly works against the equation of *woman* and *passive*. But the domesticity of that which is celebrated is one of the reasons why Jeremy Hooker suggests that the poem is 'a compromise as far as feminist convictions are concerned' – although he pertinently acknowledges that 'the duality which the poem dramatises' (by which he means its celebration of 'the very way of life ... that is shown constraining the [speaker's] grandmothers') 'greatly enriches it as a work of art and increases its psychological authenticity'.[41] More important, however, is the poem's attempt to use the imagined environment of rural Welsh space to overturn the conceptual divorce between art and the female (a divorce which I have suggested is identifiable in 'Dyddgu Replies to Dafydd'). In their engagement with the produce of the land, women are portrayed as the creators of objects that are, in the context of the poem, emphatically aesthetic achievements. Thus, Clarke talks of 'jars labelled and glossy / with our perfect preserves':

> Spiced oranges; green tomato
> chutney; seville orange marmalade
> annually staining gold
> the snows of January. (p. 11)

The foregrounding of colour here (orange, green, gold) is striking, and recalls the sensuous engagement with land in 'At Ystrad Fflur'. However, it is followed, three stanzas later, by a sense that what the poem presents as the female activity of bottling various sorts of food and drink is nothing less than an artistic rendition of landscape, seasons and weather:

> Familiar days are stored whole
> in bottles. There's a wet morning
> orchard in the dandelion wine;
> a white spring distilled
> in elderflower's clarity;
> and a loving, late, sunburning
> day of October in syrups
> of rose hip and the beautiful
> black sloes that stained the gin to rose. (p. 12)

Such activities are the answer to the 'masculine question', asked a few stanzas earlier by the gulls: "'Where" they call "are your great works?"' (p. 11). The poem's response is that they are precisely here, in the bottled renditions of environment that are no less an aesthetic achievement than the male-dominated history of art (the 'great works' of the gulls' question). To put it simply, this is a claiming of the artistic for the female – and thus an overturning of that traditional restriction of female creative work to the category of 'craft' which Kate Soper suggests.[42] As such, it is a very important move. Indeed, in the association that Clarke offers between womanhood, art and preserving things, the poem proposes a tradition of female remembrancers which, within a Welsh context, stands as a quiet challenge to the masculine tradition of the *beirdd* (bards).

Against all this, however, is the poem's profound sense of the way in which male dominance is written into the very materiality of the Welsh landscape. I have already quoted Linden Peach's observation that the inscriptions on the gravestones towards the end of the poem are part of those power structures which 'legitimise the power of men over women'.[43] Specifically, the gravestones work to sustain patriarchal dominance by registering the social achievements of the men but keeping silent about the women:

> On the graves of my grandfathers
> the stones, in their lichens and mosses,
> record each one's importance.
> Diaconydd. Trysorydd.
> Pillars of their society.
> Three times at chapel on Sundays.
> They are in league with the moon
> but as silently stony
> as the simple names of their women. (pp. 17–18)

In the record of the gravestones, the social dominance of masculine
achievement is dug into the Welsh environment itself. As such, and as
with 'At Ystrad Fflur', the landscape again becomes a historical record.
Not only are the men of Wales 'in league with the moon'; they are also
writing themselves onto the earth, and thus writing masculinity over
that landscape which the poem had earlier described as 'essentially
feminine' (p. 8). Indeed, 'Letter from a Far Country' makes it clear that
the land of rural Wales is, in certain ways, significantly antipathetic to
female presence. In the middle of the poem, the speaker recalls being in
the fields as a young girl, with 'the stubble / cutting my legs above blan-
coed / daps in a summer too hot / for Wellingtons' (p. 12):[44]

> To be out with the men, at work,
> I had longed to carry their tea,
> for the feminine privilege,
> for the male right to the field.
> Even that small task made me bleed.
> Halfway between the flowered lap
> of my grandmother and the black
> heraldic silhouette of men
> and machines on the golden field,
> I stood crying, my ankle bones
> raw and bleeding ... (pp. 12–13)

The overt reference to female blood-loss in these lines may gesture
towards the menstrual imagery that Linden Peach sought to identify
elsewhere in the poem. More immediately, however, in the violence of
stubble on human flesh, this is a blunt refusal to permit Welsh rural
space to be overwhelmed by the sensuous pleasures of sight, sound and
touch – to be dominated, in any simple way, by an aesthetics of beauty.
By contrast, the touch of the land here is undeniably harsh. Moreover,
this passage reveals the environment of Clarke's rural west Wales to be
especially punishing on *female* experience: the speaker's attempt to
move out into the male space of the field – an arena which the speaker
suggests it is a 'privilege' for her to access – is resisted by nothing less
than the agricultural life of the land itself.

* * *

The refusal to let aesthetic pleasures dominate environmental under-
standing that is identifiable here in 'Letter from a Far Country' is also
apparent from Clarke's earliest work. One of her very first poems to be

published – in the summer 1970 edition of *Poetry Wales* and then in her 1971 collection *Snow on the Mountain* – 'The Fox' begins with a contemplation of rural scenery:

> On the way we saw the red larch woods
> Blurring the mountain above Llwyn On,
> Two hills, one rising, intensely warm with colour,
> One flying free and horizontal from the plane of symmetry.[45]

These lines (the poem's opening stanza) create an idyllic interpretation of the landscape in the Brecon Beacons, with the hills essentially manifest as abstractions: one is rendered as colour, whilst the other is a geometric form. In this sense, topography is appreciated as pure aesthetic construct, rather than as lived space. However, the subsequent three stanzas of the poem work very strongly to undercut this initial approach. In stanza two, the locus of the piece having switched to Cardiganshire, the poet leaves her house (Blaen Cwrt) to walk to an area where 'the ewes shelter to give birth to their lambs'. What greets the speaker here is essentially a memento mori, with the ground in the wood littered with the bones of dead lambs. However, the scene serves a more complex purpose than merely a reminder of mortality, for Clarke makes it clear that both the ground and the 'pale bones of the past' are stained with the 'blood of birth / And life'. Life and death are inextricably mixed beneath the trees. What is crucial, however, is that the long-distance abstractions of the first stanza have vanished – even if the aesthetic sense remains, in the awareness of dark blood staining pale bones. By the final stanza, the play between aestheticism and the violence of Welsh rural life is even stronger, as the speaker finds a dead fox in a tree, where it has been hung up after being shot:

> Her beautiful head thrown back, her life stiffened,
> Her milk dry, her fertility frozen. The reds grew cold.

The final reds are not those of the fox; rather, they are the reds of the opening scene – of those 'red larch woods' which, until the poet's walk from her home, had remained 'still warm in the brain'. Close up, the rural is violent, dark and cold, whatever the beauty of those remote topographical abstractions with which the poem began.

This poem really instigates that tendency within Clarke's poetic to construct the world of rural Wales as a place of death or suffering, as well as the locus of sensuous response. As Wynn Thomas has pointed out, her 'sensuous immersion' in landscape is 'associated in Gillian Clarke's mind with a "feminine" sensibility' – something she has expressed in her sense that 'Women oftener record memories of babyhood than men and thus draw more deeply on the first physical, animal sensations of infancy, where body and mind are single, fact and imagination indivisible.'[46] Whether or not such an assertion is in any way psychologically or physiologically accurate, it certainly does tie in with the Western tradition of associating women with the bodily that is found in 'the assumption that the female, in virtue of her role in reproduction, is a more corporeal being than the male'.[47] The awareness of death in Clarke's landscapes is a kind of bodily counterbalance to the sensuous aspect of her environmental response, in the same way that I have observed a corresponding *cultural* counterbalance to it as well. Thus, in poems such as 'Ram' (*Letter from a Far Country*),[48] 'Shearing' (from the new poems in 1985's *Selected Poems*),[49] 'Hare in July' (from 1989's *Letting in the Rumour*),[50] the fifth poem in the sequence 'The King of Britain's Daughter',[51] 'Flesh' (from 1998's *Five Fields*)[52] or 'Blackface' (*Making the Beds for the Dead*, 2004),[53] death and suffering are presented as a significant principle in the Welsh rural land around which her poems so frequently revolve. For example, in 'The King of Britain's Daughter' – a sequence whose Welsh experience is, like aspects of 'Letter from a Far Country', rooted in the far west of the country on the Pembrokeshire coast[54] – when the speaker recalls her wanderings with her father, which are epitomized by his old hat, she remembers:

> mornings of forage,
> beachcombings, blackberries, pebbles, eggs,
> field-mushrooms with pleated linings …

But alongside this, she notes how her father worked his hat 'to a form / for the leveret that quivered under my hand / before it died'.[55] In the environment of rural Wales, in other words, death is close at hand, alongside the pleasures of beachcombing and blackberries. Similarly, in 'Blackface', a sheep which has been kept as a favourite dies whilst trying to give birth to a lamb, which also dies:

> What gets us is that tender glimpse
> like a sanctuary lamp
> at the door of the vulva,
> and the lamb dead in the boat of her body.[56]

For Clarke, the identification between the female and the bodily is not, it seems, just to do with birth; there is also a particular female intimacy with death – one that, so the image of the 'sanctuary lamp' would suggest, has an almost religious power.

Given the association that such poems establish between rural space and death (or suffering), Clarke's decision to engage with the UK-wide foot-and-mouth crisis of 2001 in the title sequence of *Making the Beds for the Dead* (2004) was, perhaps, unsurprising. Clearly, given the particular concerns of this sequence, there is a geographical consciousness at play here that expands beyond Wales. Thus, for example, when asking where the disease started, Clarke looks suspiciously beyond the British Isles to 'Somewhere hot and far away / where they don't fill in forms / to take a sheep to market, / don't call a beast a product, / a commodity' ('Virus', p. 56). But when the Welsh environment does appear, it is the locus for suffering and death in a way that has been prefigured in the earlier work I have been discussing in these last few paragraphs. In other words, Clarke's vision of a suffering landscape in 'Making the Beds for the Dead' does not emerge from nowhere, or merely in isolated response to a particular and acute rural crisis. What is different, however, is the sheer scale of suffering and death that is involved. As she observes in 'Cull' (p. 64):

> At Storey Arms tonight
> that lay-by under Pen-y-fan
> where we used to stop with the children
> is a theatre of death.
> The slaughtermen work
> into the night by floodlamps.
>
> There are lorries on the pass,
> the smell of blood,
> and fire in the sky ...

Here, the Brecon Beacons become a kind of hell; indeed, in 'The Vet', this connection is made explicit, with the speaker declaring that 'Night after night / we watched them die, / beasts thrown to the flames / like sinners consumed' (p. 67). As one might expect of Clarke, this is all done with significant reference to the senses: the quotation from 'Cull' simultaneously appeals to and appals both sight (floodlamps and fire) and smell (of blood). However – and this applies to the breadth of Clarke's poetry – such sensuousness is balanced by the (equally bodily) suffering and death which are, in this sequence, present in such terrifying abundance. Linden Peach is, I think, right to assert that Clarke's poetry generally ends up on 'the right side of morbidity', notwithstanding her 'cluster of recurring images – skull, shell, bone, darkness – [which] celebrate death'.[57] Here, however, that balance seems to be reversed. But as 'The Fox' would indicate, the potential for Clarke's poetry to tip towards a deeply harsh vision of the rural has been there from the beginning.

* * *

In 'Shepherd', the final poem of the sequence 'Making the Beds for the Dead', a jet 'chases' over the winter landscape, 'cresting the sill of the land / to take the Atlantic'.[58] The speaker observes the eponymous shepherd as a kind of eternal form within the land:

> In the fields
> a man and his dog
> check the sheep dawn and dusk
> as they've always done. (p. 71)

To him, the jet is of little note ('What's it to him, / the flight of kings'), bar the reminder it offers that 'the world turns' (p. 71). However, that the air of mid Wales is cut by such jets is clear from 'Night Flying' and 'In January', a pair of poems from *Letting in the Rumour* which consider fighter planes, respectively, by night and day.[59] 'In January' makes clear the symbolic provenance of at least one, in the now-decommissioned British military airfield at Aberporth:[60]

> A day of wings – jet from Aberporth,
> glittering dragonfly
> towing its shadow from the south
> over a yellow hill. It breaks the day.

That such British military machines are an assault on the experience of Welsh space is clear from the sense of destruction that this one wreaks upon the day. Moreover, the flight path of such jets over the hills of Cardiganshire means that the rural space of mid Wales becomes a place in which the political is especially obvious:

> The cities can forget on days like this
> all the world's wars. It's we
> out on the open hill who see
> the day crack under the shadow of the cross.

To be in mid Wales, in other words, is to be constantly reminded of a world at war through airborne displays of military might. Indeed, the poem goes so far as to let the dweller of the Welsh hills see the jet write the sign of suffering (the cross) onto the day. What this poem thus does is to portray rural Wales as the locus of a revelation which effectively constitutes a spiritual judgement on (British) military muscle. Moreover, in such passing of judgement, 'In January' arguably identifies Clarke as an inheritor of that earlier Welsh-language literary tradition which, in the words of Kirsti Bohata, 'recognized the threat of the ambitions of the Forestry Commission and Ministry of Defence, not to mention the Water Board' to Welsh land and Welsh identity.[61] If anything, 'Night Flying' is even blunter than 'In January'. Thus, '‘Low-flying jets by night' are 'an outrage', which turn mid Wales into enemy territory (from the jet's point of view): it becomes a 'no-man's-land' where there might be 'a sniper on a branch', 'a terrorist / taking the ditch way home', or even people 'plotting' an 'outbreak / of peace'. In short, this is to imagine Welsh space as rebellious space – either standing against the jets with force (the sniper, the terrorist) or with the 'tender subversions' of peace.

That Welsh air can be deeply political for Clarke is apparent through these two poems. It is thus unsurprising that those two staples of poetic political consciousness in Wales – conifers and water – are also apparent in her work. In the night-time world of 'Journey' (from *The Sundial*), the poem's speaker recalls her awareness of 'a load / Of logs, bringing from a deeper / Dark a damp whiff of the fungoid / Sterility of the conifers'.[62] Such sterility very much recalls R. S. Thomas's 'world that has gone sour / With spruce'.[63] Similarly, 'Clywedog' (also from *The Sundial*) observes the waters of a Montgomeryshire reservoir which the poem sees drowning farms and driving people from their homes.[64] The flooding having been completed, the poem concludes thus:

> And the mountains, in a head-collar
> Of flood, observe a desolation
> They'd grown used to before the coming
> Of the wall-makers. Language
> Crumbles to wind and bird-call. (p. 53)

This is a harsh rurality, but not one that is made so by what Kate Soper calls 'the structures, processes and causal powers that are constantly operative within the physical world' and that move living beings always towards death.[65] Rather, in 'Clywedog', Welsh rural space is harsh because it has had its culture erased from it. To put it simply, the poem sees landscape as having been returned to a non-human state ('Language / Crumbles to wind and bird-call') – and this is, for Clarke, manifestly a tragedy. Without the 'wall-makers', all is 'desolation', as if the makers of walls, farms, language had never been there. Jeremy

Hooker usefully observes an 'inwardness with nature' as 'one of the chief distinguishing features of [Clarke's] poetry'.[66] He is, I think, entirely right to note this. However, Clarke's nature is rarely purely aesthetic, purely sensuous or purely for its own sake (and this latter point means that her work cannot be classed as some sort of biocentric eco-poetry). Instead, for Clarke, to be inward with nature is automatically to be inward with the cultural, political and gender-inscribed battles of Welsh land.

5

Ruth Bidgood:
Reinhabiting Mid Wales

The environmental focus in Ruth Bidgood's poetry is substantially
bound up with what Gillian Clarke's 'Clywedog' calls 'the wall-makers':
Bidgood, in other words, is very much a poet of the built landscape –
notwithstanding the distinctly remote rural spaces on which her poetic
attention often centres. Her first collection, published in 1972, has the
following note printed on its dust jacket:

> [Bidgood's] love of and involvement with mid-Wales, which she visited first
> as a school-girl, have deepened over the years, and she hopes to make it her
> home. Many of the poems spring directly from this involvement; indeed,
> she thinks that without it none of them would have been written.[1]

The first poem of the collection – and thus the first to depict the mid
Wales to which this introductory statement gestures – is 'The Given
Time' (p. 11), a piece which displays a number of key Bidgood motifs in
her poetic dealings with the area: ruins, forest, valley, memory. The
central point of focus is a building, an abandoned house, on which
newly planted forest is beginning to encroach.[2] Bidgood's starting point
is the future, as the first stanza imagines 'the broken shape of the house'
in years to come: deep in the 'silent forest' is the 'Irregularity' of the
building, offering a contrast to the 'ordered trees' – that order
suggesting the coniferous plantation which has, since the 1950s, covered
so much of the area near Abergwesyn where Bidgood has settled and
out of which her poetry emerges.[3] But in the present, the second stanza
declares, the house is neither broken nor forgotten. Rather:

> in this time decreed as mine,
> With hardly a stone yet fallen, the house is lapped
> By the first waves of forest-land
> Whose crests bear the tiny trees.
> The house has lost its life, not yet identity –
> It is known hereabouts, stories are still told
> Of men who lived there.

Given the importance of water poetry in Wales – something that is suggested by two poems I have already considered (R. S. Thomas's 'Reservoirs' and Gillian Clarke's 'Clywedog') – it is significant that the newly planted forest is seen here as 'lapp[ing]' the house: both trees and water are notable aggressors in poetic productions of the Welsh landscape, and Bidgood combines them at this point. More central to the poem as a whole, however, is the way in which it makes use of the idea of memory to suggest that the house retains an ongoing existence, even after its abandonment: in the local community ('hereabouts'), it serves as a locus for story and recollection.

Yi-Fu Tuan talks about the idea of place as 'time made visible', whilst the anthropologists Pamela J. Stewart and Andrew Strathern argue that 'landscape is best seen as a process', as a 'form of memory'.[4] Tuan's notion is to do with the way in which the material forms of Western building function as 'architectural relics' within the landscape: thus, for example, he observes how a city may have 'temporal depth' which is 'objectified in [its] successive walls that accrue like the annual rings of an aged tree'.[5] In this context, Tuan observes that it is significant that 'Stone is the West's material for building monuments'; by contrast:

> In China and Japan wood is often used, and wood does not last as long. The Chinese civilization is old but the Chinese landscape offers few man-made structures of great antiquity ... The landscape evinces no clear story line; relics that point to stages of the past are not evident. (pp. 190–1)

In Bidgood's poem, the – significantly stone-built – physical structure of the house is very definitely rendered as a 'memorial to times past', as Tuan puts it elsewhere (p. 179). As the opening stanza makes clear, at that future point when its stones have fallen and it is 'Hardly a shape even' within the forest, it is *then* – at the vanishing point of the structure itself – that the memories associated with the house are gone ('Not a memory left, not a line of its story'). However, whilst the building still stands, the second stanza observes that it raises 'half-answers, glimpses, echoes' of those who lived there previously. Moreover, in the third stanza, it is precisely memorial which defines the poem as a whole: noting that she lives in 'the haunted present', the speaker allows the house to draw her mind back 'over nursery furrows':

> To where in the winds of the past the house rose whole,
> A shape of life in a living valley –
> Winter brightening the low rooms
> With snow-light and spark-spattering logs,
> Or spring's shadows playing like lambs,
> Racing with the sun like children over the fields.

Through the physical memorial of the house, the landscape displays what Tuan calls 'temporal depth' – it is, in the poem's terms, a place of 'the haunted present' – as the speaker moves beyond half-remembered stories to the imagination of the house as a container for life itself ('A shape of life in a living valley'). As such, the building becomes the means by which the whole life of a valley can be gestured towards and memorialized. Though darkly threatened by the 'snatching branches' of the forest to come, this was, the poem suggests – in an admittedly nostalgic gesture towards some sort of rural idyll – once a living place, full of light and movement.

What Pamela J. Stewart and Andrew Strathern's sense of 'landscape … as a process' usefully adds to Tuan's ideas is a concept of environment as a thing of fluidity. Tuan's initial comments about time and place rather put the two into conflict, when he suggests that 'Place is an organized world of meaning. It is essentially a static concept. If we see the world as process, constantly changing, we should not be able to develop any sense of place' (p. 179). By contrast, Stewart and Strathern's emphasis on landscape as process is important for suggesting the way in which human readings of landscape often focus on that which signifies alteration – particularly in the sense of how landscape is seen historically. Thus, whilst acknowledging that landscape 'often serves as a crucial marker of continuity with the past', Stewart and Strathern also argue that 'its shape at any given time reflects change and is a part of change'.[6] Such change is, they suggest, intimately bound up with 'controversy and conflict' and, as such, 'landscape as a form of memory often comes to encode past conflicts that are revealed in its own form and which people think are relevant to the present and the future' (p. 229). On one very obvious level, Bidgood's poem imagines landscape as process through its renditions both of forest growth and of the alterations that take place in a house which can variously be remembered as part of a living community, seen as currently deserted or imagined in a future state of decay. However – and more importantly – the poem also focuses on an area of profoundly important cultural conflict within the changing nature of the mid Wales environment. As Bidgood explains in her prose volume of local history about the Abergwesyn area (*Parishes of the Buzzard*):

> The decline in farming was greatly accelerated by the arrival on the scene about the time of the Second World War of the Forestry Commission, with its tempting offers to struggling farmers of plentiful 'money in the hand' – offers at first resisted, later uneasily or avidly accepted. Similar offers followed from the Economic Forestry Group, the 'private woodlands' (now Till Hill) ... Many local people were torn between gratitude for the chance of work (though this was to prove, for most, sporadic only) and a deep sadness and resentment at the disappearance of farmhouses and farmland, and the familiar beauty of bare rolling hills and great skies, under the regimented hordes of conifers.[7]

The conflict between human habitation, farming, and open countryside (on one side) and trees (on the other) – and thus the landscape changes which that conflict has instigated – is central to the recent historic experience of mid Wales. It is precisely this conflict which is captured in Bidgood's 'The Given Time'. The poem's building is not just a memorial for the lives lived in a particular place; nor is it merely a way of indicating the inevitable changes that take place in landscape – by which I mean broad patterns of alteration, development or decay. Rather, it offers up its deserted house as a way of addressing that particularly Welsh landscape conflict: the coniferization of Harri Webb's green desert. Of course, Bidgood's poem does not offer an overt colonial reading of this situation in the manner of R. S. Thomas's 'Afforestation', in which the trees are explicitly described as 'Colonising the old / Haunts of men'.[8] But the poem *does* have a clear sense of both land and community being taken over by an alien, intruding force; and it is acutely aware of the absolute devastation that the conifers create – their destruction of 'A shape of life in a living valley', as the poem puts it. As such, when it is placed within the historical context of those ordered conifers and their genesis in the work of the Forestry Commission,[9] 'The Given Time' comes into focus as a striking lament for what has been done to Welsh community by mid-twentieth-century landscape policies emanating from Westminster.[10] Indeed, the poem's rather nostalgic, idyllic construction of the past (the living valley) in terms of brightness and movement merely serves to dramatize this point, by emphasizing the contrast between what has been destroyed and the darkness of the forest that is to come. The poem itself is thus a proclamation of the need to use memory and imagination 'to break from snatching branches', lest the Welsh communities shattered by afforestation become nothing more than a forgotten 'Irregularity, among the ordered trees'.[11] From the first, in other words, Bidgood has shown herself to be, like Gillian Clarke, an anglophone inheritor of that Welsh-language tradition of political landscape writing which Kirsti Bohata has observed in the work of 'Gwenallt, Waldo Williams, Islwyn Ffowc Elis and Tryfan'. In this sense, both Bidgood and Clarke stand as female contributors to a tradition which, Bohata suggests, has historically been a thoroughly male preserve.[12]

* * *

Buildings – and particularly ruins – constitute a persistent motif in Bidgood's poetry. 'Hawthorn at Digiff', from the 1986 volume *Kindred*, is another case in point, with the poem's speaker gazing down at the eponymous house 'shivering with heat', next to the river and 'full of hawthorn':

> The tree
> grows in the midst of it, glowing
> with pale pink blossom, thrusting
> through gaps that were windows,
> reaching up where no roof
> intervenes between hearth and sky.[13]

It is interesting that the ruined house seems feverish – that 'shivering with heat' sounds unhealthy, especially in the context of the final stanza, which explains that the hawthorn, too, is 'flushed / with decay' (p. 33). Bidgood's rural mid Wales is not, it seems, a place of innocence or easy beauty. Admittedly, in a demonstration of that nostalgia which Bidgood has conceded was present in her earliest work,[14] 'The Given Time' figured the rural past as an idyll of brightness; but that image must be set in the context of the poem's presentation of destruction subsequently wrought by encroaching conifers. Just as sharply, in 'Hawthorn at Digiff', there is an impression of all-pervading sickness having infected both house and tree – a malaise that is quite in addition to the sense of decline suggested by the presence of the ruined building

itself. However, like 'The Given Time', the fallen house more particu-
larly becomes a focus for understanding the way in which the valley in
which it stands – the Irfon valley, near Abergwesyn – has changed.[15]
This is the poem's fourth stanza:

> I bring a thought into this day's light
> of Esther and Gwen, paupers:
> Rhys and Thomas, shepherds: John Jones,
> miner of copper and lead:
> who lived here and are not remembered,
> whose valley is re-translated
> by holiday bathers across the river,
> lying sun-punched: by me:
> by men who keep a scatter of sheep
> on the old by-takes. (p. 32)

Along with the important notion of the area's linguistic shift towards
English – signified by the contrast between the speaker's use of English
and a name such as 'Rhys', which stands as a synecdoche for the valley's
Welsh-language past – the sense of a place 're-translated' also echoes the
fluidity of landscape which was apparent in 'The Given Time'. Here,
however, the shift is between a past Wales to be mined and farmed, and
a current Wales to which tourists come in the sunshine and in which
farming has become minimal (the current men keep merely a 'scatter' of
sheep). Of course, as Bidgood herself makes clear in her book of local
history, the area has been a tourist attraction for some considerable time:

> In the past ..., what drew many of the visitors to the Builth area was the
> pursuit of health ... It was Theophilus Evans himself who publicised in a
> letter of 1732 to the editor of the *St James' Chronicle* the virtues of the
> 'stinking well', which he himself had tested after seeing a cheerful and
> healthy frog pop out of its noisome and unknown depths. Finding his
> scurvy greatly improved, he made known to others the healing powers of
> what was to become the Dôlycoed Well, and thus launched Llanwrtyd, or
> rather Pontrhydyfere, on a new life as the busy little spa of Llanwrtyd
> Wells, the 'Matlock of Wales'.[16]

The sense of a recreational or touristic mid-Welsh past which Bidgood
details here is not apparent in 'Hawthorn at Digiff', so Merryn Williams
is entirely right to observe, in her own critique of the poem, that it is
seemingly 'important for [Bidgood] to write about a landscape with
people, to name and bring into the light the forgotten paupers, shep-
herds and miners who lived in the valley before it became a holiday
centre'.[17] Whether or not the poem's sense of environmental history is

something of a rhetorical simplification – and the information from *Parishes of the Buzzard* suggests it might be[18] – the environmental crux of the poem at this point is the sense of two competing landscapes operating within the same mid Wales: the one, a locus of temporary recreation (for the 'holiday bathers'); the other, a place of tough work (mining, farming), which has been carried to the present by those who are no longer remembered. It is an important part of what the poem does, in its listing of the names and professions of people associated with the house, precisely to work against such forgetting – and thus to resist a merely picturesque, touristic reading of (Welsh) space.[19] Indeed, as A. M. Allchin usefully observes, 'Houses have a very special place in Ruth Bidgood's vision of things. They can act as containers which hold the memories of many generations.'[20]

Environment as 'time made visible' (to use Tuan's phrase)[21] does, then, play a significant part within Bidgood's poetic, both in terms of memorial and in the sense of understanding landscape process or conflict; and that which has been built is crucial to such a perception. However, as 'All Souls'' makes clear (from 1978's *The Print of Miracle*),[22] this is no quiet antiquarianism. Rather, it can be a powerful declaration of surviving life in mid-Welsh space, with the poem celebrating the 'lively shout of light' from the inhabited houses in the Gwesyn valley area as nothing less than a voice for those other houses which have now been abandoned. This note of celebration is important, as A. M. Allchin also suggests when he argues that 'The houses themselves are celebrated in a kind of roll-call of valley names, Tymawr, Brongwesyn, Nant Henfron, Glangwesyn, Cenfaes, Blaennant.'[23] Moreover, when the poem's speaker talks of the 'deafening darkness / of remotest hills' against which the words of the deserted houses were 'always faint', the extent to which Bidgood's sensibility tends towards the built rather than the natural becomes clear. There is, in short, no romance for the hills themselves; instead, they seem utterly antipathetic to the speech and light with which the speaker aligns herself at the end of the poem. Thus, talking of the abandoned and now silent houses in the valley, the final three lines declare:

> For them tonight when I go home
> I will draw back my curtains, for them
> my house shall sing with light.

This is memorial as activity, declaration, shout – as passionate commitment to what has been built, to the human structures on the land. Or, to put it in the terms of ecocritical discussion, it is unashamedly anthropocentric poetry. It is therefore no surprise to find Bidgood commenting, in an interview, that:

> writing about the Welsh countryside is of course different from writing out of it, which is what I do. It's an important distinction. I'm not a nature poet. John Clare is a nature poet. I use the countryside just as I use the things I find when working on local history. I'm saying something about human feelings …[24]

Thus, when Bidgood walks in the Welsh countryside, her perambulations often seem to be primarily defined by the built things she meets – such as the adit (mining tunnel) where she and her companion hide from the rain in 'Heol y Mwyn (Mine Road)', and in which they have the 'chill uneasy' revelation of the 'hill's hidden waters, falling, / falling, for ever into dark';[25] or the 'little slab-lined grave' of 'Burial Cist';[26] or even the perplexing 'short / lonely road with its traces / of ancient use' in 'Image' – a road which, 'At the head of the lead-mine valley',[27] seems to be 'coming from nowhere, ending in nothing'.[28] Indeed, in this latter example, the speaker's companion is sceptical about the road, seeing in it neither origins nor destinations ('You do not feel an onwardness / in the ancient road'). But all the same, it is the road which serves as the point from which the countryside is ultimately observed:

> Yet in evening sun
> you have come to sit beside it, far above
> old spoil-heaps and the rusty markers
> of black shafts, to watch how line on line
> the multiple horizon rears its dark
> against red sun, to hear how pure
> is the voice of the poisoned stream.

Again, it must be stressed that this interest in old structures is not an academic antiquarianism. Nor, beyond occasional moments in her earliest work, does it result in nostalgia. Rather, for Ruth Bidgood, the built environment of remote mid Wales provides its temporal and spatial frame – the means by which the area is to be navigated in both time and space.

* * *

As the final note of 'Image' suggests – that reference to the 'poisoned stream' in the 'lead-mine valley' – Bidgood's rural space is often distinctly troubled. Here, it suffers from toxicity.[29] Elsewhere it is a place of suffering, death and violence. Indeed, such an unforgiving interpretation of the rural has always been apparent in Bidgood's work. Notwithstanding its tendency towards nostalgia, 'The Given Time' is rooted in the idea of rural life destroyed. More striking, however, is 'Stone' (also from her first collection) which bluntly asserts that 'Arcadia was never here': whatever warmth there might be and whatever life – the poem notes the peat-fire with 'a summer heart' and talks of the testament of stone which 'proclaims life' – upland mid Wales is also a place in which 'Ice-needles tortured the thin soil, / spring snow lay long by the north wall', and in which 'Only stone lasts'.[30] I have already suggested that, in 'All Souls'', the countryside seems antipathetic to human work, with the hills' darkness swallowing the faint voices of the deserted farms. However, in 'Cardiganshire Story' (again from *The Given Time*), such antipathy manifests itself as nothing less than a bitter, destructive power, an actively malign force. In this poem, a fierce night on the hills kills a baby whose 'first night was his last':

> Night was the murderer,
> using all its weapons for the kill.
> One would have done, the cold
> on those hills, but night made sure,
> using rain to soak the ragged blanket,
> wind to drive home the cold and wet,
> moonless dark to make the pony stumble
> jolting the weak newborn,
> stabbing the girl with pain ...[31]

The tragedy of the child's death is one that is rooted absolutely in what the poem presents as the topography and harsh weather of rural Wales. Although the poem ends with the assertion that 'night was the only murderer' (p. 35), this is somewhat misleading: night in a warm house would not have killed the child. Rather, what finishes the child is its presence, with little protection, in the cold and wet of the Cardiganshire hills.

I have suggested elsewhere that Bidgood's mid Wales manifests a poetic of 'harsh Welsh ruralism'[32] – like that which I have already identified in the work of Gillian Clarke (see Chapter 4 above). Of course, Bidgood's recurrent attention to decaying buildings is part of this, offering a potent sense of a landscape in which something is dying (and has been dying for a long time): in addition to 'The Given Time' and 'All Souls'' one might, in this context, also turn to poems such as 'Shepherd's

Cottage', 'Carreg-y-Fran', 'Cefn Cendu' (from *The Given Time*) and to the striking later sequence 'Valley-before-Night' (from the section of new work that opens Bidgood's 1992 *Selected Poems*).[33] However, the harshness of Bidgood's mid Wales is also a matter of violence, danger, and – as 'Image' hinted – pollution. The sequence 'Valley-before-Night' (about the 'upper Camarch Valley in the old parishes of Abergwesyn and Llanafan', as the poem's head-note explains) is a case in point.[34] The opening stanza makes clear both the isolation of the place and its disturbing reputation. Thus, as one speaker explains, 'There was never a road / up the Camarch, till the Forestry came', whilst another states simply 'That is a dark valley' (p. 45). Such a combination – the isolation and the reputation for darkness – suggests the gothic, and the sequence as a whole readily fulfils this, with a series of grim deaths and peculiar apparitions. The work as a whole is divided between verse and prose sections, which interweave present, recent and long-since-past narratives of the valley's people. Few of the narratives are without some omen of danger or destruction – or at the very least, as the second stanza suggests, a sense of the valley as displaying 'a darkness of obliquity, / enigma' (p. 45). Indeed, even the narratives of the two youngest children still living in the valley are shot through with the dark colours of either present suffering or of possible fear to come. Thus, in 'Coedtrefan: Tomos' (p. 50), the story of the 2-year-old Tomos – one of the valley's four remaining children (in the house Coedtrefan) – begins with the child's night terrors, which only his father can calm, 'carrying / the tense resistant two-year-old downstairs / and out into moonlight'. Even more striking, perhaps, is 'Coedtrefan: Gwyn', a poem of 'The baby on the floor', in which the 7-month-old child is 'totally given up to laughter' (p. 52). However, the speaker seems unable to see such laughter without qualifying it with a sense of the uneasiness with which the sequence as a whole is suffused:

> He does not yet know
> ordinary from strange;
> he is not vulnerable
> to the ambiguities of dusk.

That 'yet' is crucial: in due course, the baby *will* know strangeness; he *will* be troubled by that same sense of 'a darkness of obliquity, / enigma' (p. 45) which makes the speaker of the sequence uneasy. Moreover, 'Coedtrefan: Gwyn' concludes with a sense of darkness pressing in on the baby's world ('He rolls on his back, smiling up / at plants on the sill, staring / at leaf-shapes against the darkening panes'; p. 52), whilst what immediately follows it is a description of gravestones at Pantycelyn chapel – themselves becoming subject to darkening ambiguity:

> The many stones at Pantycelyn
> grow hard to read, as moss and lichen
> impose their freer patterns
> on flowing script, grey wings and flowers.

On one level, this recalls the ending of R. S. Thomas's 'The Minister' which, as I suggested earlier, sees the objects of human endeavour as crucially subject to 'the moor's encroaching tide'.[35] These lines are, in that sense, testament to humanity's subjection to natural forces which may overrun it. However, in the context of Bidgood's poem, rather more important is the sense of 'obliquity, / enigma' that the speaker sees darkening the valley as a whole (p. 45): the non-human is here making the human unknowable, a mystery. Indeed, the transition from a baby's laughter to darkness is quickly completed when Bidgood, having produced a roll-call of valley deaths, asks:

> Who heard the *cyheuraeth* for the doomed farms?
> Who heard the *cyheuraeth* pass along the valley? (p. 53)

As the head-note to the sequence explains, *cyheuraeth* means 'howling (a death-omen, auditory equivalent of the corpse-candle)' (p. 45). And indeed, this couplet is a revisiting, from an aural point of view, of an earlier couplet which provides the visual equivalent:

> Who saw the corpse-lights dance
> for the death of the farms? (p. 47)

Death and its foretelling are keynotes in this sequence. Not only are the farms 'doomed', as these two couplets so bluntly indicate, but so are many of the valley's inhabitants. The prose sections of the sequence are particularly important in this respect, telling of deaths (some violent, some tragic) and the premonitions that preceded them. Thus, for example, after a poetry section about the house Fedw – itself a building which caused concern for a mother whose daughter (from the house Pencae) sometimes stayed there overnight – a prose section tells of a former inhabitant of Pencae:

> Morgan Dafydd of Pencae died from a wound, falling from his horse on to a little dagger which he had with him for an evil purpose.
>   At about two o'clock in the morning of that day, Rhys Rowland had seen a coffin made of light, standing outside Morgan's house. Meeting with him later, Rhys warned him, but in vain. (p. 49)

In 'Valley-before-Night', remote, rural mid Wales is a place where death is a particularly strong presence. Here, of course, there seems to be a supernatural aspect to the dangers of the Welsh environment. In 'Waterspout, 1853',[36] by contrast, the dangers are bluntly physical, with the non-human world visiting violent death on the unexpecting residents of a house called Dôlfach in the Duhonw valley to the south-east of Builth Wells.[37] The speaker (constructed as an observer of the events) describes the storm that strikes after the 'July heat' which 'grew heavier as afternoon / deepened', noting how he woke in the night 'to crazy howling, / clap after vicious clap of storm, / and growling, churning, pouring / greater far than rain'. The consequence of the storm is a stark reminder of what Kate Soper calls the 'realist concept' of nature – 'the nature to whose laws we are always subject':[38]

> Across the demented stream – a torrent now,
> tossing trees, rolling rocks, down, down
> towards bloated Wye – I saw the house Dôlfach
> split open, two contorted trees
> passing through it and on.

Lawrence Buell concludes his seminal ecocritical text, *Writing for an Endangered World*, by discussing what he calls 'Watershed Aesthetics', by which he means literary works which display 'an ecocultural understanding of peoples defined by waterways'.[39] As Buell explains, watershed thinking is part of a bioregionalist approach to environmentalism, by which he means a way of understanding:

> human and nonhuman communities within a territory of limited magnitude whose borders may not be precisely specifiable but are conceived in terms of 'natural' rather than jurisdictional units, often in terms of watershed or constellation of watersheds. Bioregionalism seeks to make human community more self-consciously ecocentric than it has been in modern times but in such a way as to incorporate, not disallow, anthropocentric concerns. (p. 297)

Bidgood's approach to community in 'Waterspout, 1853' is precisely to think it in terms of the water which flows through it. Thus, the immediate context of the poem's human drama is the storm-swollen 'Duhonw stream' which is shown dementedly charging towards the 'bloated Wye'. Indeed, even this sense of interconnected waterways is important: as Buell points out (quoting Luna Leopold), 'river systems within watersheds are dendritic, "a network of channels much like the veination of a leaf"' (p. 251). Moreover, alongside the opening image of the waterspout itself 'burst[ing] on Epynt', the poem's sense of being surrounded by water is particularly strong in the speaker's awareness of a 'growling, churning, pouring' all about his house. The community is, then, defined by the waterways and water sources amongst which it exists: for the inhabitants of Dôlfach, waterways constitute their violent physical destruction; for the observing speaker, their action leaves him mentally scarred for the remainder of his life:

> How
> could I have helped them, the five who died?
> I did not see them, and could not have heard.
> Yet whatever years are left me
> will be too few to build flood-walls
> for my once inundated mind.

The closing metaphor of the poem – the 'inundated mind' – is significant for understanding this poem in terms of watercourses and the environments they can be understood as creating: here, water bursts through into the mind itself, in a psychological reassertion of the harsh character of the landscape with which Bidgood is concerned. Watershed aesthetics are, in this poem, part and parcel of Bidgood's violent mid Wales, as waterways constitute the locus and means of human tragedy.

Bidgood's use of waterways and the valleys which they create is a returning motif in her work. 'Valley-before-Night' is, of course, a poem whose understanding of landscape is defined by a place brought together around a watercourse: the poem's movements are significantly 'up-valley and down'.[40] Moreover, like 'Waterspout, 1853', this sequence suggests a 'dendritic' understanding of water patterns ('Four miles up from Dôlaeron bridge / Cedney flows in, on its bank Pencae'; p. 47). More striking, perhaps, is 'Carreg yr Adar (Rock of the Birds)' which, again, displays tragedy – the death of a man – amongst a network of water:[41]

> The Rock of the Birds juts out
> from eastern slope to stream,
> half-bars the valley. A stony path
> creeps round it by the river.
> To the north, feeder streams debouch
> in a waste of stones. (p. 16)
>
> Here are shifting streams,
> stones studding old riverbeds:
> named streams
> dropping, dawdling, dropping
> down rocky channels

> out of the moors, ancient lands
> of stone-heavers, mound-men. (p. 18)

Environment here is seen as drainage basin, over which a jet – like those which Gillian Clarke also observed – tears 'silence open' (p. 16) and through which ancient humanity heaved its stones (p. 18). But the environmental basis is the intricate pattern of waterways. It is interesting that this way of approaching environment – through what Buell calls '"natural" ... units' – rather works against Bidgood's driving interest in that which is built by human invention. But a number of her poems are valley poems and are thus, implicitly, defined by a watercourse approach to environmental understanding. Thus, alongside a poem such as 'Carreg yr Adar (Rock of the Birds)', valleys and watercourses are simply part of the way that Bidgood thinks landscape in pieces such as – to choose just a few – 'Feathers', 'First Snow', 'Blizzard', 'Heol y Mwyn (Mine Road)', 'Towards the Blaenau' and 'Party Night'.[42] In none of these poems are valleys or waterways necessarily defining motifs; it is simply that landscape as formed around watercourses seems to be a fundamental part of Bidgood's environmental thinking about mid Wales. Indeed, it is a valley which provides one of Bidgood's most luminous interpretations of her environment – one that is in stark contrast to the unease of 'Valley-before-Night', the violence of 'Waterspout, 1853', or the frankly alarming vision of 'Slate-quarry, Penceulan',[43] in which a reassuringly beautiful field above the detritus of a quarry ('a strip of untroubled green catching the sun') is revealed to lie above a quarried-out 'chamber whose functional hugeness / amazes, whose dark hollowness / rears up close under sunny grass'. By contrast to this potentially lethal innocence, then – the danger of 'the green brittle hill' – the landscape of 'Chwefru', from the two-poem sequence 'Emblems', is the locus for a kind of transcending joy.[44] The poem begins with a recognition of the way in which the speaker's old friend 'liked that valley' (the reference being to the Chwefri valley, to the north-west of Builth Wells), whilst the latter two stanzas describe an experience in which the valley seems to open up towards heaven:

> One hot day, high upstream,
> we saw, incredulous, on a small stone
> in the river, a crowded confabulation
> of butterflies, heads together, folded wings
> raying out, uncountable angels
> on the point of a pin. Beyond, moorland
> spread away into the eye of the sun.

> There they went, rising in a whirligig,
> fluttering into the invisibility
> of huge light. I remember how his eyes
> tracked them, till tears of dazzle blurred
> stream and moor, and the butterflies were gone.

In my earlier analysis of R. S. Thomas's 'The Moor', I suggested that exposure to Welsh air was, in that poem, exposure to the sacred, with the air recalling the broken bread of the Christian Eucharist. Here, Bidgood similarly makes upland Welsh space holy in the rendering of butterflies as angels (itself a reminder of Wordsworth's vision of daffodils as a sacred 'host') and, more importantly, in her evocation of Christ's ascension. Thus, the butterflies' disappearance into 'the invisibility / of huge light' and the speaker's friend tracking them until 'tears of dazzle blurred / stream and moor' suggest the biblical ascension scene, in which Christ is 'taken up', and his disciples look 'stedfastly toward heaven' as 'a cloud received him out of their sight'.[45] At this point, in other words, Bidgood seems to place a mid Wales valley in communion with heaven itself. Such moments of transcendence are, however, relatively rare in Bidgood's construction of Wales.[46] As Bidgood herself has said, she is very much aware of the interplay of 'light and shade', but with the strong sense that 'the shade [is] necessary for the picture'.[47] Thus it is perhaps unsurprising that, in the poem 'Legacy', the poet-speaker presents her own environmental residue as a kind of pollution, in the knotweed that she has been unable to control spreading 'down-valley' from her garden:

> Further down, the Irfon curves away
> towards forests on the hill. Far across
> water-meadows, diminishing clumps
> of flowering knotweed flaunt, against
> the dark of hardly less alien spruce,
> their dubious exuberance – undiscouraged
> succubi, my sinister, unwilled,
> spectacular legacy.[48]

Although 'unwilled' (with the pun being on the notion of bequeathing something), the speaker sees her contribution to the environment in strikingly negative terms, as generative of nothing less than evil itself (figured in those demonic 'succubi'). Again, of course, there is a watershed mode of thinking here, with the poem offering up its waterway as a primary route through the landscape. But the watershed itself is overrun, as knotweed and the 'hardly less alien spruce' appear to dominate any indigenous vegetation – to the extent that they provide, respectively, both foreground and background to the picture which Bidgood creates.[49]

* * *

Writing about the tradition of the *bardd gwlad* (folk poet) in Welsh-language poetry, W. Rhys Nicholas suggests that 'the term *bardd gwlad* means exactly what it says – a poet in a rural community, reflecting the character of his society, its personalities, and its varied activities, its crafts and its diverse interests'.[50] Later in the same volume, discussing the 1932 volume *Pitar Puw a'i Berthynasau* by Thomas Jones, Nicholas emphasizes the social role of the folk poet when he states that 'The life of the whole community is reflected [in such work …]. It is the poetry of fellowship and neighbourliness' (p. 51). Such social concerns find a very significant echo in Bidgood's poetry. Indeed, this is what Jeremy Hooker seems to acknowledge when he argues that 'the *idea* of the *bardd gwlad* … is still powerful for some English-language poets in Wales' – an idea that he then links specifically to Bidgood.[51] Admittedly, one must not pursue this parallel too far. Wholly unlike the *bardd gwlad*, Bidgood clearly sees her writing as mediating to a wider world the area in which she has settled: she is on record as saying that 'I've always felt that however inadequate I might be as a voice for mid-Wales, it was up to me to speak, all the more because I was an incomer.'[52] Indeed, that incomer status also marks her off from the Welsh-language folk poets: she is an outsider, a 'latecomer' (as 'All Souls" has it), even an anthropologist collecting local stories (as she seems to be in 'Drinking Stone').[53] Finally, of course, her geographical vision goes further afield than her immediate locality; for example, the title sequence of *Singing to Wolves* is rooted in the area of three interconnected waterways on the Wales–England border (Afon Honddu, River Monnow and Escley Brook).[54] As such, it might be easier to align her work more generally with the Welsh-language tradition of *canu bro* (poetry of place). Indeed, her participation in the broad English-language traditions of place-centred poetry – which, according to Jonathan Bate, first displayed its modern form in the work of William Wordsworth – must also be recognized.[55]

However, in her poetry that deals with life around Abergwesyn and Llanwrtyd Wells, as much of what I have written so far should indicate, Bidgood echoes the idea of the *bardd gwlad* to the extent that she is emphatically writing poems of *a community in its place*. This is perhaps especially the case in a piece such as 'Valley-before-Night', with its response to living individuals, to specific landmarks (houses, farms, river, bridge, confluence of waterways) and to tales of past inhabitants. But it also builds up over the body of Bidgood's work, through the variety of narratives that centre on particular places (often ruins, such as in 'Hawthorn at Digiff') and their inhabitants, or on local tales. Thus, for example, in 'Drinking Stone' (from *The Print of Miracle*), the poet-speaker is told the story of the stone 'that each midsummer cockcrow / goes thirsty down to the stream', whilst the teller of the tale is sharply characterized by his careful laughter, which is given 'to show I [the poet-speaker as hearer] may laugh, to say / you are sure I must mock / at such old childishness'.[56] A. M. Allchin comments that such moments may suggest 'half-forgotten memories of pre-Christian rites and attitudes'.[57] Just as important, however, is the point that Bidgood's recounting of both tale and teller is a way of constructing the discourse of her locality – of 'reflecting the character of [her] society', as W. Rhys Nicholas's description of the *bardd gwlad* has it.[58] Moreover, in a telling passage at the very end of *Parishes of the Buzzard*, Bidgood writes this:

> In Abergwesyn, with its stories, its ruins, its will to go on living, 'then' marches only a shadow-pace behind 'now'. And 'to come'? The marks on hillside and valley-floor of centuries of home-building, fencing, pasturing, digging, draining, roadmaking, ploughing, growing, storing, should bring hope as well as regret, speaking as they do not only of all that is gone, but of the land's potential, and of the achievement and ever-renewed vitality of man.[59]

Such future-directed thinking again echoes the work of the *bardd gwlad* which, in the analysis of D. J. Roberts, writing about Alun Cilie, 'is an expression of the life of a whole community, to entertain *and strengthen it*'.[60] In other words, that which is told is not just for the present; it is also directed towards the vitality of the community in the future (the urge to 'strengthen it', in Roberts's terms). For Bidgood, this is the importance of acknowledging 'the land's potential' that she observes in *Parishes of the Buzzard*; it is an element of that tendency to bring 'life out of death' which Jeremy Hooker sees repeatedly in her work.[61] Thus, analysing the early poem 'Stone' – which declares that 'Stone proclaims life, affirms a future / by virtue of so many pasts' – Hooker suggests that Bidgood's work has 'a quiet, strong faith in the future'.[62] Or, as Bidgood puts it in 'Hennant' – the eponymous house being another ruin in the Irfon valley, just upstream from Abergwesyn:

> Stones are memorials, but in their disarray
> and littleness against green wilderness
> speak of beginnings ...[63]

In this context, each of Bidgood's ruins also speaks of what may be built and made again within the green desert of remote mid Wales.

However, Bidgood's poetic self-presentation as 'latecomer' recalls that she has made a choice to situate herself in the Abergwesyn area; it is not a world, as it would be for the *bardd gwlad*, to which she is native. Hers is, effectively, a liminal consciousness: as an incomer who has become deeply rooted in her chosen place, she is what might be called an 'outsider-native'. In *Writing for an Endangered World*, Lawrence Buell discusses the idea of 'reinhabitation' – a notion which has grown up within environmentalist circles to describe a specific method of committing oneself to a place. As Buell explains, 'aspiring reinhabitors' explicitly dedicate themselves to the environmental and cultural 'understanding and restoration' of a particular location, as an integral part of which process they must also '(re)learn what it means to be "native" to [that] place'. Reinhabitation is thus a 'long-term reciprocal engagement with a place's human and nonhuman environments' in which one 'welcomes the prospect of one's identity being molded by this encounter'. Moreover, as Buell makes clear, this is not 'a solitary quest'; rather, it 'must also involve participation in community both with fellow inhabitants in the present and with past generations, through absorption of history and legend'.[64] As the bulk of my analysis here should indicate, the discourse that Bidgood creates in her poetry – including the way in which it echoes aspects of the Welsh-language tradition of the folk poet – is just such a long-term engagement with the people (past and present) and narratives of mid Wales. Moreover, as both *Parishes of the Buzzard* and 'Hennant' suggest, Bidgood at least *imagines* a potential future strengthening of the area in which she lives – that 'restoration' of place to which 'aspiring reinhabitors' are dedicated. However, reinhabitation is perhaps most simply defined as 'learning to live-in-place in an area that has been disrupted and injured through past exploitation'.[65] For Bidgood, poetry constitutes a discursive participation in an environment – both of wall-makers and watersheds – that she presents as having been afflicted by activities such as coniferization ('the forest, / darkly, sourly flourishing'[66]) and the gradual loss of inhabitants (figured by the repeated ruins which appear in her work). In this sense, Bidgood's poetry of the Abergwesyn area is very much an act of reinhabitation: it is an artwork of being-in-place, amongst the conifers and the ruins; it is a vision of what grows and dies and what may grow back again in 'the last vast emptiness at the heart of Wales'.[67]

6

Robert Minhinnick:
From Pen-y-fai to Iraq

One of the focal points of Robert Minhinnick's poetic geography is a former mansion near his childhood village of Pen-y-fai in the historic county of Glamorgan. In a 1997 interview with Sam Adams, Minhinnick explained his interest in:

> a house quite close to the village where I was born, called Cwrt (Court) Colman, which I have written about for many years. It was a manor house but today it is a hotel, rather a sad and run-down hotel, and the grounds are no longer well-kept, but a lot of people in the village worked in the grounds or in the house itself, as gardeners, chauffeurs, nurserymen, domestics of one kind and another. There was a long history of people doffing their caps to the landowner, to the local gentry, but that was part of life in the community. I agree that was not common in south Wales where there were not many houses of this kind. My grandfather worked as a gardener on the estate and my mother and her sister were also employed there. I was brought up in a house on the edge of the estate and for a long time when I was a boy it was great fun to trespass on the grounds. I have always written about what I know and part of what I know is the estate.[1]

The experience of trespass that is referred to here is explored in Minhinnick's early poem 'The Gamekeeper'.[2] Recalling childhood incursions onto Cwrt Colman land, the poem's speaker remembers running from the 'English gamekeeper', 'leaving my name / Slashed white in bark' for the estate official to find. By carving his name onto an estate tree in this fashion, the youthful speaker declares that he has breached an environment that is explicitly defended against him – the poem recalls the gamekeeper's 'dogs unleashed in full-throated // Pursuit of our fleeing gang'. This self-inscription 'in bark' is thus not an act of vandalism so much as the display of a youthful urge to work against the symbolism of power and ownership which the land of the estate represents. As Sharon Zukin argues in her book *Landscapes of Power*, 'Themes of power, coercion, and collective resistance shape landscape as a social microcosm.'[3] Thus she draws attention to the significance of:

> the entire panorama that we see: both the landscape of the powerful [her eponymous 'landscapes of power'] – cathedrals, factories, and skyscrapers – and the subordinate, resistant, or expressive vernacular of the powerless – village chapels, shantytowns, and tenements. (p. 16)

Although reduced to a binary opposition at this point (between 'powerful' and 'powerless'), Zukin's general argument is clear: physical landscapes manifest the structures of social, economic and political power. Indeed, what Zukin calls 'landscapes of power' – high-status environments constructed by socio-economic elites – not only express power, they are also active forces in its continued assertion. As Martin Jones, Rhys Jones and Michael Woods explain, 'A landscape of power operates as a political device because it reminds people of who is in charge, or of what the dominant ideology or philosophy is.'[4] In 'The Gamekeeper', then, by proclaiming an incursion into the protected space of landed power, the knifed name on the estate tree is an act of resistance to just such an environmental declaration of 'who is in charge'. In the years of Minhinnick's early youth (the period to which 'The Gamekeeper' in part looks back), authority at Cwrt Colman was in the hands of the Llewellyn family – a Welsh gentry family, descended from indigenous farming stock, who had owned the estate since the first half of the nineteenth century.[5] However, in the poem's focus on an explicitly English estate official rather than on the gentry family itself, the incursions of the speaker and his gang onto Cwrt Colman land in 'The Gamekeeper' suggest a contest between local Welsh population and imported English authority figure, as well as an insurgent village spirit (albeit a childish, playful one) to set against that doffing of the cap to which Minhinnick refers in the interview. For Minhinnick, in other words, the physical environment of his south Wales landscape appears precisely as what Sharon Zukin calls a 'social microcosm', richly expressive of the historic distribution and divisions of social power in the area around Pen-y-fai.

Part of the poem's point, however, is that although as an adult the speaker continues to go uninvited onto estate land – indeed, he presents himself as nothing less than a looter of its flora ('These days I walk the same estate / Looting its creamy elderflower') – much of the excitement of trespass has now passed:

> That old man died and I
> Grew up, and trespassing is not the same
> Without his narrow shadow stooping
> Over me, his tweeds the colour of beechshade
>
> The perfect camouflage.

Without the thrill of a specific and personalized contest, the divisions of power in the landscape apparently become a much less vital affair; as the speaker puts it, in the relative calm of adult trespass, 'I miss / The danger, the fright as hot as / Nettlerash'. However, there is more to this shift in the speaker's emotional response to landscape than just the loss of a personal contest: the absence of the gamekeeper also suggests those larger changes which lie silently behind the poem. The Llewellyn family sold the Cwrt Colman estate in 1961, thus removing the long-standing gentry from the manor – a moment which Minhinnick recalls in the poem 'The Boathouse':[6]

> It's finished now. The whole place
> Closed down. Employment's found outside
> The creamery, the vinery and grange
> Farm that fed inherited wealth ...
>
> Suddenly everyone
> Had fallen asleep – nurserymen,
> Chauffeurs, kitchenmaids – the hour
> Went unstuck. (p. 25)

The adult speaker of 'The Gamekeeper' is thus no longer walking on land which encapsulates, as a living present, the social distinction between gentry estate and lower-class village. Instead, as 'The Boathouse' puts it, in the noise of removal vans and 'the barking of the country / Auctioneers', what was heard was 'A population slamming doors on a way of life' (p. 26) – in the aftermath of which the sharp division has vanished between 'The village men in feudal grouping, / Craftsmen of the estate' and the 'gentleman' whom the speaker's mother greets as he passes. In short, the speaker's changed reaction to place in 'The Gamekeeper' points towards those alterations in the social signif-icance of estate land about which 'The Boathouse' provides more explicit information. Or, to put it a different way, Minhinnick's poetic is delicately responsive to the historical shifts that have taken place in the socio-environmental operation of his south Wales landscape. At the same time, of course, Minhinnick is also in significant dialogue with a history of thoroughly *literary* landscapes in the sense that 'The Boathouse' can be seen as a wry closing up of the country house poem.

However much the Cwrt Colman estate may have a lesser emotional impact for speakers in Minhinnick's poetic present, when attention is on the past – the time of the poet-speaker's childhood and before – the estate is emphatically rendered as a primary social division in Welsh space, writing gentry power unequivocally into the landscape. Thus, in one such retrospective piece, the later poem 'Daisy at the Court',[7] to be in estate space is to be in what one of the workers (Ivor) calls a 'palace' which 'hard times don't touch' (p. 22) – this situation being symbolized by the luxury of 'a nest // Of blond apricots' (pp. 21–2) which Ivor holds in his hands. Indeed, in the early poem 'The Diary',[8] the production of such fruit is a key motif of the estate as a landscape of power (to adopt Zukin's terminology), with the speaker recounting how his grandfather had worked in:

> the steamy vinery
>
> And peach-house on a magistrate's
> Estate, your privilege
> To pick the ripened fruit
> And preserve its perfection,
> Your unfamiliar winter sweat
>
> Amidst a harvest of rare
> Odours ... (p. 38)

Vinery and peach-house – and the orangery that the poem goes on to mention – are not merely places of luxury fruit production. They are also intensely symbolic, with the poem suggesting that landed power even has the capacity to override the seasons, in the image of that 'unfamiliar winter sweat' which his hothouse work gives to the speaker's grandfather. Indeed, this winter warmth on the estate is contrasted sharply with the harsh environmental conditions outside in the village. Reading his grandfather's diary, the speaker declares that:

> it is hard
> To read of this prized work
>
> Then turn the page and find
> Your food was soup-kitchen
> Charity, your warmth the broken

Coals small boys smuggled
From the policed pits.

Whereas warmth on the estate is available to fruit – to the extent that it
will even raise a sweat in winter – in the village it is barely available to
human beings. Capacity to transcend ambient environmental condi-
tions is thus a significant marker of power – or lack of it. As such it is
important that Minhinnick describes the fruit his grandfather produced
on the estate as 'forbidden tastes / Your family must have craved / In
those thin times': for those beyond the estate, these symbols of control
over one's environment are emphatically denied (literally 'forbidden').
As Linden Peach has pointed out, discussing the poem 'J.P.' – another
early piece – Minhinnick is manifestly a poet who has 'a powerful sense
of how politics, ideology, and power relations are inscribed into "the
apparent [sic: apparently] innocent spatiality of social life"'.[9] Peach is
here quoting Edward Soja,[10] whose argument at the beginning of his
influential 1989 volume *Postmodern Geographies* is that a sense of
history has for too long been dominant in 'the critical consciousness of
modern social theory'.[11] What Soja wishes to do is to rebalance the
historical element of sociological understanding with an awareness of
the 'significance of space', thus creating 'a more flexible and balanced
critical theory that re-entwines the making of history with the social
production of space' (p. 11). For Minhinnick, as my analysis has hope-
fully suggested, the geographical politics of estate land are emphatically
caught up with particular temporal moments: 'The Diary' observes how
exclusion from the produce of the estate must have been especially hard
in what the poem calls 'those thin times', whilst both 'The Gamekeeper'
and 'The Boathouse' suggest the way in which the geographical signifi-
cance of a particular place shifts over time. In short, Minhinnick's
poetry combines temporal and spatial thinking in just the sort of way
that seems to interest Soja.

However, while Peach's use of Soja is valuable in terms of
Minhinnick's overall poetic, his interpretation of 'J.P.' itself is question-
able. The premise of this poem is another youthful incursion onto Cwrt
Colman land, with the trespassing gang of village boys being caught by
the 'jealous landowner' (the JP of the title).[12] As in 'The Gamekeeper',
it is clear that the trespass is an attempt to work against the vested inter-
ests of historic landownership, with the speaker declaring:

Llangewydd's
Square mile of history, its cwms and

> Slow decaying farms, the blaze of lawn about
> The magistrate's estate, was an inheritance
> We claimed.

In short, and in the terms set up by Sharon Zukin, this is an attempt to turn a landscape of power into 'vernacular' space – to reclaim it on behalf of those outside the socio-economic elites. Space, to put it another way, becomes explicitly contested here. But Peach too readily rushes to the conclusion that there is a straightforward colonialist dimension at play in the poem, with what he calls the 'entrenched English landowner' set against the village boys. He is right to draw a connection between the image of the landowner's panama – an archetype, perhaps, of British empire – and the idea of colonization.[13] But simply to assume that the landowner is English is an error,[14] and the poem makes no such direct connection: in this sense, 'J.P.' is different from 'The Gamekeeper' where the authority figure is explicitly identified as English. Admittedly, in 'J.P.' there is a hint of British imperial identity in the poem's construction of the 'tiny octogenarian' magistrate. But this should not be understood as automatically suggesting *Englishness*. As Kirsti Bohata has indicated, there has been clear Welsh involvement in the British empire even if 'the position of Wales within the British Empire and the United Kingdom was not, and is not, coterminous with that of England'.[15] Or to put it another way, as Bohata makes clear, it is 'entirely inadequate and thoroughly misleading' to assume that British imperial associations are incompatible with the Welsh. Thus, as the representative of that indigenous gentry family which was associated with Cwrt Colman in the period of Minhinnick's boyhood, it is entirely appropriate to see the poem's landowner, not as English, but as Welsh.[16] From such a perspective, any colonization taking place in 'J.P.' is substantially internal – in other words, it is to do with the historic operation of Welsh power over Welsh space on the part of what 'The Boathouse' calls 'inherited wealth'. In this sense, the action of the trespassing boys in 'J.P.' is a spatial attack on the history of economic divisions between Welsh people within Wales. Thus, what the poem calls the boys' 'tribal defiance' of the landowner is less an echo of 'a mythologized past in which the Welsh tried to resist the English invasion', as Linden Peach has it,[17] than a recognition of the boys' shared class difference from that of the eponymous magistrate.[18]

* * *

Minhinnick's Pen-y-fai poetry is not, of course, all bound up with what one might call the 'power landscape' of the Cwrt Colman estate. Other Pen-y-fai spaces are important to him, too – ones that are arguably vernacular (non-elite) in character – such as the stream called Nant Ffornwg and an old mill called Felingwcw, which Minhinnick renders as Cwrt-y-felin.[19] 'The Swimming Lesson', in 1994's collection *Hey Fatman*,[20] contrasts the boyhood experience of school swimming lessons – which the terrified and shamed speaker sits out 'in tropic changing rooms' – with his youthful explorations of the Ffornwg, in which the non-swimming speaker wades 'Waist-deep in that cold current' (p. 59). Crucially, the Ffornwg seems to be beyond the human authority structures that define the swimming pool, whose *brutalising chlorine* (to use the poem's terms) can only be escaped by means of 'a forged letter' (p. 59). By contrast, the Ffornwg is a place of contented discovery, where the speaker can 'happily trawl' the water for dragonfly larvae and for 'minnows thin as pine-needles', not even fearful of how 'a simple slip // Could dunk this non-swimmer / … Under the Ffornwg's dark plumage of weed, / And keep him there until the light went out' (p. 59). However, even though the Ffornwg may thus be a vernacular space, free from the human authority figures of either the school swimming lesson or the Cwrt Colman estate (the magistrate, the gamekeeper), Minhinnick seems unwilling to let it be free of authority structures entirely: as the poem indicates, his wading through the waters of the Ffornwg constitutes 'A homage paid to a primitive god' (p. 60). In a moment which recalls the sacred significance of water for ancient Celtic cultures,[21] the Ffornwg becomes a sort of religious space, with the poem gesturing towards the idea of the stream as a kind of elemental deity – a water god, effectively – in a way which is echoed by Minhinnick's comment in a later interview that 'I believe in the sacred and that it exists in the natural world.'[22] Such a move, moreover, is also a crucial means of escape from the reach of the estate, in the sense that it defines the stream not in terms of the economic landscape of Cwrt Colman, but as an environment which is subject to an entirely different model of authority (a spiritual one). As such, Minhinnick's Pen-y-fai landscapes constitute a struggle over power, not merely in the sense of who controls the land itself – the sense in which, as 'J.P.' puts it, 'Llangewydd's / Square mile of history … // was an inheritance / We claimed' – but also in terms of the very *model* of authority to which those struggles for control are subject.

The vernacular landscapes of Minhinnick's Pen-y-fai are, however, important for more than merely their involvement in contests of power.

It is significant, for example, that in the early poem 'Eels at Night',[23] the environment of the Ffornwg is a place in which the division between the human and the non-human seems to blur. Thinking which is characterized by a human/nature dualism – in which humanity is seen as distinct from the non-human environment – is a focus of particular attack for certain strands of environmentalist criticism. As environmentalist philosopher Val Plumwood explains, human/nature dualism 'situates human life outside and above an inferiorised and manipulable nature',[24] and she goes on to argue that:

> Rationalism and human/nature dualism have helped create ideals of culture and human identity that promote human distance from, control of and ruthlessness towards the sphere of nature as the Other, while minimising non-human claims to the earth and to elements of mind, reason and ethical consideration. (p. 4)

Thus, Plumwood advocates the need to overturn the consequent 'weakened sense of the reality of our embeddedness in nature' (p. 97) in order to 'establish dialogical and carefully negotiated relationships with our planetary partners of the sort that could enable us to survive in the long-term' (p. 167). Although clearly not in the business of advancing an explicit philosophical argument of the sort that Plumwood is attempting, Minhinnick's poem dramatizes one sort of movement towards a closing of the human/nature gap when the speaker, having plunged his hand into the Ffornwg's 'strange night turbulence of eels', finds himself feeling 'the slippery texture of congealing eels / Like a wound opened in myself, our common skin'. Not only does the texture of the eels seem to breach the speaker's sense of his own boundary as a single being, but – perhaps more significantly – his opening up to the non-human results in a 'common skin' between the human and what Minhinnick calls 'creatures'.[25] It is true that this opening up is construed in terms of 'wound'. But the movement of the second line quoted above seems to heal the wound into the new 'common skin' of a human/non-human combination. This moment of radically anti-dualist thinking is merely emphasized by the final stanza of the poem:

> Get an eel in the fist they say, and that's money,
> But the cold coin that I grasp now surely buys
> More than is guessable, but something like knowledge
> Of a life joined with mine, gnashing in blood's long pod,
> And a joint affirmation of the hollow flesh.

The double use of the concept of *joining*, over the poem's final two lines, indicates the direction of Minhinnick's environmental thinking here: the human/nature gap is dramatically bridged by an awareness of shared fleshliness. Indeed, Minhinnick's use of such terminology (joining, commonality) offers a striking parallel with Plumwood's terminology of partnership. However, the grasped eel is manifestly not an image of the 'dialogical and carefully negotiated relationships' with non-human partners that Plumwood is advocating. In this sense, Minhinnick's poetic shows both the sheer difficulty of moving away from any notion of what Plumwood calls 'human-self enclosure and human-centredness' and an emotional complexity which supports his statement that 'I would never write a purely "green" poem that is preacherly or evangelical, where the point is not the poem but the message.'[26] So it is perhaps not surprising to find that the poem is also anxious about the non-human itself, with the speaker displaying a profound sense of ecophobia – a fear, in other words, of the non-human. Thus, the poem's second stanza observes that:

> The terror of eels is their writhing fleece, –
> The corpse that Ffornwg shreds with slow razors.

Not only does the speaker suggest a basic dread of the stream's non-human inhabitants in the notion of the 'terror' that the eels generate, but the second line here turns the non-human environment of the stream itself into a scene of grim mutilation. Indeed, the same sort of fear manifests itself in 'Sap', another Nant Ffornwg poem from Minhinnick's first collection.[27] In 'Sap', the speaker observes the 'darkest passage' of the stream as 'A black stillwater, treacherous / Beneath a sheen of scum'. In a moment which is interestingly congruent with the association between the Ffornwg and the sacred that 'The Swimming Lesson' suggests (the experience of the sacred potentially being a matter of awe and terror), the non-human is clearly not something that may be particularly safely embraced. Moreover, in the subsequent image of a trout which rises from the Ffornwg with 'Its lean sides gleaming like / A knife', the non-human world is emphatically a thing to be approached with considerable caution. In short, there is no sense that the non-human with which the human joins in 'Eels at Night' is some kind of pastoral idyll – a point which becomes particularly clear in one of Minhinnick's poems about Felingwcw. Although beginning with an observation of a 'trench in the bedrock / Ablaze with elder's potassium- / Coloured fruit', the poem's conclusion concentrates on the 'dry midden earth':[28]

> All that survives is what people
> Disregard,
>
> The rubbish
> Of their lives an eloquent spore.

In a piece that is significantly called 'The Midden', the earth itself becomes a rubbish tip – not with any of that sense of pollution which troubles Ruth Bidgood's notion of her environmental role in 'Legacy', but rather with the suggestion that such littering is nothing less than the history of human activity.

* * *

The midden at Felingwcw provides an important link with Minhinnick's second major Welsh environmental locale – the south Wales coast near Porthcawl. Indeed, the word *midden* itself is significantly repeated in the final poem of the sequence 'The Resort', from 1985's *The Dinosaur Park*, in which the speaker, 'out on the sands, the very tip of Wales' (an apparent reference to Kenfig Sands, just to the north of Porthcawl), proclaims:

> Our culture has its midden on the sands.
> The bottles lie around the beach like empty
> Chrysalids, sea-holly holds the strewn plastics
> In a green pincer. ('On the Sands'[29])

Minhinnick's south Wales coastline is quite often littered in this fashion. Thus, 'Dawn' (from the Porthcawl sequence 'Fairground Music' in 1989's *The Looters*) observes a man who 'caresses / The beach' with a metal detector, finding 'pennies / And ruptured cans', whilst the sand displays a 'fine blue plastic / Like the skin of some creature'.[30] Similarly, in 'The Inheritors' (the first poem of '*from* A History of Dunraven' in *Hey Fatman*), the speaker remarks 'all the humdrum // Plastics of the shore',[31] and 'Questions of the Woman Who Fell' (in 2002's *After the Hurricane*) offers the witty observation of:

> Hellenic
> Ovenstick
> And an aerosol from Japan.
> We have to learn the tide's lesson:
> Avoid the literal.
> Live the littoral.[32]

In the pun which underpins both 'literal' and 'littoral', 'litter' is, it seems, inescapable. But what is perhaps most striking about Minhinnick's littered south Wales coast is the way in which it constitutes another form of gap-closing between human and non-human. Thus, the observation of a physical closeness in the tight embrace between plastics and sea-holly that I quoted a moment ago is extended by the metaphorical rendition of the human-made as natural (bottles as chrysalids in 'On the Sands'; plastic as creaturely skin in 'Dawn') and of the natural as human-made – this latter approach being apparent in the sequence 'The Resort', which observes 'An industrial sunset oiling the sea' and 'small rockpools [which] / Glitter like a switchboard'.[33] There is, at such moments, manifestly a *thinking together* of the human and the non-human. The upshot, however, is hardly Val Plumwood's called-for new awareness of human 'embeddedness in nature' for the sake of planetary survival.[34] Rather, Minhinnick's images in these poems seem far more to do with a sense that the human is now so far extended into the natural that to think of the two as distinct is simply absurd. Dualism, in short, is already overcome: the Porthcawl funfair 'has its neon midsummer'[35] – the seasons themselves having been caught up in human kitsch – whilst the 'Green Winged Orchid' of 'A Welshman's Flora' proclaims:

> Sometimes I hear the fairground at night,
> All fire and wheels and acid house,
> The videos yammering in the caravans,
> And it feels as if they're with me here,
> The Ripper, Our Shirl and Godzilla
> All trampling over the dunes.[36]

In what emerges as a kind of post-natural Wales, the human appears to be inescapable. As Minhinnick himself puts it in the poem 'Cwm y Gaer' (from the sequence 'On the Headland'):

> And everywhere the human print
> And everywhere the absence of humanity.[37]

Even where humanity is absent, the 'human print' is 'everywhere'. Nature itself, it seems, is lost to the category of the natural.[38] In other words, in these coastal poems, Minhinnick's disruption of human/ nature dualism sees nature effectively subsumed into the realm of the human – the direct opposite of Val Plumwood's model of environmentalist restoration, in which the disruption of dualism is intended to embed humanity more deeply into the natural.

Given this tendency, it is unsurprising that Minhinnick's south Wales coast is, in a more general way, persistently a place of varied human activity. In his earliest work, for example, the coastal area is a locus for

heavy industrial labour. Indeed, the very first poem of his first collec-
tion deals with ship-breaking near Cardiff, with the speaker observing
how:

> Below me in the littered dunes
> Are men attacking wreckage
> With cutting-gear of blue steel. ('Old Ships'[39])

Indeed, it is interesting to note that, in this very early poem, Minhinnick
is already thinking the natural in human terms, with the beach manifest
as 'a grey field / Quilted with burnt upholstering' (p. 12) – a far earlier
instance of that 'hybrid of the natural and the unnatural' which Ian
Gregson first identifies in 'The Hot-House' (from 1989's *The Looters*).[40]
The Cardiff focus does not continue into Minhinnick's later poetry,
which shifts its coastal concerns to the Porthcawl area. But the sense of
coast as a primary theatre of human activity is certainly sustained.
Thus, for example, '*from* A History of Dunraven' (a sequence in 1994's
Hey Fatman) charts the area of Dunraven Bay in terms of the shifting
human use of Welsh land.[41] The opening poem ('The Inheritors')
considers 'the first ones' in their coastal hill fort (on the headland of
Trwyn y Witch), and contemplates the precarious conditions experi-
enced by the area's earliest human inhabitants:

> There's not a wall, not a ditch
> You might point at and say,
>
> Here they persevered, the first ones
> In a desperate place, a cliff edge
>
> Mauve with sea-kale ...[42]

Alongside these ancient people are the contemporary 'Inheritors' of the
poem's title who, having driven up to the headland, commit suicide in
their burning car, with 'The tape turned up to max'. The rest of the
sequence suggests similar social counterpoints. The second poem recalls
a scullery-maid's painful work in the ice tower of the now-destroyed
nineteenth-century mansion (Dunraven Castle), whilst the third remem-
bers 'the king himself' sporting in 'some inscrutable pool' in the bay
(p. 34). Similarly, the fifth poem, 'A Kind of Jericho', observes shifts of
power actually taking place, with the inhabitants of the mansion
moving out, the house being handed over to 'A team of quarrymen'
who arrange its demolition, and (finally) the unnamed 'some' who
'picked for years over / The moraines of plaster the explosions built'
(pp. 36 and 37). Although Minhinnick is entirely aware of the non-

human context in which Dunraven Bay exists – he observes, for
example, the house 'quoined / On a promontory above an ocean /
Chalked by porpoises' ('A Kind of Jericho', p. 37) – his primary atten-
tion is on the way in which the ownership and use of this particular
Welsh place has been divided between different social groups and has
shifted from one human usage to another. This is, in short, history as
changing social control over land.

One of Minhinnick's other primary social spaces on the south Wales
coast is the Porthcawl funfair. The important sequence 'Fairground
Music' (from *The Looters*) is analysed by Linden Peach in terms of the
way in which the fairground itself represents the 'instantaneous nature
of postmodern society'. Commenting specifically on the ninth poem of
the sequence, 'Madam Zeena', Peach observes how 'The comparison to
a fast-food queue of the people waiting outside the palmist suggests not
only the commodification of individual futures but the postindustrial
trend toward instant gratification.'[43] Quick thrills are indeed one key
signature of Minhinnick's funfair – from the sexual abuse perpetrated
by the teacher in 'Double English' who took two pupils to the fair and,
in the darkness of the ghost train, 'put his hand on the knee / Of one of
the boys',[44] to the easy consumables of fairground rides in which chil-
dren ride 'a yellow plastic train' ('Around the World', p. 44) or the bigger
machinery of the Wheel of Fate which 'crashes' its riders downwards,
making the whole town resemble 'a film reeled back / As we rush
towards the ground' ('From the Summit', p. 51). Indeed, in this closing
image of the whole sequence, the tendency in Minhinnick's coastal
poetry to imagine the denaturing of nature is given a new twist: the
physical world is turned into an image of itself, in a movement which
recalls Jean Baudrillard's notion of the triumph of image over reality in
the era of postmodernity.[45] However, Peach lets the rhetoric of such
postmodern thinking run away with him when he suggests that the
ticket-seller in 'Ghost Train' is in a condition of 'information overload'
because she is sitting in a glass hutch with a paperback novel and, as the
poem puts it, 'headphones pulled down tight'.[46] Peach is quite right to
observe the way in which this suggests her existence within a media-
dominated world; but a book and music (even through headphones) do
not together constitute information *overload*. Far more appropriate is
Jonathan Bate's sense of the way in which, in a media-driven culture,
our ability to hear the non-human world may be drowned out by our
attention to what he calls the 'ubiquitous susurrus of cyberspace'.[47] The
girl in the ticket booth is manifestly cut off from the non-human in this

way, set apart even from the humanized natural which makes up so much of Minhinnick's south Wales coast.

Such divorce between human and non-human is, however, not especially common in Minhinnick's work. As Ian Gregson argues, Minhinnick is aware of postmodern ideas about simulation and the loss of the real whilst retaining an 'anti-postmodernist insistence on underlying realities'.[48] Far more persistent is Minhinnick's concern with rendering the non-human world as thoroughly colonized by either human activity or by a profoundly humanizing perspective. In this sense, Minhinnick's most disturbing poem is perhaps the recent piece 'The Orchids at Cwm y Gaer' – the fourth poem in 2002's *After the Hurricane* – which understands the natural in terms of the fuel rods in a nuclear reactor. Thus the speaker observes the eponymous orchids and declares:

> Once the superstitious thought
> It was Christ's blood that mottled the leaves,
> But now it's as easy to suppose
> That these eruptions, under a shadow's anglepoise,
> Are uranium rods
> Broken through from the terrible core.[49]

Indeed, in an updated echo of the ecophobia which I suggested was apparent in his early poetry, Minhinnick concludes the poem by opening up to the natural only to expect it to destroy him:

> So I open my hands to the orchids at Cwm y Gaer
> And count each breath.
> How long before the welts appear?
> How long before the cradle of nightsweats,
> Or that deep, enriched delirium, dark as dew?

Perhaps just as important, however, is the way in which this poem suggests a significant interaction between Welsh space and the wider world. The first piece in the same collection, the sequence 'Twenty-Five Laments for Iraq', is also concerned with radioactivity, considering the consequences of the first Gulf War (1990–1) and noting how it will be:

> Four billion years
> Until the uranium
> That was spilled at Ur
> Unmakes itself.
> Easier to wait for the sun to die. (p. 10)

As Ian Gregson appropriately observes, there appears to be a fairly clear environmentalist rebuke here,[50] especially when twinned with earlier lines from the same sequence which observe how:

> These soldiers will not marry.
> They are betrothed already
> To the daughters of uranium. (p. 7)

What seems to drive Minhinnick's anger at this point – an anger which, interestingly, has not generally been apparent in his rendition of human intrusion into non-human space – is the outrage of short-term techno-logical use with tragic human and impossibly long environmental consequences.[51] However, to bring this Iraq-rooted radioactive perspec-tive back to Wales, as Minhinnick does in 'The Orchids at Cwm y Gaer', is to implicate Welsh space within a global discourse that is indicative of what Gregson calls 'the policing of a world order domin-ated by the West'.[52] It is within this context that the recent poem 'The Bombing of Baghdad as Seen From an Electrical Goods Shop' func-tions, with the speaker rooted in Porthcawl, but imaginatively and visually linked to Baghdad. Thus, addressing his Iraqi friend Nazaar, the poem's speaker declares:

> And I suppose that you're at home,
> Because where else is there to be on a night like this,
> Listening to the Cruise missiles, the only
> Traffic out tonight on Palestine Street,
> While here in the window of Edwards Electrical
> Your city in the tracers' glow
> Becomes a negative of itself.[53]

Here, then, Welsh space is seen in an international context – but not in any neutral way. Rather, the view of Baghdad from a Porthcawl street can never be free of the knowledge that the destruction visible on the television – and its resounding statement about Western desires to exer-cise territorial control over non-Western states – is something in which Wales is implicated, by association with British participation in recent hostilities with Iraq. So Ian Gregson is right to suggest that Minhinnick's earlier 'territorial anxieties' are 'writ much larger in these later poems'.[54] But, more than this, such later poems are also – and crucially – an attempt to write Wales into the often-violent narratives of global politics, in what constitutes the development of a strikingly trans-cultural poetic vision.[55]

7

Mike Jenkins:
Locating the Depredations of Power

In an interview with Wayne Burrows, published in *The New Welsh Review* in 1990, Mike Jenkins rejects the interviewer's attempt to define him as a poet who has 'placed [him]self firmly in a very small camp of urban poets in Wales'. Jenkins's response is to suggest that he is far more appropriately understood as a writer who inhabits a 'borderland', both physically and poetically:

> I live on the edge of the rural and urban: my house, my village [Heolgerrig], and indeed Merthyr itself. A poem like 'An Escape' begins with the urban situation but ends with the possibility of release in the rural setting nearby. That's where I stand...[1]

Indeed, in a later conversation with David Lloyd, Jenkins refers to the previous interview with apparent annoyance, saying that:

> I did an interview for *The New Welsh Review* recently, and the whole interview was my trying to knock down all these labels. You know, 'urban poet' – I resent that. And 'political poet', and all these things people want to stick on you to keep you in one category, keep you in a particular place. I'd like to break out of all of those categories.[2]

It is easy enough to understand Jenkins's frustration: although significantly associated with the town of Merthyr Tydfil, his poetic is emphatically not just urban, with one of his major imaginative locales being what he variously calls *the common land* or *the Waun*. Just to the south of his long-time home in Heolgerrig,[3] this area – referred to as Cwm Glo on both contemporary and early Ordnance Survey maps – is

a historically various but now rural space which is overlooked by
Mynydd Aberdâr to the west and which, in turn, overlooks Merthyr to
the east.[4] In a revealing article called 'Merthyr, my adopted home', the
common land is one of the first things that Jenkins considers:

> I've long referred to this land as 'the Waun', though my wife prefers the old
> title [the common land], clinging to its possibilities.
>
> The Waun has changed so little over the years even though it's been
> invaded on occasions by motorbikers, or set fire to frequently during
> parched summers. I've learnt its history both by observation (treading it
> carefully) and reading local history. One look at the OS map will tell you a
> good deal: the countless shafts and tips which contribute to its weird
> topography. Nature's doing a fine job reclaiming much of this, with abun-
> dant wild flowers which my wife and I used to collect and press savouring
> their poetic Welsh names like *Llysiau Taliesin* (mundane *Brooklime* in
> English). The oak tree in my garden was matched by many following the
> courses of small streams. I was fascinated by their trunks and branches so
> unique with age, so wise to the storms of centuries and such a contrast to
> the strutting larches lining the top of Aberdâr Mountain.[5]

Although acknowledging its involvement with an industrial past,
Jenkins here significantly constructs the Waun as a location of nature –
nature, that is, in the third of Kate Soper's senses ('the nature of imme-
diate experience and aesthetic appreciation'[6]) – a place where he might
find wild flowers, oak trees, streams. Moreover, although he goes on to
note the political history of the place in such figures as 'the Chartists
who'd meet in the open moorland',[7] reminiscences about his children
enjoying the Waun's countryside when they were toddlers also construct
this as a familial space – giving some justification to his sense that
simply labelling him as a political writer is insufficient.[8] Of course, the
Waun certainly emerges from this passage as a place of importantly
Welsh cultural experience, through the special pleasure Jenkins finds in
experiencing its flowers through their Welsh names. Indeed, his sense
that the Welsh names are both 'poetic' and something to savour (as
opposed to their 'mundane' English alternatives) more particularly
suggests that, for Jenkins, experiencing the Waun through the Welsh
language manifests it as a place of romance – one which, furthermore,
opens up the deep time of the Welsh mythic past (*Llysiau Taliesin* obvi-
ously recalling the legendary figure of Taliesin). In short, this
interestingly various response to ex-urban space suggests a writer whose
sensibility is patently too complex to reduce to simple categories.

The significance of the Cwm Glo area to Jenkins's imagination is
also, and more importantly, suggested by the title of his second poetry

collection, *The Common Land* (1981).[9] Indeed, for a poet who feels he
has to fight off the term 'urban poet', the front cover of this volume –
with its image of trees and grassy land – is strikingly suggestive of the
countryside. Far from thinking in terms of the built environment, the
five-section title poem begins with a sense of topography defined by
watercourses, in a manner which recollects Ruth Bidgood's engagement
with watershed poetics that I discussed in Chapter 5:

> Streams are the boundaries of the common land,
> the air above them scored with mosquitoes
> in a single-pitched treble
> over the talking drum of the water,
> flight-paths for martins, who swing down
> from telephone high-wires.[10]

This is a striking poetic rendition of what Lawrence Buell is suggesting
when he talks about bioregionalist thinking as a way of understanding
'human and nonhuman communities within a territory of limited magni-
tude whose borders may not be precisely specifiable but are conceived
in terms of "natural" rather than jurisdictional units'.[11] Jenkins's sense
of what constitutes the common land is bounded not by lines of formal-
ized administration, but by the perception of non-human landscape
features (the streams). At this point, the waterways of the Waun are
thus its boundaries and its lines of travel ('flight-paths for martins'),
whilst in the third stanza – the last of the initial section – the streams
literally become a governing image, having 'ambassadors' in the form of
dragonflies.

However – and again like Ruth Bidgood in her pervasive conscious-
ness of human work in rural space – Jenkins's common land is also
crucially the location of human action. The poem's second section pulls
attention away from non-human features to where 'A flat track of grass
maps the old tram-line' (p. 21), and concludes by asking:

> Where would you enter these drift-mines now?
> Grass, the colour of sand, has made its creeping progress
> over their slag, and there are black grazes
> where soil cannot form a scab. (p. 22)

As Jenkins suggests in his prose piece about Merthyr, the topography of
the Waun has been significantly constructed by former industrial work
('the countless shafts and tips which contribute to its weird topog-
raphy').[12] So this section of 'The Common Land' is in significant
dialogue with the poem's opening – thus recognizing physical landscapes

as negotiations between non-human features and the constructions of human impact. More than that, however, these lines also emphasize the *ongoing* environmental impact of mine workings that were already disused by the time the Ordnance Survey published its 1905 1:10,560 (six inches to the mile) maps of the area.[13] Jenkins's thinking here does not exactly constitute what Lawrence Buell terms 'toxic discourse'; it is, in other words, not really a discourse of 'individual or social panic' arising from the 'fear of environmental poisoning'.[14] But it does suggest an acute sense of long-term industrial scarring. Although grass has 'made its creeping progress' over the slag of drift-mines, and the landscape appears to have sealed up the mines themselves ('Where would you enter these drift-mines now?' the poem asks), these lines also make clear that there are 'black grazes / where soil *cannot* form a scab' (emphasis added). What this particular statement catches is a sense of permanent, unalterable change – of wounds on the body of the Waun that cannot be healed, and thus of spaces where natural processes of regeneration have seemingly failed. This is especially interesting in the context of the poem's first section, in which the non-human was dominant, governing – that which defined the place. By contrast, here we find 'grazes' where nature seemingly has no dominion. Where a 'fear of environmental poisoning' (in Buell's phrase) *does* come into this second section of 'The Common Land' is in the third stanza, which seemingly raises two ghosts from the area's industrial past:

> a child with his skin turned to rags by the blades
> of the dark, a woman coughing up phlegm
> like lumps that her lungs had cut. (p. 21)

Jeremy Hooker has observed that Jenkins is much concerned with the striving and suffering bodies of working people, and this is a case in point.[15] Although the poem does not explain their presence, these two figures function as striking human casualties of the area's 'drift-mines', both of whom display serious physical consequences as a result of their environmental context. Indeed, they raise the suggestion of what Lawrence Buell calls a 'poisoned community' – a location and its people devastated by industry.[16] However, it would still not be accurate to impute to Jenkins any sense of environmental *panic*. Rather, his figuring of the Waun creates the sort of 'complex' pastoral to which Leo Marx refers – a class of literary environmental response which, according to Marx, 'manage[s] to qualify, or call into question, or bring irony to bear against the illusion of peace and harmony in green pasture'.[17] Or, to put it another way, Jenkins displays a subtle awareness of that intermingling of technology, industry, economics and ostensibly pastoral space which the title of Marx's famous volume *The Machine in the Garden* so succinctly captures. The sort of 'borderland' which Jenkins inhabits here is, then, not merely to do with situating this poem in a vision of land between mountain and town; rather – and, I would argue, rather more importantly – it is to do with his discourse of that land itself as 'complex' pastoral.

The rest of 'The Common Land' continues to exemplify this complexity. The third section sees the landscape of 'slag-heaps', 'thick moor grass', 'fence and forest' run through by a 'young man' on a dirt bike, filling the land both with a 'blast of exhaust' and with his bike's noise. Indeed, as the poem observes, 'He is the hub of the scene now', with the importance of the streams that was suggested in the first section being fiercely contested as a result. As Martin Jones, Rhys Jones and Michael Woods put it very neatly, 'many subtly different "places" may be constructed as existing on the same territorial space'.[18] This sense of multiple space is precisely the condition of Jenkins's common land: territory that is dominated both by watershed and industrial impact is also a space for (air-polluting) play – whilst, in the next section, the Waun becomes a park in which people can escape from the constrictions of the built environments nearby to engage in sexual activity:

> Weekends and the sun transform the place
> to parkland. While cows' tails whip and ears twitch
> furiously independent of their solid bulk,
> so couples disappear into a ridge of shade,
>
> into coils of ivy and crawling bramble. (p. 22)

Drawing on the work of Henri Lefebvre, Dolores Hayden observes that 'Space is shaped for both economic production – barns, or mine shafts, or piers, or a factory – as well as for social reproduction – housing for the workers, managers, and owners, a store, a school, a church.'[19] Jenkins is acutely aware of such complex social shaping of space; as such, to Hayden's list, one might add from this poem the social spaces of park and playground, alongside the economic spaces of mines and slag heaps. Indeed, that this is a space of highly various identities is suggested in the above passage not only by the apparent disjunction between the 'solid bulk' of the cows and the furious, seemingly independent activity of their ears and tails, but also – and more importantly – by the hint of metamorphosis stalking the description of couples 'disappear[ing] into' shade, ivy and bramble. Moreover, in one final move of environmental multiplicity, Jenkins counters both the gentle pastoral of the opening section and the suggestion of ordered nature in the notion of 'parkland' through the poem's fifth and final section, which creates the common land as a place of violent, destructive weather:

> When storms come, the sky
> wants to uproot the whole hillside,
> the rain has sharp claws, and tufts of reed
> bow in submission. (p. 23)

Welsh space that has been both beautiful and ordered is here, in addition, full of the awe and terror of the sublime.

* * *

Although Jenkins's engagements with the Cwm Glo area are vitally important to his overall poetic – the remarkable sequence 'The Last Coal' is a later return to it, as is 'Sensing the Waun'[20] – so are his treatments of Merthyr itself. Amongst his earliest work to deal with this subject are '"China"' and 'Guest Memorial', both of which are included in *The Common Land*.[21] Like 'The Common Land' itself, '"China"' is sharply aware of pollution in the landscape. The poem's title refers to what its explanatory note describes as 'A slum and outlaw area in 19th century Merthyr Tydfil' and the opening stanza quickly characterizes the place as a kind of waste tip for the whole town:[22]

> A cess-pit of a place, some called it,
> where all the waste in streams collected
> in the bowels of the town ...

The opening image here is replete with a sense of environmental degradation, imputing the notion of sewage to the 'waste' that follows in the subsequent line: China, the poem seems to say, was basically Merthyr's sewer. More importantly, perhaps, in the poem's penultimate stanza, the human toll of such living conditions is suggested in the roll-call of mortality which Jenkins details:

> Babies died as the rain's talons pierced;
> babies died as the sun swam in Pontsarn pool;
> babies died in the river's choking throat,
> in the rusted lungs of miners.

Merthyr's iron industry had seen the town's population expand bewilderingly fast – from 7,700 in 1801 to 46,378 just fifty years later.

Unsurprisingly, as Geraint H. Jenkins suggests, living conditions were appalling:

> By 1841 Merthyr figured among the fifty largest towns in Britain and its workplaces hummed with activity. But, in general, life for most people was a daily battle against deprivation, disease and death ... In 1852 the average life expectancy in Merthyr – a rumbustious, populous town likened to Sodom and Gomorrah by Nonconformist ministers – was seventeen and a half.[23]

As he makes clear, cholera was a particular scourge and 'from 1832 ... pruned families with terrifying swiftness' (p. 199) – thus the particular link in '"China"' between water and death ('the sun sw[imming] in Pontsarn pool'; 'the river's choking throat').[24] Indeed, it might be argued that such a connection encapsulates the precise opposite of the sort of idyllic water-defined imagery with which 'The Common Land' began. For '"China"', in other words, what water brings is rubbish and effluent, not some kind of rural beauty. Nor do the watercourses of nineteenth-century Merthyr have dragonflies as their ambassadors; rather, the ambassadors that these waters send out are disease and death. This is, to put it another way, watershed aesthetics again – but, like Ruth Bidgood's 'Waterspout, 1853', the waters concerned bring devastation. In fact, in the image of 'the river's choking throat', water even seems to have brought devastation upon itself. Moreover, to the extent that this particular image suggests a suffering human body, the sense of inter-connectedness between tormented environment and tormented people in historic Merthyr becomes especially striking.

However, it is not merely nineteenth-century sanitation (or lack of it) which draws Jenkins's attention in this poem. As the second stanza makes clear:

> [China] grew under the shadow of mill-smoke
> which fisted outwards over canal arches.

This image of smoke 'fist[ing]' out over the town – a significantly human image, emphasizing the smoke's origin in human activity – is a potent symbol of Merthyr's status as the 'epicentre of the iron industry' from the late eighteenth century until the middle of the nineteenth, where, as Geraint H. Jenkins puts it, 'flaming labyrinths dominated the industrial landscape'.[25] The 'contaminated community' of China is thus not contaminated merely by the unidentified general waste of a townful of people in an era before decent sanitation.[26] It is also contaminated by the specific material conditions inherent in the development of industry in the south Wales coalfield – a development symbolized in Merthyr by the four great ironworks of Dowlais, Cyfarthfa, Plymouth and Penydarren.[27] Moreover, whereas in 'The Common Land' the impact of industrialization on the Welsh environment was seen, in human terms, in the bodies of merely two representative characters, here its effects are linked to an entire community. And this move crucially joins together the poverty of the community in question – Jenkins presents 'Whole families huddled under a roof / the black barges passed over' (in other words, under the arch of a canal bridge) – with the environmental suffering that is the consequence of an inability to emulate the 'self-insulating propensities of the rich'.[28]

This final economic note is important, because Jenkins's shadow of smoke hanging over the development of China should not be seen as a simple case of 'techno-dystopian thinking' (to use Lawrence Buell's useful phrase).[29] To put it more bluntly, the image of a community growing up under a pall of fumes is not just about pollutants emanating from Merthyr's ironworks. Rather – and perhaps more importantly here – it is also to do with registering landscape as the manifestation of socio-economic power. To revisit Sharon Zukin's arguments, which I quoted in my discussion of Robert Minhinnick's Pen-y-fai poetry, the physical environment is a 'social microcosm', displaying the 'landscape of the powerful' alongside the 'expressive vernacular of the powerless'.[30] Environment as formed by human beings is a constant reminder of – and a continuing attempt to assert – 'who is in charge' or 'what the dominant ideology or philosophy is' (as Martin Jones, Rhys Jones and Michael Woods put it, in their useful summary).[31] In '"China"', then, the pall of smoke which hangs over the life of one particular area of Merthyr is an environmental reminder of the then-dominant power of heavy industry in the town. It is, to put it another way, a symbol of that to which the town and its inhabitants were subject. Similarly, the canal bridge under which Jenkins has 'Whole families' sheltering is a further demonstration of what Zukin sees as the ultimate dominance of economic power over the built environment. As she puts it, 'in the struggle for expansion in the built environment, and control over the uses of space, economic power predominates over both the state and vernacular culture'.[32]

The building of canals in the south Wales coalfield was 'the great enterprise of the 1790s', serving the need to connect 'the iron districts with the ports'.[33] Like the smoke, then, the canal in '"China"' – as an expression of the flow of goods and, thus, of capital – is a blunt physical reminder of power in Merthyr life under iron kings such as the Guest

(Dowlais) and Crawshay (Cyfarthfa) families. Moreover, it is, for this reader at least, significant that Jenkins concentrates on a canal *bridge*, in the sense that both smoke and waterway thus hang over the heads of the people as iconographic manifestations of a literally higher power – below which lie the desperate lives of the vernacular that Jenkins captures in huddled families and dying babies. Jenkins is, of course, notable for his socialist commitments. As the introductory notes to a 2002 selection of his work make clear, Jenkins 'is still active in left-wing circles in the valleys of south-east Wales, particularly with the group known as Cymru Coch [*sic*: Cymru Goch], the Welsh Socialists'.[34] A poem such as '"China"', with its imagery of the lowest socio-economic classes suffering beneath the fist and flow of economic might, suggests a left-wing perspective that is entirely congruent with such affiliations. Moreover – and as a striking counter to the poem's iconography of subjection – in his telling final image of the 'tavern voices' of China 'soaring / like buzzards hovering over Merthyr', Jenkins also points towards what Sharon Zukin calls the 'collective resistance' which can respond to 'Themes of power' in the shaping of 'landscape as a social microcosm'.[35] Notwithstanding all the sufferings which the poem has suggested, by their association with the brutal beauty of birds of prey, the despised inhabitants of this area 'of appalling living conditions, of cruelty, inhumanity and despair, where crime flourished and the forces of law and order feared to go' are elevated to a sort of grandeur which simultaneously recognizes their potential violent strength.[36] That higher power to which both smoke and canal bridge pointed may be threatened by something higher yet, soaring above it and ready to stoop.

The way in which Jenkins makes power inescapably visible and mate-rial is also apparent in the next poem in *The Common Land*, 'Guest Memorial' – a poem responding to the figure of Sir Josiah John Guest (1785–1852; known as Sir John Guest), ironmaster at Dowlais and Member of Parliament for Merthyr.[37] Here, the first two stanzas again emphasize the economic and political element of landscape:

> The workers' terraces
> like so many pigeon-lofts
> at the base of Dowlais.
>
> John Josiah Guest, feudal industrialist
> with strips of plot
> he called his votes.[38]

South Wales mining communities were, of course, famous for the pigeon lofts which dotted the landscape – something to which the poetry of both Idris Davies and Gwenallt responds.[39] The poem's 'pigeon-lofts' are, in other words, an image replete with precise local significance; they are a sharp physical and social marker of historic south Wales working-class environments. However, what Jenkins does is to parallel the workers' 'pigeon-lofts' with their own houses, thus emphasizing the small size of the houses when set against the sheer bulk of the ironworks themselves. Indeed, by doing this, he also appears to suggest that, as the pigeons are to the workers, so the workers are to the owner of Dowlais. The poem's imagery of environmental organization – particularly here in relation to size – is thus a statement of the dizzying discrepancy in power relations between workers and industrialist owner. Moreover, even the grammatical possessive in *'workers'* terraces' (emphasis added) is absolutely undercut by the second stanza, which gives those selfsame terraces straight back to the 'feudal industrialist' and turns them into 'his votes'.[40] To Sir John Guest, the houses thus cease to be material structures of human habitation and become bound pledges of support – currency, in short, of political control. Indeed, just like the terraces at the start of the poem, so also in the penultimate stanza the town library is given to the people and then abruptly taken away: Guest, Jenkins writes, 'built the library and stole away / their time to use it'.[41] In a world of immoral power (the poem directly critiques Guest by presenting him as a thief), workers are permitted no genuine control over space – whether that be public or private. For the poem, in other words, the most important memorial to Guest is the oppression of economically subordinate people that has been inscribed in/as the physical environment of historic Dowlais. It is the history of such oppression which Jenkins attempts to recover and memorialize in 'Guest Memorial' – in an effort to critique and counter the appropri-ation of local historic identity by those monumental celebrations of the powerful to which the poem's title literally refers.[42]

Having offered up a vision of ordinary people denied power over space in 'Guest Memorial', 'Chartist Meeting (Heolgerrig, 1842)' crucially figures the opposition to such denials, as Jenkins has the people of nine-teenth-century Merthyr create a kind of vernacular, resistant arena in the land above the town when a thousand people listen to the Chartist leader Morgan Williams.[43] Here, with the working people brought together outside the landscapes of power which '"China"' and 'Guest Memorial' so sharply picture, Williams sees 'in the burnt hands a harvest of votes' (p. 20), as the poem puts it. In other words, this area becomes as explic-itly politically inflected as that around the Dowlais ironworks in 'Guest

Memorial' – with the upshot that Jenkins's poetic renders the nineteenth-century south Wales coalfield as a landscape crucially polarized between the arenas of different classes. It is, in this sense, important that from the resistant, vernacular meeting place where the workers congregate in 'Chartist Meeting', Jenkins observes how:

> way below them
> Cyfarthfa Castle was set like a diamond
> in a ring of green,
> and the stalks of chimneys
> bloomed continuous smoke and flame.

Both Cyfarthfa Castle, built symbol of the Crawshay family's economic might,[44] and the 'continuous smoke and flame' of immense capital actually-in-the-making remain in view as two landscapes – Chartist meeting place and icons of industry – effectively confront one another. Perhaps it is no surprise that Jenkins renders this particular environment in a particularly confrontational fashion: as John Davies observes, 'Of the violent outbreaks associated with Chartism, the most serious occurred in Wales.'[45]

* * *

Although poems such as '"China"', 'Guest Memorial' and 'Chartist Meeting (Heolgerrig, 1842)' are concerned with Merthyr's past, they also represent approaches to landscape and environment which echo into that section of Jenkins's work which engages with the town's present. 'Gurnos Boy' is a case in point. Published in *A Dissident Voice* (1990) but subsequently revised in *Graffiti Narratives* (1994)[46] – the version I discuss here – 'Gurnos Boy' is a dramatic monologue, spoken in Merthyr dialect, by a character from the tough Gurnos estate on the northern edge of the town.[47] Talking about the area in which he lives, the speaker declares:

> Ower streets wuz named arfta trees
> t' make em sound natural, innit?
> But yew mostly ave Nature b'yer
> when yew tread in-a shit,
> or see dogs umpin in threes!

The importance of language in constructing the environment – something to which Jenkins's reaction to Welsh flower names in the Cwm Glo area has already pointed – is emphasized in the opening line of this quotation. Here, language has been imposed by authority structures – those responsible for road naming – in an apparent attempt to define urban space in terms of pastoral innocence. Of course, the counter to this comes from an entirely different linguistic position – that of the dialect speaker, the resident, for whom the local environment is far from a thing of natural beauty. The situation that the speaker depicts is clearly not a case of environmental pollution comparable in severity to that which is depicted in '"China"'. But it is important that Merthyr is again associated with a lack of cleanliness, as the urban experience of nature is reduced to stepping 'in-a shit'. Moreover, as in the earlier poem, environmental degradation again finds a focal point in ideas of water which, here, is overrunning the speaker's home:

> The state o' ower ome is beyond:
> we got ot an cold runnin water
> down-a walls an windows an a pond
> in-a livin-room, which we oughta
> convert into a tidy sauna.

This is water as unruly force, degrading living conditions by having become uncontainable – a kind of domesticated parallel to Jenkins's early poem 'The Floods' in which the River Taff becomes a 'marauding army, // knowing no boundaries, looting shops, soaking / … ownership through furniture and carpet / and claiming lives'.[48] Finally, and once more echoing '"China"', the built environment of 'Gurnos Boy' is clearly understood as encapsulating disparate levels of power, with the speaker threatening violence against 'them posh people … / in theyr big ouses with burglar larms'. This is an emphatically vernacular, sharply resistant response to the 'big ouses' which symbolize socio-economic power. Seeing the south Wales landscape as the inscription of class difference, Jenkins crucially lets his poetry give voice to those to whom the spaces of power are denied. In this case, of course, in the construction of the poem's dialect speaker, such *giving voice* is literal.

The combination in 'Gurnos Boy' of a sense of environmental destitution or poisoning and the critique of those lineaments of power which the urban landscape shows in material form is, I think, the two-part key to Jenkins's environmental response to Merthyr. Perhaps the archetypal expression of the former tendency is the start of the sequence 'Empire of Smoke', with its speaker's declaration that:

> I was born in the crater of this town
> below a ring of tips and heaps
> which glower down.[49]

Not only is the topography of the valley-town reduced to something like a bomb site in the word 'crater', but it is a crater which is ringed by oppressive (glowering) industrial detritus. Moreover, in the poem's second stanza, that perception of natural growth as unable to cover industrial scarring which was apparent in 'The Common Land' is rendered even more bleakly. Thus, considering the 'inheritance' of Richard Crawshay's 'empire of smoke' – an explicit recognition of the power that was implicit in the pall of smoke in '"China"' – the poem's speaker sees 'at Dowlais Top':

> a black planet of scattered mounds
> where hardly a tuft of grass
> can take root; where sheep
> turn grey, branded by the soil ...

Here, then, it is not just that nature cannot imprint itself on certain areas blasted by former industrial activity; rather, the filth left by industry is still imprinting itself onto nature in the way that the very 'sheep / turn grey'.

For a more recent poem with this environmental perspective, one might point to 'The Big Ole' from the collection of dialect monologues *Coulda Bin Summin* (2001).[50] Here, the town is made filthy not by industry (or at least, not directly). The background to the poem is the post-industrial reuse of a former industrial site – the 'Big Ole' of the poem's title – the context being given by the speaker of 'When-a Wind Blew Black' (from the same collection) who explains, with bitter irony, that Dowlais Top has a 'lovely Big Ole / t' keep fillin now-a coal's ewsed up' (p. 17). What fills the hole is a 'ewge tip', as the eponymous 'Big Ole' is sold by the council 'f'ra quid' ('The Big Ole', p. 59).[51] The upshot is that the councillors rejoice over the income from the consequent land-fill tax, while the community of Dowlais Top suffers from 'daily sickness' – a sickness that is figured in 'footie an rugby fields' turned into 'giant bins' as rubbish is redistributed by the wind and, more disturbingly, in the consequences seen in stanzas four and five:

> When-a gas come right up
> from-a sewers an children
> spewed theyer guts out,
> oo wuz askin-a questions?
>
> When-a froth begun t' ooze
> from-a nearby drains,
> it wuz like-a tip spreadin
> poison tentacles round us.

According to Lawrence Buell, the 'toxic discourse' of contemporary culture – by which he means the discursive qualities of cultural products which express the 'fear of a poisoned world' – is 'an interlock[ing] set of topoi', one of which is to do with what he calls 'Traumas of pastoral disruption', or the 'horrified realization' that one is part of a locale, a community that has been environmentally contaminated.[52] Here, however, apart from the 'footie an rugby fields', there is no sense of any green space being disrupted. This is not, in other words, some shattering of 'the rose-colored lens of pastoral-utopian innocence'.[53] Rather, as 'When-a Wind Blew Black' suggests, its history as the location of the 'boggin Opencast' renders such innocence utterly alien to Dowlais Top ('Send us all yewr bloody cack / we on'y come from Dowlais Top / we're ewsed t' crap up yer: / ad it f' yers we ave'). Those final 'poison tentacles', however, do suggest what Greg Garrard, summarizing Buell, describes as 'the "gothicization" of squalor and pollution characteristic of the environmental exposé'.[54] In short, in his exposure of the horrors of yet another era of environmental abuse, Jenkins manifests Merthyr as a kind of gothic space.

'The Big Ole' also brings us back to Jenkins's other major Merthyr topos – that of the built environment as an expression of power relations. Not only does the 'ewge tip' bring 'daily sickness' to the residents of Dowlais Top, but its very presence as a material fact in the landscape is testament to the twin power of state officials (the opening stanza indicates that it is the council which sells the land) and economics (in the iconography of the landfill tax which the councillors celebrate at the end of the poem) over and against a powerless local community. That community, it seems, is absolutely unable to get the dangers of the tip considered: as the speaker puts it, when the contamination starts to become apparent, 'oo wuz askin-a questions?' The tip, in short, is exemplary of powerful officialdom and powerless community – and the poem crucially offers up to a member of the community thus abused a chance to speak out, to protest, in the 'authentic' voice of local experience. Unsurprising perhaps, given his documented affiliation to socialist causes, Jenkins's poetic is thus not merely a *display* of what Sharon Zukin calls the 'social microcosm' of landscape.[55] Rather, it constitutes *a crucial act of solidarity* with those whose suffering, exploitation and oppression is variously inscribed into the environments of south Wales.

A parallel situation to that of 'The Big Ole' is apparent in the first poem of 'All Ail Ower Bran' New System' (again from *Coulda Bin*

Summin) in which the speaker *explicitly* reads the new Merthyr road system as a landscape of power:

> Got more lights 'n Blackpool 'lluminations!
> Got more signs 'n Spaghetti Junction!
> Fancy routes with numbers
> even-a maps don' register,
> just so-a bloody councillors
> cun get straight outa town.[56]

Here, the new road layout manifests the control and desires of the political classes, with the upshot, interestingly, being another layer of pollution ('Whool town's like the Church / o' the Present Day Exhaust Fumes'). Moreover, it is also undertaken at the expense of community heritage, with the poem noting that 'Bethesda Street [is] practiclee gone'. This particular situation is explained more thoroughly in 'Bethesda Brought Down' (from 1999's *Red Landscapes*) and 'Bethesda Has Gone' (from 2004's *The Language of Flight*).[57] Both of these poems set the 'council's philistine force' ('Bethesda Has Gone') against the cultural symbolism of Bethesda Chapel. Demolished for the sake of the council's new road – which 'struts above roofs of terraces' ('Bethesda Brought Down') – the chapel is symbolic of community heritage not only as the place 'where Joseph Parry played' but also, in 'its second life', as the locus for arts, crafts and radical politics ('Bethesda Has Gone'). As Dolores Hayden makes very clear, one way

> to analyze the production of space historically is to look at power struggles as they appear in the planning, design, construction, use, and demolition of typical buildings, especially dwellings ... Camille Wells, social historian of architecture, puts it this way: 'most buildings can be understood in terms of power or authority – as efforts to assume, extend, resist, or accommodate it'.[58]

Admittedly, Bethesda Chapel was not a dwelling; but, as a chapel, it was what Hayden calls a *typical building* in a Welsh context. In the terms that these road-related poems of Jenkins's offer, then, its demolition and subsequent absence – just as much as the building and subsequent presence of the new road – are testament to the power of officialdom over the community (vernacular) urge which, in the words of 'Bethesda Has Gone', declared that 'Bethesda had to be saved'. Indeed, in their particular construction of the council as 'philistine' and its road as arrogantly strutting, these poems are a striking protest against such power as institutionalized thuggery. No wonder, perhaps, that Jenkins eventually reaches the point at which, in 'Gulag Gurnos, Stalag Merthyr',[59] landscapes of power become what Martin Jones, Rhys Jones and Michael Woods call 'Landscapes of control and exclusion':[60]

> At the top of a pillar
> are the red spikes
> of a Medieval weapon.
> Regeneration schemes happen
> behind steel meshing
> seen before on pubs, barracks
> along the Falls.

Here the built environment is no longer displaying merely symbolic levels of power, but is '*physically* exerting power'[61] to protect the economic interests of 'Regeneration schemes'. Indeed, the landscape of Merthyr has become such a contested space in this context that Jenkins's key cultural associations not only manifest it as a prison camp (*Gulag, Stalag*) in which all symbols of officialdom have to be protected from the prisoners (the poem notes the 'Ranks of green lances / around schools and hospital') but also parallel it, in the reference to 'the Falls', with that archetype of the contested environment, Northern Ireland.[62] The upshot is that Merthyr effectively becomes a kind of militarized zone, its space and its people both controlled and divided by wire, spikes and steel.

* * *

Wynn Thomas has pertinently suggested that Mike Jenkins's is an 'important work of cultural reclamation and political rehabilitation in Merthyr'.[63] I would add to this by arguing that Jenkins's engagement with the often problematic complexities of Merthyr's environments, both urban and ex-urban, is a crucial part of that process. However, as a coda to this chapter, it is important to acknowledge that Jenkins – whilst he has avowedly and 'sometimes very movingly served as *bardd gwlad* to a community that has been left stripped of its memory and its dignity, along with the wealth it at one time so liberally produced for the greedy world to take'[64] – also extends his poetry beyond the particularities of Merthyr into a more general imagined Welsh space, as well as into other specific locations (Welsh and otherwise). Significantly, at such points, the sort of concerns and commitments we have seen in his Merthyr poetry surface again. Thus, for example, in 'Returning to the Nant' (from 1990's *A Dissident Voice*), his vision of Nant Gwrtheyrn –

a tiny former quarrying village on the Llŷn Peninsula – makes clear the way in which the material formation of the place is a manifestation of the disparate power structures in its industrial history:

> In the Nant, workers' terraces
> linked arm-to-arm, with rooms
> the size of the manager's hearth …[65]

The workers' community is celebrated here through the sense of warm camaraderie suggested by the houses being 'linked arm-to-arm'; simultaneously, however, the poem protests the profound environmental inequality to which that same community is subject – with the manager having as large a space for his fire as the workers have for whole rooms. Moreover, in the present, the environment of the locality constitutes nothing less than a 'mourning' for the relative powerlessness of vernacular community over economic conditions. Thus Jenkins writes of Nant Gwrtheyrn's closest neighbouring village:

> Llithfaen: a place of granite.
> But 'Ar Werth' signs
> are flags of mourning.

As Roger Geary explains, 'Employment opportunities in rural Wales have never been plentiful and deteriorated further during the recessions of the 1970s and 1980s.'[66] Jenkins's vision of houses for sale here thus grieves for the erosion of community under the pressures of unfavourable economic conditions in ex-urban Wales in the later twentieth century. More specifically, it grieves for the erosion of a *Welsh-speaking* community, as the poem's telling use of the phrase 'Ar Werth' indicates.

This latter point is made more sharply in 'House for Sale' (the previous poem in the same collection), which deals with the potential purchase of a Welsh house by a non-Welsh-speaker. Crucially, the buyer of the ironically described 'Idyllic home with quaint local name: / "Tŷ Haf" meaning *Get away from stress*' is told to

> Learn the essentials of the native tongue:
> how to say 'Llanfair P.G.'
> How to smile *I'm-part-of-the-land*
> as they gibber … nothing personal,
> they're talking about TV. (p. 72)

In the sale of the house, control of the vernacular environment thus passes out of the hands of those who speak the indigenous language, which Jenkins satirically reduces to 'gibber' about nothing significant.

Moreover, the house's name – which really means 'sumer [*sic*: summer] house/home' (as Jenkins's footnote explains, p. 73) – implies that the property is to be bought as a holiday home. Thus the concluding stanza reads:

> Tŷ Haf
> Stryd Wag [empty street]
> Ghost Town. (p. 73)

The control of its built environment by people who want only seasonal accommodation is exposed as reducing Welsh space to a landscape of empty streets and ghost towns, whilst simultaneously destroying Welsh-language culture. As the poem puts it, 'No neighbours for miles / except in summer, / when you'll find that language / is no problem at all' (p. 72).

This is precisely the condition that Roger Geary describes in writing about the arson attacks on holiday homes and other English-owned properties which took place in Wales, from 1979 to the early 1990s, under the symbolic banner of the group Meibion Glyndŵr (Sons of Glyndŵr).[67] Thus, Geary observes that 'By 1988 Welsh Office statistics revealed that there were more than 20,000 holiday homes in Wales with the majority located in the northern and western Welsh speaking areas.' The upshot, as Geary indicates, was an inflation of property prices 'to a level … well beyond the reach of local people', and the creation of 'virtual ghost villages', with second homes 'left empty for the greater part of the year' – a situation that 'must have seemed particularly unjust', as he puts it, 'when local authority housing departments had over-subscribed waiting lists of local people'.[68] Alongside the influx into Wales, from 1981 to 1990, of around 600,000 permanent settlers – 'nearly all from the rest of the UK' (p. 82) – the consequence was, in many heart-land Welsh-speaking areas, 'the dilution and destruction of a linguistically distinct common culture' (p. 83). It is out of this context that Jenkins's poem sharply observes one of 'the benefits' of a Welsh second home to be 'Fires all year round' (p. 72). Like the imagery of buzzards at the end of '"China"', this clear reference to the arson attacks of Meibion Glyndŵr thus stands as a suggestion – admittedly very much in passing but certainly with no condemnation – of that 'collective resist-ance' to power which Sharon Zukin identifies as one of the crucial forces in the social formation of landscape.[69] It is within such a spirit of oppos-ition that, in the much lighter context of 'Yr Wyddfa Speaks Out!',[70] the mountain rejects the name given to it by the 'trip-trap trailing termites / carrying their backpacks / [who] tread me down' (p. 34). Observing the tourists' T-shirts which declare "'I've climbed Snowdon'", Yr Wyddfa asks:

> who's this 'Snowdon' anyway,
> some kind of Lord?

In these lines, an icon of the Welsh environment recognizes itself only in its Welsh name, as Jenkins uses an identification between language and land to challenge the appropriation of Welsh space by the socio-economic power of anglophone tourism. For Mike Jenkins, in other words, a poetry of the Welsh environment is significantly a poetry of resistance – recurrently giving voice to, speaking out for or standing in solidarity with those places and communities which have been (in the terms of 'Yr Wyddfa Speaks Out!') *trodden down* by the depredations of power.

8

Christine Evans:
Creating Sacred Space

Christine Evans moved to north Wales in 1967, and is particularly asso-
ciated with the island of Bardsey where she spends part of each year,
having 'married into the last of Bardsey's farming families'.[1] Bardsey is
a recurring presence in Evans's poetry, and her fourth collection, *Island
of Dark Horses* (1995), is focused entirely on the island, its inhabitants
and its history.[2] The question of how Evans represents Bardsey in this,
her most developed work on the subject to date, is the issue that I shall
address here. What concerns me specifically is the way in which *Island
of Dark Horses* locates this particular Welsh space within a mythical
framework – by which I mean the way in which it forms the various
physical and human geographies of the island into what Yi-Fu Tuan
calls *mythical space*.

   In *Space and Place*, Tuan explains that mythical space is a 'concep-
tual schema' which operates by attributing assumptions, qualities and
importance to various physical points, features and directions in the
physical world. Mythical space is thus '*construed* space' – effectively, a
conceptual ordering of the environment – 'which depends on the power
of the mind to extrapolate far beyond the sense data'.[3] For Dorian
Llywelyn, in his study of Welsh land, national identity and spirituality,
it is this sort of process which creates a sense of place, as 'locations ...
are charged with human significance and positive values and associ-
ations'.[4] The process of construing location as mythical space, Tuan
suggests, operates in two quite distinct ways:

In the one, mythical space is a fuzzy area of defective knowledge surrounding the empirically known; it frames pragmatic space. In the other it is the spatial component of a world view, a conception of localized values within which people carry on their practical activities.[5]

According to Tuan, there are thus two types of mythical space. The first is rooted in the imaginative construction of locations which have not been experienced first-hand: 'When we wonder what lies on the other side of the mountain range or ocean, our imagination constructs mythical geographies that may bear little or no relationship to reality' (p. 86). Meaning, in other words, is injected into the blank spaces of unexplored regions by our imaginings, thus forming what Tuan calls 'Worlds of fantasy' (p. 86). By contrast, in the second type of mythical space, a society's world view fuses with its physical geography to impute meaning to the places in which its people live and work, and to the locations which exist around, below, and above them. Place, in short, is rendered as conceptual pattern.

One of the key manifestations of such patterning is what Tuan terms 'Oriented mythical space' (p. 91), in which meaning is ascribed to locations according to their various directions out from a central point: 'man is the center of a cosmic frame oriented to the cardinal points and the vertical axis' (p. 88). The 'cosmic frame' which surrounds the human is a web of significances that are distributed according to physical orientations, such as up and down or east and west. For example, Tuan observes that, for the ancient Greeks:

> East and west came to be sharply differentiated. East, the place of sunrise, was associated with light and the sky; west, the place of sunset, with darkness and the earth. The right-hand side was identified with the east and the sun, the left-hand side with the 'misty west' (*Iliad*). Pythagorean thinkers coupled 'right' with 'limit,' and 'left' with the evil of the 'unlimited.' Isles of the Blest, and later in the Middle Ages the Fortunate Islands, were located in the west. These were idyllic places in which men lived effortlessly, yet such places also connoted death since dead heroes went there. (p. 98)

In other words, in oriented mythical space, the cardinal points of north, south, east and west are given specific attributes. Physical orientation becomes meaning-bearing, and particular directions are filled with what Dorian Llywelyn calls 'positive values' or 'human significance'.[6]

This sort of mythical space is markedly present in Christine Evans's construction of Bardsey. 'At the End of Summer' starts with the following lines:

> It was easy, looking over towards Ireland
> To understand the myth of Avalon.
> At our backs the colours of endurance
> The Sound brusque, a military blue, but
> West – translucent, milky-pale, vermilion –
> The ebb-tide sliding into place like syrup.[7]

Evans's sense of geographic meaning is, here, divided along a broadly east–west axis. As in the medieval ideas which Tuan notes, the west is the location of mystery and romance (what Evans calls 'myth')[8] – specifically Avalon, place of healing and magic,[9] or, in Geoffrey of Monmouth's terms, 'The Fortunate Island' itself.[10] Admittedly, this is not quite how the poem begins. Rather, as the first two lines of my quotation indicate, the poem actually starts by suggesting that if one looks towards the west it is easy to understand *the idea* of a magical island. By the end of the stanza, however, the west is being painted in the misty yet rich colours of romance – 'translucent, milky-pale, vermilion' – which indicates that, even if she only started off by *thinking* of dreams and legends as she looked west, Evans is now figuring the west explicitly in terms of mystery. Moreover, as Tuan observes, the islands of the west 'connoted death since dead heroes went there',[11] and it is precisely such a connection between the west and death that is captured in the poem's second stanza:

> Walking on the headland after hearing
> Muggeridge on the radio, at eighty
> Welcoming the thought of death, we watched
> The slow sun settling for the night ... (p. 62)

Watching the west – here, the direction of the 'settling' sun – it is no surprise that the thoughts of the poet-speaker turn to death: within the post-medieval Western tradition, this is part of what the west *is* in mythical terms. In short, Muggeridge 'Welcoming the thought of death' is nothing other than the mythical turn west. For Evans, then, conceptualizing the west construes it both as mystery and as death. Indeed, all of this westward character is emphasized by comparison with the opposite direction of the mythic compass. As the first stanza of the poem indicates, the east, towards mainland Wales, is characterized by *endurance*, *brusqueness*, even a sense of *militariness*. The east, in other words, is practical and stoic. The west, by contrast, is the place of romance to which we depart (perhaps finally) through a seascape that is 'translucent, milky-pale, vermilion'.

Evans's spatial myth here is apparently very straightforward: the Bardsey of mythical geography sits between the romance of the west and the practicalities of the east. The island is thus a kind of centre, poised between the conceptual alternatives that are mapped onto opposing cardinal points. Indeed, as the poem's final stanza indicates, Bardsey seems to negotiate between conceptual extremes:

> We stood close together, facing out.
> I could not guess where his thoughts lay.
> Perhaps as well. Our own myths fade
> Slower, more tenderly that way. (p. 62)

At this point, the island is construed as a place where mystery is possible ('I could not guess where his thoughts lay') – but where the mysterious (Evans's 'myths') will still inevitably fade. It is caught between the arena of myth and the arena of practicality. However, the penultimate stanza of the poem suggests a rather different perspective:

> The long arm of the mainland down to Aber
>   Was shadow-pleated and against the hills
> Small gibberish of stars was signalling.
> I could blot it all out with one finger
> While we seemed effortlessly floating outward
> Towards the shining, that mesmeric edge. (p. 62)

In these lines – which begin by looking out eastwards, down along the Welsh coast as far as Aberystwyth – the poem's speaker seems unable to understand the view towards the mainland (it is 'gibberish'), whilst the idea of blotting out the eastward view suggests the desire to refuse the potential communication suggested by 'signalling'. The mainland, in short, is rejected as incomprehensible. By contrast, the island itself seems to be floating towards 'the shining … mesmeric edge' of the west, towards the romantic space of 'translucent, milky-pale, vermilion' in which the first stanza located the mystery of Avalon itself. Far from being a midpoint, in other words, these lines associate Bardsey emphatically with the romance of the west.

In the terms set up by 'At the End of Summer', then, Bardsey is a midpoint in two senses: as a place from which one can look out west towards mystery and east towards practicality; and as a space in which mystery is both extant and fading. But, simultaneously, it is not really a midpoint at all. Not only is it the place from which the mainland east is rejected, but the island itself also displays a clear drift westwards, out 'Towards the shining, that mesmeric edge'. For Evans, in short,

Bardsey's mythical geography is significantly characterized by contra-
diction, a quality of mythical space that Yi-Fu Tuan highlights:

> Mythical space is an intellectual construct. It can be very elaborate.
> Mythical space is also a response of feeling and imagination to funda-
> mental human needs. It differs from pragmatic and scientifically conceived
> spaces in that *it ignores the logic of exclusion and contradiction*. Logically a
> cosmos can have only one center; in mythical thought it can have many
> centers, although one center may dominate all the others. Logically the
> whole is made up of parts, each with its characteristic location, structure,
> and function. The part may be essential to the functioning of the whole,
> but the part is not the whole in miniature and in essence. In mythical
> thought the part can symbolize the whole and have its full potency.[12]

Mythical space, in other words, is simply not bound by the dictates of
the rational. Thus it is perhaps unsurprising that, in Evans's poetic,
Bardsey has contradictory functions – that its myth of place develops
along lines that are elaborate and alogical.

* * *

Although just one element of Bardsey's complex mythical construction
in *Island of Dark Horses*, the notion of midpoint – that idea of Bardsey
as centre – is important and is worth pausing over. Indeed, given
Bardsey's physical location as both remote and peripheral – that is,
removed from the mainland – this is a construction that is especially
notable because it is, arguably, so counterintuitive.

Perceiving a place as being located at the middle of things is,
according to Tuan, a classic definition of *home*. As he indicates in the
chapter of *Space and Place* which considers 'Attachment to Homeland',
'Human groups nearly everywhere tend to regard their own homeland
as the center of the world.'[13] For Evans, Bardsey has a kind of gravita-
tional pull; it is the centre towards which things will tend. Specifically,
in the terms set up by 'Through the Weather Window', Bardsey has a
definite centripetal force. In this poem, the poet-speaker is pictured on
a boat, getting off the island just before the weather breaks (thus the
title of the piece):

> The forecast's bad again, farewells snatched.
> *A hell of a swell – we'll make a run for it.*
> *Cross before the flood comes.* (p. 69)

Out on the Sound – the stretch of water between Bardsey and the main-
land – the speaker experiences the power of the sea and, in particular,
the currents that run around the island:[14]

> The boat rolls, and dips, and rises
> as the ocean's grey skin heaves ...

> If the engine cut, we would be carried
> backwards by the heave and kick, the
>   bunching muscle
> of the current. (p. 69)[15]

What Evans particularly observes here, then, is the power of a current which would heave the boat back to Bardsey and away from the mainland were the boat's engine to fail. As Tuan makes clear, in most conceptual geographies, all things focus or pull back onto the homepoint; home is, as he puts it, the 'center of the world'.[16] Thus, the action of the current is entirely to be expected if Bardsey is indeed 'home' in the conceptual geography that *Island of Dark Horses* sets up. However, it is worth noting that, at this point, the island does not actually have any pull in and of itself; instead, it is as though other forces in the world – here, the current – are acknowledging Bardsey's centrality by trying to pull the boat back towards it. Later in the poem, however, and at a particular moment in the middle of the Sound, Evans indicates that:

> There is a moment, sudden as
> slack water, when the island's pull
> falls away. (p. 69)

Whether or not this is a common experience for those travelling away from Bardsey in the material world itself, in the mythical geography that Evans's poetic establishes, the island explicitly has, by this latter point, an inward pull of its own. The description of 'the island's pull' is unequivocal in its simple possessive: Bardsey has a kind of gravitational force.

Such physical qualities find a psychological parallel in a poem called 'Keeping in Touch', in which Bardsey is a place of potential convergence, a point where things come together. Writing about a woman called Viv, Evans observes that:

> This island won her with its fullness
> a seamless ripening that took her in
> and whispered here might be the place
> for the bright strands to converge (p. 65)

Admittedly, Bardsey is only the place where things *might* converge. However, the particular description that Evans chooses – the sense of Bardsey as a place of potential convergence for 'bright strands' – is important. As Yi-Fu Tuan explains:

A people who believe they are at the center claim, implicitly, the ineluctable worth of their location. In diverse parts of the world this sense of centrality is made explicit by a geometrical conception of space oriented to the cardinal points. Home is at the center of an astronomically determined spatial system. A vertical axis, linking heaven to the underworld, passes through it. The stars are perceived to move around one's abode; home is the focal point of a cosmic structure.[17]

Admittedly, in 'Keeping in Touch', there is no 'geometrical conception of space' linking stars, heaven, underworld and home. But there *is* a psychological–emotional equivalent of this, in the sense of Bardsey being construed as the place where the 'bright strands' of Viv's life may converge. In other words, Bardsey has the archetypal home-value of being a 'focal point'; it is a *coming-together place*. Or, to put it another way, this coming-together value is its 'ineluctable worth' – the 'ineluctable worth' that Tuan ascribes to homelands.

As a whole, 'Keeping in Touch' is about promising to stay in contact with Bardsey folk from the distant 'starlessness / of Milton Keynes', as the poem puts it (p. 66). Its emotional direction, in other words, is very firmly turned towards Bardsey as the mythical centre of Evans's conceptual geography. Indeed, this is clear from the poem's opening stanzas:

> *This is Viv, in Milton Keynes ...*
>
> I always think of her against the shining
> west, her eyes the sweet clear green
> of goosegogs not yet fully ripe –
> green with the force of light behind.
>
> Easy to imagine them at moonrise
> turning emerald and luminous.
> She is topaz and amber
> earth quickened by fire
>
> but drawn back always to cold shores
> where light brings out the shades
> in rocks and people, and confirms
> that all shades fit. (p. 65)

Here, the poetry crucially suggests the notion, proposed earlier, of the island having some sort of gravitational pull: Viv is 'drawn back always' to the island's 'cold shores'. But in these lines, Bardsey becomes even more significant than this. As I have already noted, Yi-Fu Tuan asserts that mythical geography denies the logics of exclusion and contradiction when he says that 'In mythical thought the part can symbolize the whole and have its full potency.'[18] Precisely such a process is in play here: at this particular physical point, at what we have learnt is the centre of things, we find that 'all shades fit'. In other words, all the different shades and flickers of experience find a place here. Bardsey is not just home; it is nothing less than the part which contains the whole. Moreover, these various 'shades' are not merely the experiences of the present. Rather, in the ghostly connotations of the word, Bardsey becomes a place in which both the past and the present combine. Indeed, such temporal implications find a strong parallel in Brenda Chamberlain's assertion, in *Tide-race*, that Bardsey is 'a land that hoards its past and merges all of time in the present', or – more striking still – that 'past and future merge into the living moment on and about this sea-rock'.[19] In short, that which is dead 'fits' here, as does all the variety of the present.

It is, however, necessary to reiterate Tuan's notion that mythical geography is wrapped around by contradiction. Because, although Bardsey has a gravitational pull and the centrality attributed to homes, although it is the part that contains the whole, it is also emphatically an edge. In 'Keeping in Touch', the poet-speaker envisages Viv:

> Riding the white mare above the booming caves
> aware of living at the edge of knowing
> what tides of sea or sky
> would leave within her reach tomorrow (p. 65)

Being on Bardsey is an experience of being on the 'edge of knowing' – here, apparently, because of the unpredictability of what the physical world will do. Elsewhere in the collection, Bardsey is more than merely the sort of psychological edge that is identifiable here. At the start of 'Island of Dark Horses', the long final poem which gives its title to the collection as a whole, the island is nothing less than a kind of last refuge – so far out, in fact, that in the poem's first narrative the island is only really visible from a distance. This first narrative is a fictional extension of the story of Garmon following the defeat of Benlli, king of Powys. Evans's helpful notes explain the context:

> *Benlli*: King of Powys, possibly Irish ... After an attempt by Garmon to convert him to Christianity (but possibly unrelated to it) he was defeated in an uprising led by Cadell in 474. The island's Welsh name [i.e. Enlli] may be connected [to the name 'Benlli']; the more usual derivation is 'island in the current'.

Garmon: linked with Pen Llyn [*sic*] (Abersoch church, Llanarmon) but I have invented the story of his coming to the island. (p. 94)

The poem renders this latter story in the following way:

> After the burning
> of Benlli's city, they were marked men,
> Garmon and his brothers.
> Men moved aside for them.
> Mothers hid their babies' faces.
>
> None could shut out the cries,
> the roar of flame and the smell of fat.
> So he led them north, seeking cleansing ...
>
> At last they reached the rocky place
> where the land looks out before it drowns
> to the whaleback island waiting
> against sunset. As dusk thickened
> the wind dropped, winter wave-swell
> fell away and a strange light
> grew and strengthened on the ocean,
> a phosphor glow unlike the moon
> that turned to mist and curdled
> low on the water. They paddled out
> through rafts of silent birds.
>
> Two nights later, fire was seen
> soon after nightfall, and in summer,
> to the lowbrowed shelters on the hill
> came other men of faith and power ...
> and it was turned to Insula Sanctorum. (pp. 73–4)

In this section, Bardsey is effectively a hideaway for a group of 'marked men'. It is a place for the cursed, on whom the innocent – here figured in the babies whose faces are hidden by their mothers – may not look. This is a markedly different conceptualization of the island from the sense, previously discussed, of Bardsey as the centre of the world. Here, by contrast, it is the last refuge of the marked, the cursed. Rather than being what Tuan calls a 'focal point',[20] it is a place beyond even the land that you reach at the last:

> *At last* they reached the rocky place
> where the land looks out before it drowns
> to the whaleback island waiting
> against sunset. (p. 73; emphasis added)

If one takes these lines literally, Bardsey is beyond the last place: it is beyond the 'At last' with which the stanza begins. Indeed, it is even beyond the drowning of the land itself. Thus, beyond what the poem presents as the death of land, beyond the drowning of that which is solid, that is where Bardsey is to be found – so beyond the certainties of solid ground that, figured as a whale, it may not even be land at all. Bardsey becomes land beyond land, a place beyond places. It is in this sense that Evans describes Bardsey as 'waiting / against sunset': rather than the 'misty west' [21] being to the west of Bardsey (as it was in 'At the End of Summer'), it is now *Bardsey itself* that is wreathed in the darkening colours of sunset, surrounded by the peculiar glow and the odd mists of the enchanted island. This is a far cry from the notion of homeland: here, Bardsey is the west-point, wrapped in mist; it is the place for those excluded from normal life – the place for both the cursed (the 'marked men') and the sacred (the 'men of faith and power').[22]

It thus makes considerable conceptual sense when, at the end of this first section of the collection's title poem (in the final lines quoted above), the reader is effectively left looking into the island from the outside, seeing fire spring up in the darkness and shelters outlined against the hillside. Indeed, the readerly experience of Bardsey here is little different from the possible vision of Avalon experienced by the speaker and her companion in 'At the End of Summer': it is a place out on 'that mesmeric edge', where something is 'shining' (p. 62). At this point, the reader is outside, peering into the island's mystery – emphasized by that final reference to its becoming a place of particularly sacred mystery, 'Insula Sanctorum' – not inside, within the island homestead, gazing out. However, given what I have already argued about the complex mythical patterning of Bardsey that Evans offers in this collection, it is unsurprising that *Island of Dark Horses* does indeed figure this latter experience. For example, the poem 'Window, Dynogoch' (p. 11) is rooted in Evans's house, and presents the poet-speaker looking out through a small window and seeing the rocks which:

> dark-slimy-haired, uncouth,
> hump and crawl and haul themselves
> back out of the warm shallows on to land.

Indeed, and in stark contrast to the Bardsey of far-off fires which is apparent in 'Island of Dark Horses', the contemporary fires of the Bardsey lighthouse in 'Window, Dynogoch' are a homely presence within which the speaker sleeps and wakes in her island house ('All night

the lighthouse prints its sixteen squares / on the whitewashed wall and on
our faces / throwing dark's doors wide / over and over, to welcome the
waker'). Subject to the changing contexts of particular historical circum-
stance, Bardsey is thus far from static: the ancient destination of the
excluded who turn it into 'Insula Sanctorum' is mythically different from
the island of the contemporary farmer-resident who lives under the
welcoming beams of the lighthouse. A place of paradoxical doubleness
(both homely *and* mysteriously remote), Bardsey is crucially a shifting
field, its space constituted across time as well as across (for example) the
cardinal points of the compass. As Doreen Massey puts it, 'Space is not
static'; rather, it is four-dimensional, bound up with the temporal to such
an extent that it is best thought of as 'space-time'.[23]

Later in the final poem (in the section 'Lauds'), many contradictions
come together in one especially resonant stanza, which encapsulates
much of Evans's complex mythical geography of Bardsey:

> *Andros*, Pliny called it; *Edri*
> to ancient Greek mapdrawers of the western edge.
> A world of waves and pouring air
> the lighthouse's long steady stroke
> in the flux of the sea.
> An island where so many came to die.
> Fragment of land, and a whole place, peopled,
> generous with truths between the tide's
> twin ceremonies of dark and light. (p. 75)

According to this stanza, Bardsey is emphatically marginal (it is quickly
characterized as part of what has been perceived as 'the western edge').
It does not have the centralizing stability of home (it is 'in the flux of
the sea'). However, it *is* central because it is caught between extremes,
between the 'twin ceremonies of dark and light' (in other words, it is
also a midpoint). It is, moreover, a manifestation of the western isles, in
their function as the place where 'dead heroes' go:[24] for it is to Bardsey
that 'so many came to die' – these 'many' being 'men of faith and power'
(p. 74), as the first narrative of the poem tells us. As such, Bardsey fulfils
the mythical responsibilities of the western isles by being the location of
death for the saints (Christian heroes). In short, Evans's Bardsey is a
complex paradox: it is caught between centre and edge; in here and out
there; dark and light; home and mysterious elsewhere.

* * *

It is in this final sense of the island as a place of otherworldly mystery that *Island of Dark Horses* crucially forms Bardsey not merely as part of a geo-mythical framework but as a mythical space itself. Yi-Fu Tuan's primary distinction between two types of mythical space is thus worth reiterating:

> Two principal kinds of mythical space may be distinguished. In the one, mythical space is a fuzzy area of defective knowledge surrounding the empirically known; it frames pragmatic space. In the other it is the spatial component of a world view, a conception of localized values within which people carry on their practical activities.[25]

My analysis in this chapter has, so far, concentrated substantially on Tuan's second type of mythical space, in which specific geographical points are subject to conceptual interpretation. However, implicit in much of what I have suggested about Evans's rendering of the west in particular has been the notion of mythical space of the first sort – what Tuan calls 'fuzzy' space. 'Fuzzy' space is manifest in the construction of places that are fundamentally 'Worlds of fantasy' (p. 86), essentially romantic locations – of beauty, terror or mystery – which are built on wondering what, for example, lies out there over the sea, beyond specific geographical knowledge.

It is by creating just such a sense of 'fuzzy' space that Evans establishes Bardsey itself as mythical space – as a place of either mystery or, at the very least, of the hazily perceived. Such a move is identifiable in the story of Garmon's approach to Bardsey in the first section of 'Island of Dark Horses', which is thus worth quoting again:

> At last they reached the rocky place
> where the land looks out before it drowns
> to the whaleback island waiting
> against sunset. As dusk thickened
> the wind dropped, winter wave-swell
> fell away and a strange light
> grew and strengthened on the ocean,
> a phosphor glow unlike the moon
> that turned to mist and curdled
> low on the water. They paddled out
> through rafts of silent birds. (p. 73–4)

Bardsey is created as mythical space here because it is formed as a place over which hovers the question *What precisely is out there?*, behind the mystery of the 'strange light' and the 'phosphor glow'. It is, in Tuan's terms, something of a *world of fantasy* – a place that is, for the people approaching it (in whose perspective we exist at this point in the poem), 'built on meager knowledge and much yearning'.[26]

Moreover, it is not merely from a distance that Evans turns Bardsey into a place of mystery. For example, the poem 'Sounding' deals with the experience of being on the island under the cover of fog. In this environmental context, the field of immediate perception is significantly reduced and the wider vistas of the island are gone. The upshot is that nearly everything is turned into fuzzy space – into space that generates the question *I wonder quite what's in (or out) there*. Listening to the foghorn, the speaker says:

> Timing it makes the moment
> Momentous, makes me recall
> Contractions. And, after each
> A glistening bag of quiet sounds
> Opens, drying off around us.
> Swaddled, the ground stretches and chuckles;
> Glows in the tent of our seeing.
> Somewhere in the sleeping cloud a warbler
> Tries the rusty wheel of its song.
>
> Twelve paces from my nose, the whole world
> Blinks, or suddenly beyond a reef
> Or a startle of foxgloves
> Dissolves back into wet, thick air.
> The sea croons, silky, pacified. (pp. 28–9)

The imagery in the first stanza here is striking: the experience of physical space is significantly gendered, with the sounds of the island under fog coming to the speaker like a birth, whilst the timing of the foghorn 'recall[s] / Contractions'.[27] Such gendering of place suggests a generative quality for Bardsey – although that which is born crucially emerges out of mystery. This is because the contextual space that surrounds the immediate in this poem is *literally* fuzzy: the ground is 'Swaddled' and 'Glows'; the world 'Dissolves'. What Evans catches here, in other words, is a very literal manifestation of Tuan's idea of places that are conceptually imprecise and which thus have the quality of haziness that produces them as myth. What the poem does is thus to turn Bardsey into a realm of guesswork (out of which things are born). Fuzzy space is so close in on the speaker that she seems able to do little more than achieve rudimentary orientation: she is aware of the sea crooning; she has a sudden vision of foxgloves; a bird sings 'Somewhere'. But there is little more detail than this. The upshot is that Evans can turn Bardsey into a locus not only for the generative, but also for a kind of beautiful yearning – an equivalent to the western vista of 'translucent, milky-pale, vermilion' that was manifest in 'At the End of Summer' (p. 62). Thus, later in 'Sounding', she writes:

> This afternoon
> I trod a causeway through the clouds
> That flexed and quivered like a great swan's wings
> From the ridged spine of the mountain.
> Dry grass crunched underfoot like snow.
> Thistledown lifted on a thermal
> And a well-shaft opened to the light
> A shower of gold sparks dancing on the water
>
> Unfathomable depth below
> And in the shifting veils right over me
> A growing incandescence like a torch
> Approaching, or a great vague face
> Bending into focus. (p. 30)

Under the influence of fog, the island becomes a place where divinity itself draws downwards, in the images of the sun as a 'growing incandescence' and of a 'great vague face / Bending into focus'. Bardsey thus becomes a mythical space of profound desire – articulated in the sense of a glowing presence which is nothing less than a manifestation of transcendence. Interestingly, however, Evans seems to want to throw all this off as the poem ends. By the final stanza of 'Sounding', the speaker's thoughts are tending away from fuzziness and towards the clarity of 'late-summer vistas', as she wonders:

> What brinks, what late-summer vistas
> We are all ripening towards
> As we wait to see, wait
> For the sun
> To burn a way through. (p. 31)

As the poem concludes, then, the speaker muses on what clarity and wide vision will bring to the island instead of the closed-in, mythical space of foggy visions in which she has temporarily existed. For Evans, it seems, Bardsey can never be left to rest in just one state; it is a location whose conceptual identity is always on the move.

Such an observation is an appropriate reminder that, alongside the mythical patterns which Evans creates for Bardsey, *Island of Dark*

Horses also frames the island as what Tuan calls 'pragmatic' space – in other words, as a place of workaday, physical activities such as farming and play.[28] Thus, for example, in 'Myxomatosis', the island is a place of disease and consequent death:

> he had to keep on
> killing rabbits that summer on the island,
> a moment's sharpness in his hands
> seeming kinder than three days' long dying
> in that heat. (p. 47)

Similarly, the poem 'Gannets' is a fascinated celebration of non-human life, as the speaker watches birds diving for fish:

> Gannets fall
> as if fired back
> by sky they have stretched
> with their slow, strong wing-beats.
> …
> Over and over they plunge
> straight down into the dark
> to spear a glimpsed magnetic glitter.
>
> Watching makes us hold our breath. (pp. 12 and 13)

In both of these pieces, much of what matters is not Bardsey as a space configured into a particular schema or rendered in suggestive lack of clarity. Instead, the island here becomes the locale for a manifestation of the explicitly physical: sickness; heat; the 'sharpness' of a twisted neck; a particular wing-beat; the shape of a bird's plunge towards water; the appearance of fish below the surface of the sea. Indeed, even the reaction of the speaker in 'Gannets' is resolutely bodily: breath is held as the birds perform their acrobatics.

Evans's strategies of mythical formation thus never erase the materiality of the island; they never deny Bardsey's sheer physicality. What they do achieve, however, is an ongoing argument for the value of the place. For example, in 'Sounding', when the poet-speaker experiences something like a divine revelation in the natural world (for Evans, a distinctly rural space of mountain, grass, thistledown and water; p. 30), Bardsey is manifest as heir to the Romantic landscapes of Wordsworth and Coleridge, in which nature is valuable precisely because it is a locus for spiritual awakening. Indeed, Evans's deified sun in this poem can be seen as an inheritor of Wordsworth's famous angelic host of daffodils – as a moment of eternity breaking through into the temporal world.

Thus, in a striking demonstration of contemporary Romantic thought, Bardsey becomes a place of potential revelation: it sees what the religious historian Mircea Eliade calls an 'irruption of the sacred', by which he means that '*Something* that does not belong to this world has manifested itself apodictically.'[29]

Of course, it is arguably the case that such a move is inherently problematic – that it renders Welsh space as a sort of formulaic Celtic twilight (a misty place where mystery is manifest); or, at the least, that it merely *makes use of* Welsh environment less for its own sake than as a way of achieving spiritual rebirth, in the manner of the English Romantics, who, as Belinda Humfrey points out, 'used Welsh locations to convey spiritual transformations and creative revelations'.[30] However, whereas the relationship of the English Romantics with Wales was broadly that of the visitor or tourist,[31] Evans's poetic engagement with Welsh space is that of the insider, the resident. Thus, in 'Meeting the Boat', the poet-speaker is portrayed as an islander who watches outsiders arrive for one sort of short stay or another:

> Saturdays, we sit outside the boathouse
> to wave goodbye … and watch the next lot land. (p. 9)

For the poem's speaker, Bardsey is not merely an inspiring but inevitably passing scene on a visitor's itinerary. Rather, the sense of divine contact that occurs in 'Sounding' emerges alongside (or even in spite of) the familiarities and repetitions which are bred by long-term residence – familiarities and repetitions which the speaker of 'Island of Dark Horses' articulates thus:

> This is a real place, small enough
> to see whole, big enough to lose
> our own importance. Brings us back
> to our senses. *Here we dig and sow and gather*
> *walk and swim and watch birth, blossoming*
> *and rot* … (p. 80; emphasis added)

The experience of transcendence in 'Sounding' is, then, crucially distinct from the false or naïve epiphany of the visitor – that unrealistic 'bubble of expectations' which, as Evans puts it in 'Meeting the Boat', 'we might see punctured by a sharpening edge / of sense, if they [visitors] stay long enough' (p. 9). Evans avoids the touristic trap of merely *using* the place for inspiration. In this sense, the closest parallel to Evans's work is probably that of Brenda Chamberlain who, in the final pages of *Tide-race*, renders Bardsey as hallowed ground – it is 'a soli-

tary place but blessed by the sun'[32] – but does so as self-conscious resi-
dent rather than Romantic tourist. Thus, Chamberlain is emphatically
aware of the moment at which she shifts from being a seasonal visitor
to a permanent inhabitant of the island ('Today, we became islanders';
p. 138), just as she presents herself as intimately involved both in the
social politics of the island and the often-communal demands of its
work. From such a perspective, any sense of Bardsey as 'blessed' space
is hard-won and is achieved alongside the hardships of island life.[33]

More generally, Evans's strategy of giving the island a mythical dimen-
sion which suggests the romance of the western isles again renders
Bardsey as a location with intrinsic value beyond the simply physical. It
effectively construes the island as more than a Site of Special Scientific
Interest or a National Nature Reserve (as it was declared, respectively, in
1953 and 1986)[34] – however important such designations might be – in
order to create it as a place where, at the least, mysteries may survive a
little longer than they do on the mainland. Of course, an environmen-
talist reading of such a position is likely to frown on its implicit rejection
of intrinsic value in the natural world as sufficient reason for a place to
be worth protecting. Evans's approach, by contrast – and in addition to
any value the collection may impute to the purely physical aspects of
the island – offers additional, conceptual reasons to value Bardsey. I
have argued elsewhere that anthropocentric reasons for defending
(preserving) certain environments are not to be rejected,[35] and I would
definitely want to reiterate that here: it makes pragmatic sense, at the very
least, to marshal as many arguments as possible for the defence of sites
which are, as Bardsey is, of major environmental importance (evidenced
bureaucratically by the two designations cited earlier in this paragraph).
To broaden the argument, it is also worth pointing out that the mythical
values imputed to Bardsey in *Island of Dark Horses* mark the collection
as broadly complementing the work of the Bardsey Island Trust, which
was, according to Justin Wintle, formed 'to protect the island's natural
and spiritual heritage'.[36]

Clearly, the mythical element that I have detailed here is not the
famous sense of Bardsey as place of Christian pilgrimage, the island of
20,000 saints – that history which Peter Hope Jones defines as the first
of Bardsey's 'Metaphysical images'. Nor is it what Jones sees as the
second of the island's metaphysical lives – the sense of 'the peace and
quiet which the island affords' that functions 'as an antidote to the
noisy pace of mainland life'. Rather, the mythical aspect that I have
outlined here is most closely related to Jones's third category of Bardsey

metaphysics – what he calls a 'shadowy, parallel-world aspect of meta-physics' – in which the island has accrued an identity 'based on truth or half-truth coupled with vivid imagination' to become the epitome of 'the "island in the west" so beloved of mediaeval romancers'.[37] Of course, as I have argued, Evans's mythical geography is rather more complex and contradictory than this simple correlation. But the main point here holds good: by giving the island mythical value, Evans's poetic marks Bardsey out as special – and thus, by implication, as a space to be protected. In Mircea Eliade's terms, such differentiation of space is the way in which a particular space is made sacred:

> For religious man, space is not homogeneous; he experiences interruptions, breaks in it; some parts of space are qualitatively different from others. 'Draw not nigh hither,' says the Lord to Moses; 'put off thy shoes from off thy feet, for the place whereon thou standest is holy ground' (Exodus, 3, 5). There is, then, a sacred space, and hence a strong, significant space …[38]

From this perspective, the way in which Evans renders Bardsey mythi-cally as different from the space around it – as what Eliade would call an *interruption* within that surrounding space – effectively makes the island a kind of 'holy ground'. This is not to suggest that *Island of Dark Horses* is either a specifically Judaeo-Christian or more generally a reli-gious text. Rather, its enactment of a mythical geography works to construe the island as sacred in the broadest of senses – as somewhere that is set apart; or, as Eliade puts it, as a 'strong, significant space'. In the terms set up by the geo-mythology of *Island of Dark Horses*, the value of Bardsey is not just an environmental issue; rather it is to do with nothing less than the identification of sacred space within the geography of Wales.

9

Ian Davidson:
'the form and function of the world'

Like Christine Evans, Ian Davidson is particularly associated with
north Wales. In the 'Afterword' to his 2004 volume of poetry *At a
Stretch*, he explicitly positions himself 'in north Wales between the
mountains and the sea' – although his stated interest in the ways in
which the 'local inter-relates with the global' also echoes the transcul-
turalism of Robert Minhinnick which I have previously discussed.
Indeed, Davidson's notion of 'simultaneously existing in a number of
different locations from a number of different perspectives' suggests a
refusal of place as a stable, readily bounded, or single entity that goes
some way beyond Minhinnick's transcultural engagements.[1] Again like
Evans, Davidson has centred a volume of poetry on an island in the
north-west of the country: in his case, Anglesey and its environs, in the
seventeen-poem sequence which constitutes the 2003 collection *Human
Remains & Sudden Movements*. Thus, although the title of this volume
is, on one level, a pun on the phrase 'the quick and the dead' (albeit with
the components reversed), it is perhaps more important to note that the
eponymous notion of *Human Remains* also refers to the experience of
an archaeological dig at Trearddur Bay on Holy Island (Ynys Gybi), off
the western edge of Anglesey itself.[2] The title's *Human Remains* are thus
ones which emerge specifically from the Welsh environment. It is this
volume that particularly interests me here – especially the way in which
it manages to create a kind of abstract vision of Welsh space which, at
the same time, renders the Welsh environment as a significantly cultural
and political entity.

Davidson's construction of Welsh space in politicized terms has been apparent from his earliest work. His first solo collection (1989), *No Passage Landward (Environmental Studies)*, includes the pieces 'Taking the Piss' and 'The Industrial Heartland', both of which sharply note signs in English that declare Welsh space out of bounds. Thus, in the Anglesey poem 'Taking the Piss',[3] the poem's speaker observes –

> Black and white rings
> on the lighthouse
> and NO PASSAGE LANDWARD
> a sign spells out we scramble
> round a few rocks the English
> saying private

– whilst 'The Industrial Heartland' is blunter still:

> Scratch scratch the kids write on old slate ends
> picked up on the footpath. I deface in full view
> a monoglot sign saying of course private. (p. 12)

Although I was unwilling to concede Linden Peach's argument that Robert Minhinnick's poem 'J.P.' was to do with a colonization of Welsh space by English power,[4] Peach's suggestion might be more fruitfully applied in this case. The cultural significance of the monoglot sign – manifestly monoglot *English*, given that it says *private* rather than the Welsh *preifat* – is captured by the sense that its declaration of private space is entirely expected ('of course'). English-language culture in north-west Wales – Davidson indicates that the poem emerges from an experience of Dinorwig, above Llyn Peris, in Caernarfonshire[5] – is thus presented as a business of exclusion and rejection *as a matter of course*, keeping everything else out of the Welsh space to which it has laid a claim. It is precisely this that 'The Industrial Heartland' goes on to emphasize by observing 'Other favourite signs' which include 'keep out keep off / no public right of way'. Moreover, in the poem's final stanza, English appropriation of Welsh space succeeds in reducing Wales itself to a kind of toy:

> climbers in stripy pants clinging to the sheer walls
> bulked with apparatus their shrill English voices echo
> my home is a playground.

I have considered English power over Welsh land for pleasure purposes in my chapter on Mike Jenkins, and Davidson here echoes Jenkins's concerns. But the final note of Davidson's poem is different both from the treading down of Wales's most famous environmental landmark in

Jenkins's 'Yr Wyddfa Speaks Out!' and from the deserted streets created by the purchase of holiday homes at the end of his 'House for Sale'. Rather, for the early Davidson, the end of 'The Industrial Heartland' suggests Welsh space as effectively trivialized, as an environment reduced to nothing more than a plaything. Although she does not consider such activities explicitly, Sharon Zukin's study of gentrification suggests a parallel situation, in which the 'social values of existing users' of an area with relatively low economic status 'exert a weaker claim' on the landscape in question 'than the cultural values of potential gentrifiers' who effectively come into an area with money to spend and thus redesign it to their taste.[6] The environment of Davidson's Wales is, here, precisely redesigned to the taste of the English climbers, who thus render it as the 'playground' on which note the poem ends.

* * *

The poetry in *Human Remains & Sudden Movements* is far more oblique than that in *No Passage Landward*. Indeed, annotations on Davidson's copy of *No Passage Landward* indicate a later ambivalence towards his emphatically blunt landscape politics in that early volume. One suggested change to 'The Industrial Heartland', for example, deletes 'English' from the poem's penultimate line. This removes both the implication of English identity from the climbers and, as a consequence, the specifically English reduction of Welsh space to trivia from the whole of the final stanza. Similarly, in the collection's opening poem (significantly titled 'The Country's Up for Grabs'), an apparent reference to the activities of Meibion Glyndŵr ('the flicker of flames') has been entirely deleted.[7] Such tendencies towards a less overt form of landscape poetics have, I think, come to significant fruition in the north Welsh spaces of *Human Remains & Sudden Movements*.

To understand Davidson's more recent approach, it is useful to turn again to the work of Yi-Fu Tuan, who suggests that:

Places and objects define space, giving it a geometric personality. Neither the newborn infant nor the man who gains sight after a lifetime of blindness can immediately recognize a geometric shape such as a triangle. The triangle is at first 'space,' a blurred image. Recognizing the triangle requires the prior identification of corners – that is, places. A neighborhood is at first a confusion of images to the new resident; it is blurred space 'out there.' Learning to know the neighborhood requires the identification of significant localities, such as street corners and architectural landmarks, within the neighborhood space.[8]

A known place is, according to Tuan, understood through its construction out of particular landmarks – out of specific objects which can be connected together to form a 'geometric personality', much like a triangle. Familiar places such as home, town, region and so on are produced conceptually by linking together the specific 'significant localities' that make them up. In Tuan's analysis, it is this process of recognizing and then connecting precise points of significance which changes an area (a 'neighborhood') from 'blurred space' ('a confusion of images') to *defined space*. This sense of *defined space* also seems to drive Lawrence Buell's understanding of place and 'place sense', in his observation of 'the complex network of sensations and value commitments' that are vitally caught up with a sense of place.[9] In short, a known space – a 'place', in Buell's terms – is formed from a network of physical points of significance.[10]

In *Human Remains & Sudden Movements* there is a tendency to point out – in a way which initially suggests Tuan's ideas about place formation quite precisely – landmarks within the environment. For example, in the very first poem of the sequence, what we are confronted with primarily is a set of physical formations.[11] In the opening stanza, Davidson presents images of a pool 'spreading in the cool morning' and of 'water between ... banks'. The delineations of shaped space appear immediately, as the poem establishes a sense of three-dimensionality: the horizontality of the spreading pool; the banks which rise in the vertical against the water and set its horizontal limits as a result. In fact, as the poem progresses, this sense of three-dimensional space becomes stronger through various references to 'dropped arches', 'tall monuments // casting shadows', 'a bulky pinnacle' and 'a heap of / rock'. Davidson further notes that 'from holes in the / ground many spikes rise commemorative', and observes 'a series of / rectangles each one over and / under or to one side the fit not // perfect'. Geometric formations pattern the poem, just as they pattern the landscape that is being depicted. We are, in other words, presented with a scene that is full of landscape markers: arches, holes, pinnacles and rectangles. Thus, the space suggested by the poem emphatically has shape – or, at least, contains shape(s).

Such shape, however, does not necessarily point towards a coherent image of a place. For example, although the speaker observes, at the end of the poem's fourth stanza, 'I can see my house from here', 'here' is not clearly located in relation to the other objects observed within the poem. This ambiguity is, in part, created by the particular tradition out of which Davidson's poetic emerges – that radical tradition of twentieth-century poetry in which, amongst other things, to quote Charles Olson's famous essay 'Projective Verse' (first published in 1950), 'the conventions which logic has forced on syntax [have been] broken open'.[12] Thus, when the poem's speaker indicates that he can see his house from 'here', the fact that the poem is syntactically ambiguous means that it is difficult to be sure whether 'here' relates to the opening topography of the pool and water (for example) or to the syntactically closer 'bulky pinnacle' of the previous line:

> the tall monuments
>
> casting shadows brain
> damage from a bulky pinnacle
> I can see my house from here a
>
> sphere of influence

The difficulties inherent in simply reading the poem's syntax – and thus of reading its landscape – are strong at this point. Specifically, in these lines, is there a conceptual parallel between 'the tall monuments // casting shadows' and 'brain / damage from a bulky pinnacle'? Or should the break in sense be read from after 'brain / damage', resulting in an interpretation which suggests that 'from a bulky pinnacle / I can see my house from here'? The issue is undecidable, and the place of the poem is, in this sense, distinctly ambiguous: the 'corners' of Tuan's triangle may be established – in Davidson's poem, the arches, holes, rectangles and spikes – but the way in which they should be connected is far less clear. To put it simply, it may seem that the reader is very much in the position of Tuan's 'new resident' to whom a neighbourhood is still a 'confusion of images'.[13] As such, what Davidson achieves is a rendition of Welsh land as a fundamentally abstract collage of shapes – thus suggesting a significant affinity with what Harriet Tarlo has called 'radical landscape poetry', which is characterized by a 'formal and ideological shift away from more traditional forms of landscape writing'.[14] Indeed, even when the concluding lines of the poem finally draw a link between two points (lighthouses), thereby suggesting the bounds of a particular coastal area –

> from lighthouse
>
> to lighthouse no more than a heap of
> rock where the birds come to roost beyond
> the fold around the tides meet

– the space thus enclosed is immediately characterized in terms of shape (a rocky heap).[15] Physical shapes within the environment appear to be a persistent concern. By contrast, drawing such shapes together to form a navigable space – in which spatial relationships between points are clearly established – is a far more occasional matter.

* * *

The particular approach to the construction of space and place that dominates the first poem of *Human Remains & Sudden Movements* – that sense of rendering Anglesey as a collage of shapes – is apparent throughout the sequence as a whole. Shapes thus seem to be figured within the environment as things worth experiencing in their own right. As a result, there is a basic pleasure in Davidson's rendition of the Welsh environment in what might be seen as the physicality of things – things, in other words, as material forms. For example, poem three observes 'the superstructure / of pier mighty columns across a / stretch', rendering Bangor Pier and the bridges across the Menai Strait – the features which, according to Davidson, are fused together into the images offered in these lines[16] – primarily in terms of a sense of structure, with the emphasis on the impressive bulk of columns and the suggestion of a bridge's wide span. Similarly, poem nine starts with the simple observation of 'pleats on the chimney pot'. However, when this phrase leads onto the following remark about 'levelling / the view finder', it is unclear whether the view finder in question is directed towards the chimney pot or towards the 'human remains' ('out // of sight', in any case) which immediately follow. As with the first poem of the sequence, in other words, the emphasis in poem nine seems to be more on the particular physical forms that the environment contains than on an attempt to connect them together to create a conceptually navigable area. A similar approach is again identifiable in poem six, which notes:

> fractured column to column like a
> curtain the fold of the
> base stone the road and the railway

That shapes and (human) formations are part of this landscape is readily apparent (columns, base stone, road, railway). How they relate to one another spatially, however, remains unclear. Moreover, as poem one suggested, when connections *are* made, they are typically limited in

scope or are incomplete. In that previous poem, although the final lines
linked together two lighthouses in a way which created the sense of a
bounded (and then characterized) space, this process in no way resolved
the spatial interconnections between the physical structures that were
identified by the rest of the poem. Similarly, in poem seven, the opening
line observes 'at the bottom of the steps a lighthouse', whilst further on
we see 'figures / approaching the chapel on a sand dune': steps and
lighthouse are obviously in close proximity, and there are sand dunes
somewhere near a chapel. But topographical connections are pursued
to no greater extent than this. Indeed, Davidson's refusal of specific
place names (apparent throughout the collection) rather fuels this:
lighthouse and chapel become almost generic markers of a coastal
Welsh identity, rather than particular places between which one might
know how to walk.[17] The Anglesey area with which *Human Remains &
Sudden Movements* is concerned thus primarily emerges from the
sequence not as a readily navigable space, but as a collection of physical
forms – columns, stones, span, chimney pot, road, railway, human
remains. It is unsurprising that, in the final poem of the sequence (poem
seventeen), Davidson concedes:

> I wrote specifically as if I could do otherwise
> the totality escapes me the folds that matter makes up

Davidson's approach to the landscape of his sequence is thus, on one
level, a matter of fragments; as he puts it here, 'the totality escapes me'.
And it does the reader: the environment of the Anglesey area emerges
as a mass of images, which are rarely drawn into anything more than
limited or passing spatial coherence. However, the fragments that are
observed are vital: in their attention to landscape details, 'Davidson's
recurrent, partial observations' (as I have described them elsewhere[18])
are a significant challenge to that limited environmental responsiveness
which Lawrence Buell suggests is typical of human beings (the 'envi-
ronmental unconscious' in its 'negative aspect', as he puts it). They are,
in Buell's words, 'breakthroughs' in environmental awareness 'achieved
in grasping the significance of the unnoticed detail'.[19]

However, it would also seem to be the case that, in his greater attention
to such detail than to spatial interconnections, Davidson tends towards
that sort of 'specialized intellectual curiosity' which Lawrence Buell
considers one of 'the many causes of foreshortening' of environmental
vision (p. 22) – and which results in an inability to produce the 'distilled
and panoramic image, dependent on knowledge of how the various

biotic and geological constituents interlink: the ability to read landscapes from the mountaintop, so to speak' (p. 17). Indeed, even when Davidson approaches a moment of spatial distillation, as he seems to do at the end of poem one – that rendition of the area between two lighthouses as 'a heap of / rock' – it is, as I have suggested, quite insufficient for resolving the spatial connections between the mass of 'biotic and geological constituents' (in Buell's terms) which the rest of the poem has collected together. From this perspective, what Davidson's poetic provides is a kind of hyperfocus – an obsession with individual items which lacks that sense of systemic interconnectedness which has been claimed as central to the environmentalist vision (the Barry Commoner principle that 'Everything is connected to everything else'[20]).

Davidson's poetry does, however, put up an explicit defence against such a critique. Following his assertion that 'I wrote specifically ... / the totality escapes me', the opening stanza of poem seventeen concludes with the statement that 'little becomes more': in other words, *even if the totality is unavailable, the specific details that I have given you will add up to more than their individual parts*. Indeed, at the very end of the collection, as poem seventeen draws to its close, Davidson observes:

> viable processes a peasant way of life or concrete taking the shape of
> whatever it's poured into ... lift
> thine eyes up to the hills ...

The sense here is of human life poured into a specific location and shaped in a particular way as a consequence – an understanding of the link between humanity and environment that Buell calls 'the theory of people and cultures as ecocontextual products'.[21] In other words, even if it does not seem to give great weight to localized spatial interconnections, Davidson's poetic is manifestly sensitive to larger environmental forces, not just to the minutiae of individual shapes in a given place. Thus, in its evocation of Psalm 121,[22] poem seventeen suggests the notion of how a culture may form significant elements of its consciousness around the landscape within which it dwells. (Specifically, here, the reference is to the ancient Jewish sense of hill country as a place of spiritual significance.[23]) As such, the poem proposes a formative relationship between the environment of north-west Wales and 'a peasant way of life'. The effect of this association – which suggests that one social group bears the particular imprint of the land itself – is to lay claim to a very specific social interpretation of Wales's north-west as the domain of the rural poor. Although these lines are clearly making a connection between people and land, this is not that 'very unsettling racial essentialism' which Ian Gregson decries in what he sees as Gillian Clarke's organic 'equation of language and land', and which leads, as he puts it, 'to the ideology of blood and soil'.[24] Rather, Davidson is gesturing towards an argument about environmental conditioning as an emphatically social process: that a particular mode of human life is formed, at least in part, in response to the environment in which it takes place. Indeed, it is interesting to note that the particular link which Davidson proposes between 'a peasant way of life' and north-west Wales is strongly suggestive of historic class distribution. As *A Vision of Britain Through Time* ('A vision of Britain between 1801 and 2001') indicates, lower-class working-age males – classes 4 and 5, which the study defines as 'semi-skilled and unskilled manual workers' – have consistently made up a larger percentage of the population in Anglesey and Gwynedd (the latter, of course, comprising much of historic Caernarfonshire and Merioneth) than has been the average for England and Wales as a whole.[25] In this sense, north-west Wales is thus significantly distinct from Wales as a whole in which, until well into the twentieth century, lower-class working-age males made up a *smaller* percentage of the population than was average for England and Wales as a whole.[26] Davidson's suggestion is that such social conditions are emphatically bound up with environmental context. In other words, his poetic at this point rises above the particularities of individual physical formations within a landscape to assert the involvement of broad topographical patterns in the social processes of identity formation in the Welsh north-west.

It is precisely this sense of the potential cultural implications of landscape which ensures that Davidson's poetic, although not particularly concerned with spatial interconnection, is manifestly aware of far more than just fine-grained environmental detail. Or, to put it a different way, an awareness of the interrelations between land and its inhabitants is crucial to this sequence as a whole. The *Human Remains* of the collection's title suggest the marks which human communities have made on the landscape of the Anglesey area – and this explains, at least in part, those shapes which Davidson persistently documents. Thus, poem nine observes 'the walls the edge human / remains', and goes on to evoke processes of archaeological uncovering with the observation that 'the mound becomes the // shape of what it was'. Such notes are significantly explained by poem thirteen which records a monument crashing to the ground and then offers the following apparent commentary on this process:

                    shards of
                    previous civilisations

At least some of Davidson's shapes and forms are thus records of human civilization that have been written into and onto the environment of north-west Wales. Some are or have been covered over because of their age: poem nine notes 'human remains out // of sight of the public'.[27] Others are readily apparent: in poem six, 'the road and the railway'; in poem seven, 'at the bottom of the steps a lighthouse'. As Davidson puts it in poem fifteen, this is a poetry which engages with both 'the form and function of the world'.

                              * * *

It is this latter sense of the 'function of the world' which is crucial in moving *Human Remains & Sudden Movements* beyond an exclusively Welsh context, as the sequence seeks to identify large-scale socio-environmental processes into which its immediate surroundings might fit. This is, in other words, part of that tendency towards understanding environment in terms of multiple locations and perspectives to which Davidson gestures in his 'Afterword' to 2004's *At a Stretch*. Indeed, the decision to avoid place names throughout *Human Remains & Sudden Movements* suggests a similar desire to avoid being restricted to a sense of place as a stable, single entity. Rather than restricting the poetic focus to the Anglesey area which provides the collection's specific topographical root, emphasis may thus be thrown either onto other places entirely or onto generic-level theories of place construction. All of this becomes apparent from the very beginning of the collection in a fragment of poem one that I have already quoted:

                    the tall monuments

                    casting shadows brain
                    damage from a bulky pinnacle

If the syntactic break within this section takes place after 'casting shadows', what is being suggested here is a sense of the potential darkness that can be created in human lives by structures within the landscape. In this context, what immediately precedes these lines becomes significant:

                    fascist
                    memorabilia a spreading pool
                    of fact

There is an explicit concern with matters of political impact here, which may even imply that the opening topography of the sequence as a whole ('a pool / spreading in the cool morning') is as much metaphorical as it is literal. Or, to put it another way, Davidson refuses to block the emergence of those *general* political associations which his *particular* topographical observations may suggest. It is thus unsurprising that stanza seven of the opening poem observes 'people / written over': the 'series of / rectangles each one over and / under or to one side' with which the poem was concerned in stanza six – presumably archaeological uncoverings – are not without human impact; they are not, in short, apolitical formations. Instead, they represent the ways in which one form of human life may be obscured, suppressed or overwritten by another, and their persistence in the formations of the landscape – their status as the collection's eponymous *Human Remains* – is thus a record of cultural-political cycles. For Davidson, in other words, the landscape becomes very literally a text: the environment is a page onto which political processes are written.

It is precisely this perspective that is embedded in the other part of the collection's title – the reference to *Sudden Movements* – as the fourth stanza of poem two indicates:

> Most sudden movements can cause bruising the
> Marxist party or clearing land of its
> people for other purposes and that's why the
> big house is big

What concerns Davidson here is the way in which 'sudden movements' such as 'the / Marxist party' or 'clearing land of its / people' can 'cause bruising' – bruising, it seems, to either the land or the people who live on it. The collection's eponymous *Sudden Movements* thus seem to be political changes of one sort or another. As such, it might be said that what Davidson appears to advocate here is a kind of quietist or conservative approach to politics, by which I mean a distinct wariness of change. In the terms of the poem, this constitutes a disinclination to sanction those 'sudden movements' which might 'cause bruising'. However, it seems that what concerns Davidson at this point is not so much *any* change, as change which results in the oppression of the sort of people to whom the final poem of the collection gestures in its reference to 'a peasant way of life' – people, in short, who have historically had strictly limited social power. This is why the final clause quoted above is so important: the big house in the landscape is not a neutral phenomenon; more precisely, its size within the landscape is not merely a matter of physical proportions. The big house is the size it is, and it looms as large in the landscape as it does, because it has availed itself of structures of power – structures of power which, in such matters as land clearances, have written a history of wealth's repeated and often-violent subjugation of poverty into the texture of the landscape itself.

For a British reader, the notion of land clearance to which Davidson refers here perhaps most immediately suggests the political-environmental history of Scotland in the early nineteenth century. But it also suggests, on a generic level, the processes which create and sustain those dominating environmental forms that Sharon Zukin calls 'landscapes of power'.[28] However, whilst poem two manifestly reaches out to both general and non-Welsh socio-environmental issues at this point, the issue of the big house simultaneously registers the explicitly Welsh nature of Davidson's work. Given the prominent presence of Plas Newydd on the eastern side of the island, this idea is specific to the collection's Anglesey context.[29] But Davidson is also responding more generally to the way in which the *plas* – the 'big house' of the poem – has been a key environmental manifestation of the power and wealth that have been bound up with landownership across significant areas of Wales. As such, Davidson's observations here on the link between estate power and social suffering echo those important Welsh critiques of landlordism which John Davies notes as beginning with the pamphlets of S.R. (Samuel Roberts) in the mid-nineteenth century (*Ffarmwr Careful of Cilhaul Uchaf* of 1850 and *Diosg Farm* of 1854) in which 'landlordism was [seen to be] at the root of the problems of rural Wales'.[30] Specifically, the material, economic and class dominance of large estates was seen by such work to have 'soiled, and burdened, and slandered, and humiliated, and degraded, and trampled underfoot'[31] – *bruised*, in Davidson's terms – the actual farmers who worked estate land. Thus, for Davidson to strike the note he does here indicates a responsiveness to the particularly important history of landownership in Wales – and its consequent significance to the social production of Welsh landscape. As John Davies indicates, 'In 1887, only 10.2 per cent of land in Wales was owned by the person who farmed it' – a significantly smaller percentage than was the case in either Scotland (14.0%) or England (16.1%).[32] At this point, then, the big house functions in Davidson's poetic precisely to symbolize the historic status of estate power over rural Welsh land.

As this moment in poem two suggests, the landscapes of Davidson's poetry are significantly bound up with the discourse of politics – both in

terms of the specific history of the Welsh environment and in relation to
procedures of place formation in general. The production of Davidson's
landscapes, in other words, is very much part and parcel of the produc-
tion of human discourse. It is thus not surprising that poem two starts
with those entirely human ideas 'The longitude and the latitude', and
goes on to take note of 'contour lines'. More significant, perhaps, is the
way in which this poem meshes such concepts with the observation that,
on a mountain, 'higher still no vegetation grows'. In other words, an
attempt to suggest the phenomenal realities of the environment is intim-
ately bound up with a form of discourse *about* the environment –
specifically, the pictorial discourse of mapping. Similarly, poem twelve
suggests an interconnection between the processes of art and the phys-
ical world itself:

> take material pulverise it ...
> add water make it art

On an initial level, what Davidson indicates here is that the materials of
the phenomenal world are 'pulverise[d]' in the making of art (literally,
in the creation of certain pigments). However, in the context of a
sequence so intimately bound up with a coastal topography, this image
also suggests the poetic process of the collection itself: the physical
shapes of land are broken down and mixed together, water (the sea) is
added, and the art form is thus created. Davidson's sense of place, in
other words, knows that landscapes are never simply *given* when they
enter human discourse; rather, he sees landscapes as works of art which
take existing physical phenomena ('take material') and shape them into
something new. In Lawrence Buell's phrase, what Davidson seems to
engage with is thus a 'mutual constructionist understanding of place-
ness'.[33] This is an awareness that, although archaeology (for example)
may uncover the concrete realities of that 'mound' which, as poem nine
indicates, 'becomes the // shape of what it was' as it is unearthed, such
shapes are never free of cultural patterning and associations as soon as
they enter forms of human discourse.

However, Davidson's concern with large-scale environmental
processes comes to perhaps its sharpest focus in that desire to globalize
the local to which he refers in the 'Afterword' of *At a Stretch*. In poem
seven of *Human Remains & Sudden Movements*, Davidson considers the
coastal topography on which the collection is centred and observes:

> sandbags like
> maggots on a dead body figures
> approaching the chapel on a sand dune
> caves such as the Taliban might use to
>
> conceal weaponry

The environment of Davidson's north-west Wales is, at this point, inextricable from its wider-world resonances. Specifically, in the reference to the Taliban, the poem evokes the global politics of the current conflict in Afghanistan (which began in October 2001), in which the UK has been significantly implicated as a partner to the USA. One landscape, in this sense, is connected to another by the imagined similarities which the poem brings to bear: in other words, the Welsh caves of the poem's immediate observation may be just like those in which the Taliban hide their weapons. In the terms offered by poem sixteen, this is 'the global breeze' that blows 'through the bar area' – that 'bar area' signifying *pub*,[34] or (to put it another way) *local*. Just as was the case with Robert Minhinnick's later poetry, Wales is crucially embedded in the wider world. The result is a kind of double vision – an awareness of the global resonances of local topographic formations which suggests precisely that unwillingness to see place as a singular or stable entity which is identifiable in the 'Afterword' of *At a Stretch*. This is a way of thinking about place which, in Doreen Massey's terms, suggests the 'multiplicity of social relations across all spatial scales'.[35] Thus, poem eight observes what seems to be a built structure and notes:

> kalashnikov through the doorway
> petrol down the vent shaft
> mainly pigeons
> he shook his angry head

To pick up a term that I have earlier associated with Robert Minhinnick, this structure is, precisely, transcultural: the reference to pigeons seemingly establishes it as part of the association that poem one sets up between bird-life and Anglesey ('no more than a heap of / rock where the birds come to roost'), whilst the phrase 'kalashnikov through the doorway' simultaneously locates it in terms of the Afghanistan conflict to which the previous poem referred. It is, moreover, an acutely political space, indicating the uses to which features within the landscape may be put in the pursuit of power, and thus operating as a contemporary parallel to the historic land clearances noted in poem two. To put it simply, it is such moments which reveal the full extent of what poem fifteen means when it refers to 'the form and function of the world': that, for Davidson, the forms of Welsh place (a cave in poem seven; a built structure in poem eight) may be political spaces of thoroughly global scope.

10

Afterword:
'a landscape with everything in it'

Carolyn Davies and Lynne Bebb have written a short book about the artist Kyffin Williams that I leaf through every so often with my 3-year-old son. Targeted at schools, *Kyffin Williams: Painting the Mountains* reproduces a variety of Williams's renditions of the Welsh environment in all their jagged drama: a storm at Trearddur Bay (one of the locations, of course, behind Ian Davidson's *Human Remains & Sudden Movements*); the rough sweep of the Llŷn Peninsula; the harsh edges of Crib Goch.[1] However, as part of their splendidly clear commentary, Davies and Bebb point out that Williams's concern is not just with Welsh landscape as natural formation. Rather, as they put it:

> Kyffin uses the Welsh word, *cynefin*, when he thinks of his beloved landscape and everything in it: the mountains; the ridges and screes; the lakes; the rivers and waterfalls; the castles; the farms and cottages; the animals, and of course the people. There is no English word quite like it – it means the area in which you belong, the place in which you feel at home. (p. 18)

In other words, for Williams, as well as being a matter of non-human objects and forces, the Welsh environment that was his home is also emphatically a human thing. Indeed, it is this latter quality that my son particularly responds to: he seems especially interested by those paintings in the volume which feature squat buildings, uneven stone walls and farmers out in the snow with their dogs.

When they write about his use of the word *cynefin*, what Davies and Bebb are specifically referring to is a moment in Kyffin Williams's 1998 volume *The Land & the Sea* in which he states that:

Everywhere in Gwynedd I see the stone farmhouses and cottages and the meandering stone walls that tie them all together into a fascinating unity. I have always loved to paint these buildings, maybe because of the people who lived in them or the abstract patterns they create. I am always conscious of the Welsh word *cynefin* which does not mean just landscape but a landscape with everything in it.[2]

On one level, this immediately suggests some of the specific concerns raised by the poets with whom I have engaged in this study. Perhaps most strikingly, Williams's interest in the 'abstract patterns' of the Welsh environment quickly recalls Ian Davidson, whose similar concern with the shape of things is so important to his rendition of the Anglesey area in *Human Remains & Sudden Movements*. But also, the interest in 'farmhouses and cottages', for example, suggests Ruth Bidgood's persistent engagement with the built structures in the area around Abergwesyn. More important, however, is the general principle which Williams suggests in his use of the word *cynefin* and his notion of producing, in his paintings, 'a landscape with everything in it'. This is, I think, precisely what draws together the diversity of geographical and social concerns in the poetry that I have examined here: it is all centrally interested in rendering the physicality of the Welsh environment as a vitally *human* space. In this sense, it sets itself against that long-standing and specifically English artistic approach to Wales which I referred to in my analysis of R. S. Thomas in Chapter 3 – the 'English topographical tradition' which, according to Wynn Thomas, renders Welsh space as nothing more than 'scenery and ... natural resources' (as R. S. Thomas himself put it). Professor Thomas has noted how Mildred Eldridge (R. S. Thomas's first wife) was much influenced by this tradition – which, he suggests, was strongly apparent in the mid-twentieth-century *Recording Britain* volumes to which Eldridge's drawings and watercolours of Wales were such important contributions. Thus, he observes that Eldridge's work shows a tendency to render human figures 'so lightly' that they 'seem wispy outgrowths of the [Welsh] landscape itself'.[3] By contrast, the human forces in the Welsh environments that I have examined in this volume show no such tendency to 'wispy' half-presence. The 'critically important distance' which my discussion in Chapter 3 observed between R. S. Thomas and the 'English topographical tradition' appears to have been significantly propagated by later anglophone poets writing from Wales.

Linden Peach has usefully observed the 'abiding concern' of 'contemporary poetry from Wales' with what he calls 'the sociopolitical construction of space', and it is this sort of tendency that I wish to suggest particularly holds together the poets I have addressed in this book.[4] In the words of Wynn Thomas, drawing on the analysis of Jeremy Hooker, 'landscape is turned by Anglo-Welsh poets into a subtle language for the expression of social feeling'. The specific point that Thomas is making is that the Welsh landscape has become a way of exploring, far more than the concerns of the individual and isolated 'I', the 'shared experience' of Welsh lives.[5] Indeed, in a recent interview, Jeremy Hooker has again emphasized this sense of collective experience as a trait he particularly discovered in Wales when he came to live here in 1965.[6] What I am suggesting, in other words, is that, in the poetry I have examined in this volume, Welsh environments are inextricable from the operations of Welsh culture. Thus, they function as a way for Gillian Clarke to address differing gendered experiences of Welsh place; for Robert Minhinnick to examine conflicts of class, changing over time, around the collective life of a south Wales estate; or for Ian Davidson to explore the various records of human construction which are scattered over the Anglesey area. This is not, of course, to suggest that the poets I have been concerned with somehow abandon a sense of the materiality of the environments out of which they write. Mike Jenkins is deeply concerned with the physical character of the common land near Heolgerrig, rendering it as a 'complex' pastoral combination of streams, wildlife and old mine workings; Christine Evans's notion of Bardsey as a kind of centre-point with its own gravity is substantially the consequence of an awareness of tidal currents around the island; and Ruth Bidgood's is a poetic which is crucially bound up with valleys and watercourses. Moreover, although explicitly biocentric tendencies are rare – by which I mean specific arguments about the value of the earth for its own sake – this does not mean that the poets I have addressed are blind to matters of green concern, such as environmental damage. Mike Jenkins, perhaps in particular, is aware of the fierce history of environmental degradation which surrounds Merthyr. Indeed, it might also be worth noting that, whilst Wynn Thomas's summary of Jeremy Hooker suggests that, in English-language poetry from Wales, landscape has become a '*subtle* language for the expression of social feeling' (emphasis added), subtlety is sometimes far from the primary note being struck, with Ian Davidson's early anger about the English appropriation of Welsh space for pleasure purposes being a case in point.

This complex environmental ideology is, then, precisely what I think Kyffin Williams is suggesting when he talks about the implications of the word *cynefin*. Of course, in their rendition of environment as acutely social space – as a product of social discourses – the poets I have considered may well lie outside the concerns of much of what has, to date, been the focus of that environmental critique of literature which has gone by the name of ecocriticism. As I have explained elsewhere,[7] the ecocritical tendency has been to focus on the American nature-writing tradition from which it took its initial inspiration, with an emphasis on praising key authors and their treasured places rather than, to quote Michael P. Cohen, on seeing particular environments 'as contested terrains the way environmental historians see them'.[8] By contrast, that social aspect which much ecocriticism has seemed to lack is almost forced upon the reader of those poets whose work I have addressed in this book. Welsh environment – understood as abundantly physical in its valleys, rivers, tides and natural resources (the latter, for example, lying at the root of Merthyr's development) – is simultan-eously formed, inescapably, under the sign of culture: Bardsey as sacred; Cwrt Colman as the site of class contest; Abergwesyn as a record of human building. This is a far cry from Welsh space understood as mere scenery. Rather, it suggests precisely what Kyffin Williams means when he refers to the word *cynefin*: an environment that is both abundantly non-human and supremely social; or, as Williams puts it, in that phrase of such resonant clarity, 'a landscape with everything in it'.

Notes

Notes to Chapter 1

1   As J. N. Kennedy explains, land for Coed y Brenin was first obtained by the Forestry Commission in the early 1920s from the 'Vaughan family of Nannau', after which it took its initial name of Vaughan Forest. Planting started in 1922. Then, in 1935, 'to commemorate the Silver Jubilee of King George V, the forest was re-named Coed y Brenin (King's Forest)': J. N. Kennedy, 'Forests', in Herbert L. Edlin (ed.), *Cambrian Forests*, 2nd edn (London: HMSO, 1975), p. 9. It should be noted, however, that not all Coed y Brenin land is newly afforested. As a 1950 booklet indicates, 'When the land was acquired, some of the valley bottoms and many of the lower slopes of the hills carried natural woodland of oak, ash, alder and birch': see Forestry Commission, *Britain's Forests: Coed y Brenin* (London: HMSO, 1950), p. 4.

2   Describing Coed y Brenin in the 1970s, J. N. Kennedy indicates its predominantly coniferous nature, writing that 'Sitka spruce is the dominant species within the forest but there are fine stands of Douglas fir, Norway spruce and Corsican pine.' The use of a 'wider range of species' – including 'Beech, oak, wild cherry and lime' – was, Kennedy notes, restricted to 'good sheltered sites' or areas where 'the soils are better' ('Forests', p. 10). A set of leaflets apparently dating from the late 1970s indicates that coniferous plantation in Coed y Brenin totalled 6,230 hectares; broadleaved plantation, by contrast, totalled just 80 hectares: see Forestry Commission, *Coed y Brenin* (n.pl.: Forestry Commission, n.d.), leaflet 6. As the Forestry Commission's recent survey of Welsh woodland indicates, its own woodlands in Wales remain heavily dominated by conifers, which account for 73.6% coverage: see Forestry Commission, *National Inventory of Woodland and Trees: Wales* (Edinburgh: Forestry Commission, 2002), 19 Nov. 2007 <*http://www.forestry.gov.uk/PDF/niwales.pdf/$FILE/ niwales.pdf*>, p. 17.

3   R. S. Thomas, *The Bread of Truth* (London: Rupert Hart-Davis, 1963), p. 17.

⁴ Kirsti Bohata, *Postcolonialism Revisited* (Cardiff: University of Wales Press, 2004), p. 94.

⁵ The amount of coniferous plantation in Wales in the period in which Thomas's poem was published is indicated by William Linnard's observation that 'The proportion of coniferous high forest increased from 33% of the Welsh woodland area in 1947 to 70% in 1980. *The increase was most rapid between 1947 and 1965, when the actual area under conifers almost trebled*': W. Linnard, *Welsh Woods and Forests: A History* (Llandysul: Gomer, 2000), p. 211 (emphasis added).

⁶ That Thomas's approach draws on an earlier Welsh-language tradition of political landscape poetry has been observed by Kirsti Bohata (*Postcolonialism Revisited*, p. 84).

Notes to Chapter 2

¹ Lawrence Buell, *Writing for an Endangered World: Literature, Culture, and Environment in the U.S. and Beyond* (Cambridge, MA: Belknap, 2001), pp. 2–3. Greg Garrard notes that ecocriticism is concerned with both literature and a broader cultural field – the latter a more recent development: 'Many early works of ecocriticism were characterised by an exclusive interest in Romantic poetry, wilderness narrative and nature writing, but in the last few years ASLE [the Association for the Study of Literature and Environment] has turned towards a more general cultural ecocriticism, with studies of popular scientific writing, film, TV, art, architecture and other cultural artefacts such as theme parks, zoos and shopping malls.' See Greg Garrard, *Ecocriticism* (London: Routledge, 2004), p. 4.

² See Cheryll Glotfelty, 'Introduction: literary studies in an age of environmental crisis', in Cheryll Glotfelty and Harold Fromm (eds), *The Ecocriticism Reader: Landmarks in Literary Ecology* (Athens, GA: University of Georgia Press, 1996), pp. xvi–xviii, for a basic outline of the emergence of ecocriticism – a movement which, in the mid to late 1980s, brought literary study (somewhat belatedly) into the general greening of the humanities that had been taking place since the 1970s. The main professional focus for ecocriticism is the Association for the Study of Literature and Environment (ASLE), a US-based organization with around 1,000 subscribing members: the spring 2006 issue of *ASLE News* indicated that the organization at that point had 'about 1000 active ... members, including nearly 150 people from other countries [i.e. not the USA]'; in 2004, overseas members were from twenty different countries: see Amy McIntyre, 'News from the managing director', *ASLE News*, 18, 1 (2006), 3, and Annie Ingram, 'ASLE treasury is the healthiest it has ever been', *ASLE News*, 16, 1 (2004), 5. ASLE also has affiliate organizations in Canada, Australia and New Zealand, India, Japan, Korea, continental Europe and the UK. ASLE itself was only formed in Oct. 1992, so its growth has been fast: for details on the founding of ASLE and its initial growth see 'Conferences', *American Nature Writing*

Newsletter, 4, 2 (1992), 7, and Cheryll Glotfelty, 'Letter to *ANWN* subscribers and ASLE members', *American Nature Writing Newsletter*, 5, 2 (1993), 1. First published in the spring of 1989, *The American Nature Writing Newsletter* predated ASLE, although the two became affiliated on the latter's formation: see [Alicia Nitecki and Scott Slovic], 'From the editors', *American Nature Writing Newsletter*, 4, 2 (1992), 2. The *Newsletter* became *ASLE News* in 1996. The main ecocritical journal is the twice-yearly *ISLE: Interdisciplinary Studies in Literature and Environment*, which was first published in spring 1993 and was adopted as the 'official journal of ASLE' from its winter 1996 issue: see Patrick D. Murphy, 'Editor's note', *ISLE: Interdisciplinary Studies in Literature and Environment*, 2, 2 (1996), p. iii, and Cheryll Glotfelty, '[Letter]', *American Nature Writing Newsletter*, 7, 1 (1995), 1–2.

3   Garrard, *Ecocriticism*, p. 3.

4   Jonathan Bate, *The Song of the Earth* (London: Picador, 2001; orig. 2000), p. ix.

5   On the notion of alienation from the earth see, for example, Bate's assertion that 'Our grandparents were intimate with house and well. We move from house to house and our water comes from reservoirs, not wells. That is progress, but it is also alienation' (*Song of the Earth*, pp. 264–5).

6   As John Barnie has pointed out, 'The pressure to write for "the cause", whether that cause was Communist Russia, Republican Spain, or nearer to home Welsh nationalism, was a prevailing one in the twentieth century … In the more totalitarian regimes it led to many blighted careers; everywhere it produced a great deal of bad verse.' Indeed, Barnie continues by suggesting that 'The pressures of eco-poetics and eco-criticism are similar. Simon C. Estok quotes Richard Kerridge as saying that "Most of all, eco-criticism seeks to evaluate texts and ideas in terms of their coherence and *usefulness* as responses to environmental crisis" (my emphasis). The next step is prescription, telling poets what to write, and the step beyond that, poets believing the prescription, and poets and critics and readers colluding in agreeing that because the "message" is approved, the poem is good.' See John Barnie, 'Touch the snake', *New Welsh Review*, 74 (2006), 21.

7   Indeed, it would be personally dishonest: my own ecocritical interests are manifest in my membership of both ASLE and its British affiliate, ASLE-UK.

8   Raymond Williams, *Keywords: A Vocabulary of Culture and Society*, revised edn (London: Fontana, 1988; orig. Flamingo, 1983), p. 219.

9   Simon Schama, *Landscape and Memory* (London: HarperCollins, 1995), p. 7.

10 In making this parenthetical observation, I wish to recognize what Kate Soper's seminal work *What is Nature?* calls the 'extra-discursive reality of nature' even though we, as human beings, can only approach it, understand it, and present it to ourselves through discourse. As Soper puts it: 'I recognize … that there is no reference to that which is independent of discourse except in discourse, but dissent from any position which appeals to this truth as a basis for denying the extra-discursive reality of nature.' See Kate Soper, *What is Nature? Culture, Politics and the Non-Human* (Oxford: Blackwell, 1995), p. 8.

11 Schama, *Landscape and Memory*, p. 7.
12 This statement also sets my work apart from much ecocriticism, which often seems concerned – by stark contrast – to pursue a literature that will, somehow, supply to the reader the world as it is beyond the text, that will 'make the presence and reality of the natural world available to us by proxy': Dana Phillips, *The Truth of Ecology: Nature, Culture, and Literature in America* (New York: Oxford University Press, 2003), p. 7. The first chapter of Dana Phillips's volume deals with this ecocritical tendency in some detail.
13 Schama, *Landscape and Memory*, p. 10.
14 Buell, *Writing for an Endangered World*, p. 3.
15 Ibid., p. 2. Buell's phrase 'acts of environmental imagination' is extremely useful as a description of environmentally directed literature. However, it is worth indicating that, however unintentionally, it is also a phrase which acknowledges – in the notion of *imagining* – the emphatically constructive process that Schama details in relation to the concept of landscape.
16 The phrase 'extra-discursive reality' is Kate Soper's: see n. 10 above.
17 In the opening chapter of his *The Truth of Ecology* – a book which is sharply critical of a number of naïve tendencies within ecocriticism – Dana Phillips writes that 'Confusing actual and fictional trees, or trying to conflate them (however rhetorically and provisionally), would seem to be a primitive error ... in the sense that it occurs at a level of such fundamental philosophical importance as to lead anyone who makes it astray, sooner rather than later. In short, it is a critical error. To cite ... [an] observation made by Barthes, it overlooks the fact that while "the work is a fragment of substance, occupying a part of the space of books (in a library for example), the Text is a methodological field." It is "held in language," not "in the hand"' (p. 10). In other words, whereas the physical stuff of mountains and forests can be held 'in the hand', the poem that is written about them – and thus its landscapes – is only ever 'held in language'.
18 Drawing on the work of the philosopher Daniel C. Dennett – and citing his remark that 'The environment contains an embarrassment of riches, much more information than even a cognitive angel could use' – Dana Phillips argues that human beings are far from being cognitive angels and that our literary work is thus entirely unable to make anything like full or true 'copies' of the environments in which we find ourselves (*Truth of Ecology*, p. 15).
19 Leslie Norris, 'From Leslie Norris', *Poetry Wales*, 7, 4 (1972), 120 (emphasis added).
20 Jonathan Bate suggests the difficult issue of artistic legitimacy before the world when he talks about '"truth to nature" as a criterion of aesthetic judgement' (*Song of the Earth*, p. 34). The problem here is that Bate's phrase may be considered to imply a nature which will somehow *reveal itself* as a yardstick without any discursive intervention. But, as Simon Schama observes, wilderness 'does not name itself' (*Landscape and Memory*, p. 7); in other words, there will always be discursive intervention in appeals to the nature of the world. Thus, any such debate over literary 'truth to nature' must register itself as a

debate over differing judgements on the world. Which is not in any way to deny the externally existent world, or its thoroughgoing importance. Rather, it is to *embrace* that world as something about which judgements are always in active discussion. Debates over planetary environmental health or crisis are a case in point. Each linguistic move in such debates remains discursive. But insofar as any linguistic move is a response to extra-textual experience – manifest in appeals to, for example, personal/lay experience of environmental phenomena, scientific research or examples of real-world consequences if the action suggested by a particular linguistic judgement on the world is followed – then the physical world remains involved in the formation of those linguistic moves which constitute the clash of differing judgements. In short, even if one accepts that 'language is a self-enclosed system' which is always discursive and thus inevitably 'split off' from nature' – to cite Jonathan Bate's assessment of so-called hermeneutic approaches to the relationship between language and world – this is in no way to imply that such an understanding locks one into a circle from which, as Bate claims, one cannot 'look out from the text to the planet' (*Song of the Earth*, pp. 247 and 248).

21 Williams, *Keywords*, pp. 219 and 224.

22 This last example may seem a little odd; it is, however, suggested by Lynette Roberts's notion that there is a particular quality to Welsh light – 'the white sunlight of Wales' which 'glazes every building, stone and tree' – and which is, to quote Patrick McGuinness's useful summary of Roberts's position, 'an explosive revealer of forms'. Roberts's suggestion for the source of her very particular Welsh light is as follows: 'The rain, the continual downpour of rain, may also compensate us indirectly, by giving us that pure day which precedes it, which everyone in Wales must know. During those intervals the rain water is reflected back to us through a magnetic prism of light. The sea, which surrounds two-thirds of Wales, throws up another plane of light. And a third shaft of light reaches us at a fuller angle through the sun.' See Lynette Roberts, *Collected Poems*, ed. Patrick McGuinness (Manchester: Carcanet, 2005), p. xxvi. As my analysis in ch. 8 suggests, the experience of light – through fog, for example – is important to the environmental construction of Bardsey in Christine Evans's poetry.

23 Soper, *What is Nature?*, p. 155.

24 It is significant, however, that Soper qualifies these observations somewhat by noting that 'the elasticity of these limits is very much in dispute even among the ecologists themselves' (*What is Nature?*, p. 159).

25 Bate, *Song of the Earth*, p. 34.

26 Schama, *Landscape and Memory*, p. 11.

27 Buell, *Writing for an Endangered World*, p. 3.

28 Buell's note explains that, in *The German Ideology*, Marx argues for the effective disappearance of 'the nature that preceded human history', whilst *Capital* describes 'nature as becoming "one of the organs" of man's activity' (*Writing for an Endangered World*, p. 268, n. 7).

Notes to Chapter 3

1. As Conran explains, 'For a year or so after the end of the Second World War in 1945, Anglo-Welsh poetry of the thirties and forties was still very much in place ... Yet ten years later the scene was in ruins.' See Tony Conran, *Frontiers in Anglo-Welsh Poetry* (Cardiff: University of Wales Press, 1997), p. 177.

2. Ibid., p. 188.

3. Ibid., p. 187.

4. That Thomas's work had gained major status within Welsh anglophone poetic life by the beginning of the 1970s is suggested by the publication of the 'special R. S. Thomas' number of *Poetry Wales* in the spring of 1972. Indeed, it is in this issue that a letter from Harri Webb proclaims Thomas as '*Prifardd* [chief bard] of English-speaking Wales': see Harri Webb, 'From Harri Webb', *Poetry Wales*, 7, 4 (1972), 123. That year also marked the publication of *H'm* – Thomas's first collection for four years, and generally accepted as representing a new direction in his work. In terms of establishing the position at the start of the period with which this volume is predominantly concerned – the period, that is, which follows the Second Flowering of the 1960s – my interest here is in Thomas's first poetic phase, up until and including the 1968 collection *Not That He Brought Flowers*. (It is worth noting that *Not That He Brought Flowers* is itself a 'transitional' volume, caught between the sort of work that predates and that which follows Thomas's crucial move to Aberdaron in 1967: see Meic Stephens (ed.), *The New Companion to the Literature of Wales* (Cardiff: University of Wales Press, 1998), p. 721.)

5. The other major energizer of anglophone Welsh poetry in the 1960s was Bryn Griffiths. He was responsible for founding the London-based Guild of Welsh Writers in 1964. In the same year, and as 'the first published consequence of this new enterprise', he brought together a brief selection of eleven contemporary London-based Welsh poets in the periodical *London Welshman*: see [Bryn Griffiths] (ed.), 'London Anglo-Welsh: a brief anthology', *London Welshman*, 19, 7 (1964), 19–22. Three years later, he was the editor of the major anthology *Welsh Voices: An Anthology of New Poetry from Wales* (London: Dent, 1967). As Tony Conran explains, Griffiths's work was primarily London-based, in contrast to Stephens's location in Wales itself: see '*Poetry Wales* and the Second Flowering', in M. Wynn Thomas (ed.), *Welsh Writing in English*, A Guide to Welsh Literature, 7 (Cardiff: University of Wales Press, 2003), pp. 225–30.

6. Stephens is careful to acknowledge that his own formation of *Poetry Wales* as a 'nationalist publication' and his sense that 'political questions must be asked in any consideration of Anglo-Welsh verse these days' showed R. S. Thomas's influence. Moreover, even though he thought that Thomas's 'brooding on rural decay and [on] the spineless attitudes of his countrymen' was a potential 'emotional dead-end', he acknowledged that it was 'salutary for the time being': Meic Stephens, 'The Second Flowering', *Poetry Wales*, 3, 3 (1967–8), 6.

7. Ibid., 6 and 7.

[8]   Matthew Jarvis, 'Repositioning Wales: poetry after the Second Flowering', in
      Daniel Williams (ed.), *Slanderous Tongues: Welsh Poetry in English 1970–2005*
      (Bridgend: Seren, forthcoming).

[9]   Conran, '*Poetry Wales* and the Second Flowering', p. 229.

[10] See, variously: John Tripp, *Diesel to Yesterday* (Cardiff: Triskel, 1966) and John
      Stuart Williams and Meic Stephens (eds), *The Lilting House: An Anthology of
      Anglo-Welsh Poetry 1917–67* (London: Dent; Llandybïe: Christopher Davies,
      1969). For the poems discussed here, see *Lilting House*, pp. 168–70 ('Welcome
      to Wales') and pp. 167–8 ('The Diesel to Yesterday'); *Diesel to Yesterday* is
      unpaginated, but the poems are (respectively) the eleventh and tenth in a
      volume of sixteen pieces.

[11] Tony Conran identifies Webb's poetry as one of two 'bodies of work' which
      dominate the 'early issues' of the magazine; the other is Conran's own 'trans-
      lations of Welsh poetry' ('*Poetry Wales* and the Second Flowering', p. 230).

[12] Harri Webb, 'The Boomerang in the Parlour', *Poetry Wales*, 1, 1 (1965), 14.

[13] The *Oxford English Dictionary* indicates that the word *prodigal* suggests both
      'recklessly wasteful' and 'lavish'.

[14] I have argued elsewhere that there is an emphatic and significant notion of
      future potential for Wales in this poem, and that it is an element which is
      crucial to an overall interpretation of the piece. However, my sense is that such
      potential is not reflected in the environmental vision of the poem; rather, it
      comes from the poem's idea of cultural memory (Wales as 'a land whose
      memory / Has not begun'), which parallels Australia as a place 'Where nearly
      all the songs have yet to be sung' (Jarvis, 'Repositioning Wales').

[15] Brian Morris, *Harri Webb*, Writers of Wales (Cardiff: University of Wales
      Press, 1993), p. 62.

[16] Ibid.

[17] In Stephens's note to 'Above Tregaron', he indicates that the poem was written
      in 1963 and that it was 'the earliest of HW's poems to deal with "the Green
      Desert" of mid-Wales': see Harri Webb, *Collected Poems*, ed. Meic Stephens
      (Llandysul: Gomer, 1995), p. 400. 'Above Tregaron' was first published in
      Webb's collection, *The Green Desert: Collected Poems 1950–1969* (Llandysul:
      Gomer, 1969), p. 36. Stephens also observes that the connection between Wales
      and desert initially appeared in Webb's journalism, in a 1962 edition of *The
      Welsh Nation* (Webb, *Collected Poems*, p. 401). In a piece about restoration of
      national pride through resistance at Tryweryn, Webb refers to 'the spreading
      green desert of the Empty Centre': see [Harri Webb], 'The breed of the spar-
      rowhawk', *The Welsh Nation* (Oct. 1962), 3.

[18] The road to which the poem refers is apparently the minor road which runs for
      around fourteen miles between Tregaron in the west and Abergwesyn in the
      east and which, for a while near Abergwesyn, runs alongside the Irfon river.

[19] As Meic Stephens's notes to this poem explain, the Irfon and Camddwr are
      'rivers in upland mid-Wales' (Webb, *Collected Poems*, p. 400).

[20] John Davies, *A History of Wales*, revised edn (London: Penguin, 2007), pp. 156
      and 157. However, it must be recognized that the area 'Between Irfon and

Camddwr' to which the poem explicitly refers is around a dozen miles away, as the crow flies, from the place of Llywelyn's death.

21 For twentieth-century tendencies to identify life in the Welsh uplands with notions of 'the Welsh remnants of the original pre-Celtic tribes', see M. Wynn Thomas, 'R. S. Thomas: war poet', *Welsh Writing in English: A Yearbook of Critical Essays*, 2 (1996), 87–90. The afforestation that Webb feared in the area between the rivers Irfon and Camddwr did indeed take place. A comparison between the 1974 and 1982 editions of the 1:50,000 Ordnance Survey map 'Elan Valley and Builth Wells' shows the dramatic increase in size of what the map calls the 'Towy Forest': see 'Elan Valley and Builth Wells', Sheet 147, 1:50,000 (Southampton: Ordnance Survey, 1974 and 1982), NGR (National Grid Reference) SN 75, SN 76, SN 85, and SN 86. For the coniferous character of these woodlands, see the 1996 edition of the same sheet.

22 Stephens, 'Second Flowering', 6.

23 Bryn Griffiths, 'A Note for R. S. Thomas', *Poetry Wales*, 1, 2 (1965), 23.

24 R. S. Thomas, *The Stones of the Field* (Carmarthen: Druid Press, 1946), p. 14.

25 See 'Beet', *Encyclopædia Britannica*, 2007, Encyclopædia Britannica Online, 6 Dec. 2007 <*http://search.eb.com/eb/article-9014114*>. For the growing of root crops on Welsh hill farms in the years shortly before Thomas wrote 'A Peasant', see A. W. Ashby and I. L. Evans, *The Agriculture of Wales and Monmouthshire* (Cardiff: University of Wales Press, 1944), p. 101.

26 Terry Gifford, *Green Voices: Understanding Contemporary Nature Poetry* (Manchester: Manchester University Press, 1995), p. 45.

27 Yi-Fu Tuan, *Space and Place: The Perspective of Experience* (Minneapolis, MN: University of Minnesota Press, 1977), p. 110.

28 Ibid.

29 Thomas, *Stones of the Field*, p. 40.

30 Tuan, *Space and Place*, p. 107.

31 Gifford, *Green Voices*, p. 47.

32 Thomas, *Stones of the Field*, p. 24.

33 M. Wynn Thomas, 'For Wales, see landscape: early R. S. Thomas and the English topographical tradition', *Welsh Writing in English: A Yearbook of Critical Essays*, 10 (2005), 8. Professor Thomas indicates that this mode of understanding Wales had originated in the 'proto-Romantic travellers of the late eighteenth century in search of the picturesque and sublime', matured in the 'great writers and artists of the English Romantic movement, including Wordsworth, Shelley and Turner', and was manifest in the twentieth century in the 'artists of the Neo-Romantic movement, some of whose leading figures settled for a period in [Wales]' (9).

34 Thomas, 'For Wales, see landscape', 11; for a reproduction of Eldridge's drawing, see 'For Wales, see landscape', 12. The connection with 'Country Church (Manafon)' was suggested by Professor Thomas in a personal communication to the author.

35 R. S. Thomas, *Song at the Year's Turning: Poems 1942–1954* (London: Rupert Hart-Davis, 1955), p. 92.

[36] Thomas, 'For Wales, see landscape', 14.

[37] R. S. Thomas himself declared that 'the true Wales is still to be found in the country' (translation provided in Jason Walford Davies, '"Thick ambush of shadows": allusions to Welsh literature in the work of R. S. Thomas', *Welsh Writing in English: A Yearbook of Critical Essays*, 1 (1995), 99–100). As Jason Walford Davies goes on to explain, Thomas 'criticizes the Anglo-Welsh for conveying an imbalanced view of Wales as an industrial land, and stresses that the rural tradition reaches back through the centuries to a more essential Wales' (100).

[38] R. S. Thomas, *Autobiographies: 'Former Paths', 'The Creative Writer's Suicide', 'No-one', 'A Year in Llŷn'*, trans. and ed. Jason Walford Davies (London: Dent, 1997), p. 148.

[39] R. S. Thomas, *Not That He Brought Flowers* (London: Rupert Hart-Davis, 1968), p. 33.

[40] The story of Jacob wrestling with an unnamed figure is recounted in Genesis 32: 22–32. In the Bible, the figure is identified both as God and angel (Genesis 32: 30 and Hosea 12: 3–4).

[41] R. S. Thomas, *Pietà* (London: Rupert Hart-Davis, 1966), p. 41.

[42] Christopher Morgan, *R. S. Thomas: Identity, Environment, and Deity* (Manchester: Manchester University Press, 2003), ch. 3. See particularly Morgan's discussion of 'The Parish' (from the 1961 collection *Tares*) in which he asserts that 'in these lines is the paradox central to Thomas's writing on nature: destructive, consuming power in league with transcendent beauty' (p. 73).

[43] Thomas, *Song at the Year's Turning*, p. 92.

[44] Thomas, *Pietà*, p. 24.

[45] Tuan, *Space and Place*, p. 110.

[46] Thomas, *Not That He Brought Flowers*, p. 26.

[47] In referring to Welsh geographical areas throughout this book, I use the historical county names. As the authors of *The National Gazetteer of Wales* explain, 'There has been a tendency in recent years to use administrative areas in a general geographical context. It should be remembered that each administrative geography has been created (usually by an Act of Parliament) to facilitate the provision of a particular public service (or set of services). None has been invested with a wider geographical or cultural role ... Popular geography is better based upon the fixed, and more historically and culturally relevant, framework of the Counties of Wales.' See 'Administrative Wales', *The National Gazetteer of Wales*, 6 Dec. 2007 <*http://homepage.ntlworld.com/geogdata/ngw/admin.htm*>.

[48] Einion Thomas, *Capel Celyn: Deng Mlynedd o Chwalu: 1955–1965/Ten Years of Destruction: 1955–1965*, 1st bilingual edn, English text by Beryl Griffiths (n.pl.: Cyhoeddiadau Barddas and Gwynedd Council, 2007), pp. 18 and 93.

[49] As Alan Butt Philip explains, 'despite the calling of two national conferences on [the Tryweryn] question in Cardiff and Welsh opposition at Westminster, the Conservative Government persuaded the House of Commons to approve

the scheme, which was contained in a private bill sponsored by Liverpool City Council. By obtaining authority for its plans in this way, Liverpool did not have to secure the consent of the Welsh local authorities affected by the scheme, and it was this that so incensed the Welsh public.' Philip goes on to observe the 'inability of the almost unanimous Welsh M.P.s to prevent the passage of Liverpool's bill', and notes that 'The Tryweryn valley was given up to Liverpool by vote of the Commons on 31 July 1957', with the voting '175 in favour of Liverpool's bill and 79 against (excluding tellers)': see Alan Butt Philip, *The Welsh Question: Nationalism in Welsh Politics 1945–1970* (Cardiff: University of Wales Press, 1975), pp. 77 and 297. According to the *Western Mail*, '20 of the 36 Welsh M.P.s took part in the division on the third reading of the Bill. Of these only one ... voted for the Bill ... Of the other 16, [five] abstained. The remainder were absent or paired': David G. Rosser, 'MPs table censure on Brooke', *Western Mail* (2 Aug. 1957), 1. (For initial advice on the subject of Tryweryn, I am grateful to Dr Owen Roberts, Aberystwyth University.)

50 As Douglas Pringle makes clear in his book *The First 75 Years: A Brief Account of the History of the Forestry Commission 1919–1994* (Edinburgh: Forestry Commission, [1994]), the Forestry Commission was established in 1919 as the centralized state forest authority of the United Kingdom (pp. 3–5). As such, although the 'Commissioners were to operate at arms-length from Government' (p. 7), the character and scope of the Commission's work were, from the start, ultimately determined by Westminster policy (see, for example, pp. 14 and 17). However, with the passing of the Forestry Act of 1945, 'The Government decided ... that forestry policy was of sufficient importance to be made a direct Ministerial responsibility' and, as such, 'The Commission became a Government Department' (p. 32). Indeed, George Ryle (a former Deputy Director-General of the Forestry Commission) notes the persistent failure of the Commission in its first forty-five years to achieve any significant decentralization away from London: see George Ryle, *Forest Service: The First Forty-Five Years of the Forestry Commission of Great Britain* (Newton Abbot: David & Charles, 1969), pp. 33 and 103. Unsurprisingly, the Forestry Commission has persistently been seen in Wales as 'one arm of a centralized, often arrogant and alien, London government': Kirsti Bohata, *Postcolonialism Revisited* (Cardiff: University of Wales Press, 2004), p. 86.

51 Jim Perrin, 'Land & freedom', *New Welsh Review*, 74 (2006), 11; emphases in original.

52 Lawrence Buell, *Writing for an Endangered World: Literature, Culture, and Environment in the U.S. and Beyond* (Cambridge, MA: Belknap, 2001), p. 6 (emphasis added).

53 Thomas, *Not That He Brought Flowers*, p. 26.

54 Ian Davidson had previously published a joint collection, with John Muckle, called *It is Now as it was Then* (London: MICA in association with Actual Size, 1983).

Notes to Chapter 4

1 Gillian Clarke, *The Sundial* (Llandysul: Gomer, 1978), pp. 22–3.

2 Ystrad-fflur is at NGR SN 746 657. The abbey is thus right at the western edge of what was, for Harri Webb, the green desert – 'the last vast emptiness at the heart of Wales' (Brian Morris, *Harri Webb*, Writers of Wales (Cardiff: University of Wales Press, 1993), p. 62). (Throughout this volume, six-figure National Grid Reference (NGR) identifiers are used to locate small features, such as individual buildings, on contemporary Ordnance Survey mapping at a scale of 1:10,000 and greater. Four-figure and two-figure NGR identifiers are used for larger landscape features.)

3 K. E. Smith, 'The poetry of Gillian Clarke', in Hans-Werner Ludwig and Lothar Fietz (eds), *Poetry in the British Isles: Non-Metropolitan Perspectives* (Cardiff: University of Wales Press, 1995), p. 271; M. Wynn Thomas, *Corresponding Cultures: The Two Literatures of Wales* (Cardiff: University of Wales Press, 1999), p. 200; Linden Peach, *Ancestral Lines: Culture & Identity in the Work of Six Contemporary Poets* (Bridgend: Seren, [1993]), p. 85.

4 Yi-Fu Tuan, *Space and Place: The Perspective of Experience* (Minneapolis, MN: University of Minnesota Press, 1977), p. 10.

5 See Miranda Green and Ray Howell, *Celtic Wales: A Pocket Guide* (Cardiff: University of Wales Press and The Western Mail, 2000), p. 7, which classes the torc as one of the key 'common features of material culture' to be found across the 'chronologically and culturally diverse set of communities' to which the term 'Celtic' is applied.

6 Ibid., pp. 7 and 28. Green and Howell identify the ritual deposit of high-status goods in watery sites as another key marker of Celtic culture (p. 7). They discuss such deposits in Wales at Llyn Fawr and Llyn Cerrig Bach (pp. 27–9).

7 Tuan, *Space and Place*, pp. 16–17.

8 Torcs found in Wales include, for example, those in the Llanwrthwl hoard, the Milford Haven torc hoard, and the Heyope ribbon torcs. See 'Gold torc from the Llanwrthwl hoard', *Gathering the Jewels*, 6 Dec. 2007 <*http://www.gtj.org. uk/en/item1/25857*>, 'The Milford Haven torc hoard', *Gathering the Jewels*, 6 Dec. 2007 <*http://www.gtj.org.uk/en/item1/25848*> and 'The Heyope ribbon torcs (Bronze Age)', *Gathering the Jewels*, 6 Dec. 2007 <*http://www.gtj.org.uk/ en/item1/25853*>. As the commentary on the Llanwrthwl gold torc indicates, 'Gold torcs were worn as symbols of wealth and high status during the Middle Bronze Age in Wales.'

9 Tuan, *Space and Place*, p. 12.

10 'In the thirteenth century, [the abbey's chapter house] became a virtual burial vault for the Deheubarth dynasty of princes, the descendants of the Lord Rhys': see David M. Robinson and Colin Platt, *Strata Florida Abbey; Talley Abbey*, 2nd edn (Cardiff: Cadw, 1998), p. 55.

11 'The medieval Welsh love poet, Dafydd ap Gwilym, was buried at Ystrad Fflur' (Clarke, *Sundial*, p. 23). By the publication of her *Selected Poems*, Clarke is more cautious and her note observes that 'Ystrad Fflûr [*sic*] (Strata Florida)

Cardiganshire, is *traditionally held to be* where Dafydd is buried': Gillian Clarke, *Selected Poems* (Manchester: Carcanet, 1985), p. 111; emphasis added.

[12] For parallel Welsh and English texts of these poems, see Rachel Bromwich (trans. and ed.), *Dafydd ap Gwilym: A Selection of Poems* (Llandysul: Gomer, 1982), pp. 26–9, 52–5, and 136–9.

[13] John Davies, *A History of Wales*, revised edn (London: Penguin, 2007), p. 139.

[14] Geraint H. Jenkins, *A Concise History of Wales* (Cambridge: Cambridge University Press, 2007), p. 87.

[15] R. S. Thomas, *The Stones of the Field* (Carmarthen: Druid Press, 1946), p. 14

[16] Clarke, *Sundial*, pp. 20–1.

[17] Thomas, *Corresponding Cultures*, p. 198. In a similar way, Thomas usefully observes that, in 'At Ystrad Fflur', 'Clarke quietly claims, in the name of her female self, not only the place where Dafydd ap Gwilym is buried but also the traditions of praise poetry and *canu bro* (poetry of place), which had previously been virtually a Welsh male preserve.'

[18] The error of 'minister' for 'minster' is corrected in Clarke, *Selected Poems*, p. 22. For Dafydd ap Gwilym's construction of green space in terms of a building see, for example, 'Y Deildy' ('The Leafy Hut'), which figures the space 'amidst birch and hazel' as a 'house of leaves that God the Father made', even giving it a 'vaulted roof'. In such terms, the poem also declares that 'a living-room is better if it grows', whilst the forest is effectively identified as a church for lovers ('love's altar is the forest glade'). See Bromwich, *Dafydd ap Gwilym*, pp. 10–13.

[19] Louise H. Westling, *The Green Breast of the New World: Landscape, Gender, and American Fiction* (Athens, GA: University of Georgia Press, 1996), pp. 31 and 33.

[20] Kate Soper, *What is Nature? Culture, Politics and the Non-Human* (Oxford: Blackwell, 1995), p. 99.

[21] Thomas, *Corresponding Cultures*, pp. 198–9.

[22] Soper, *What is Nature?*, p. 100.

[23] Ibid.

[24] Quoted in Westling, *Green Breast of the New World*, p. 27.

[25] Ibid.

[26] Gillian Clarke, *Letter from a Far Country* (Manchester: Carcanet, 1982), p. 25.

[27] Clarke moved to Blaen Cwrt in 1984; see Jeremy Hooker, *Imagining Wales: A View of Modern Welsh Writing in English* (Cardiff: University of Wales Press, 2001), pp. 150–1 and 224. However, her association with the house goes back to 1969: 'I bought Blaen Cwrt in 1969. We used it for holidays and weekends in its ruinous state and very slowly restored it' (personal communication from Gillian Clarke to the author).

[28] See David T. Lloyd (ed.), *The Urgency of Identity: Contemporary English-Language Poetry from Wales* (Evanston, IL: TriQuarterly, 1994), p. 25.

[29] Westling, *Green Breast of the New World*, p. 25. Westling draws attention to Genesis 3:17–19, in which God declares to Adam, 'cursed is the ground for thy sake; in sorrow shalt thou eat of it all the days of thy life; Thorns also and thistles shall it bring forth to thee; and thou shalt eat the herb of the field; In the

sweat of thy face shalt thou eat bread, till thou return unto the ground' (King James Version).

30 Neither historic (i.e. County Series) nor contemporary large-scale Ordnance Survey maps of Login, Carmarthenshire, show a dwelling called Bryn Isaf. However, as Clarke has explained, 'Bryn Isaf was known as Lower Hill' (personal communication to the author), and this farm is indeed mapped at Login (NGR SN 163 234), close to Capel Calfaria (NGR SN 165 233), to which the poem also refers. Fforest Farm (NGR SN 024 394) is on the coast at Newport Bay, Pembrokeshire.

31 Personal communications from Gillian Clarke to the author.

32 Linden Peach, '"The imagination's caverns": identity and symbolism in the work of Gillian Clarke and Christine Evans', in Belinda Humfrey (ed.), 'Fire Green as Grass': Studies of the Creative Impulse in Anglo-Welsh Poetry and Short Stories of the Twentieth Century (Llandysul: Gomer, 1995), p. 151.

33 Jane Aaron and M. Wynn Thomas, '"Pulling you through changes": Welsh writing in English before, between and after two referenda', in M. Wynn Thomas (ed.), Welsh Writing in English, A Guide to Welsh Literature, 7 (Cardiff: University of Wales Press, 2003), p. 287.

34 Clarke, Letter from a Far Country, p. 8.

35 Writing about Clarke's poem 'Llŷr', Wynn Thomas talks about the 'unbending masculinity of so much of the history of Wales – "Land of my fathers" as the Welsh national anthem proudly hymns it', and observes the 'desiccated Puritan culture of rural areas' as part of this tendency: see M. Wynn Thomas, 'Place, race and gender in the poetry of Gillian Clarke', in Katie Gramich and Andrew Hiscock (eds), Dangerous Diversity: The Changing Faces of Wales; Essays in Honour of Tudor Bevan (Cardiff: University of Wales Press, 1998), p. 9. Or, in the words of R. Merfyn Jones, 'the Welsh identity, whether expressed in the figure of the nonconformist minister or the miner, rugby playing and socialist, resonated with masculinity': see R. Merfyn Jones, 'Beyond identity? The reconstruction of the Welsh', Journal of British Studies, 31, 4 (1992), 349. Similarly, in discussing Clarke's poetry, K. E. Smith also refers to the sense that 'the very myths of Welsh distinctiveness have attached themselves to male archetypes, such as the medieval bard, the Nonconformist minister or the coalminer': see Smith, 'Poetry of Gillian Clarke', p. 274.

36 Peach, '"Imagination's caverns"', p. 153. In one of Peach's less satisfactory moments of analysis, he gestures towards unspecified 'ambiguous references' in the creation of menstrual symbolism.

37 Westling, Green Breast of the New World, pp. 10 and 27.

38 Peach, '"Imagination's caverns"', p. 152.

39 Jeremy Hooker, 'Ceridwen's daughters: Welsh women poets and the uses of tradition', Welsh Writing in English: A Yearbook of Critical Essays, 1 (1995), 135.

40 Jeremy Hooker perceptively appreciates this particular balance, albeit from a slightly different angle, when he writes that 'Letter from a Far Country' 'celebrates motherhood, as well as showing the limitations it imposes upon the woman as an independent creative being' ('Ceridwen's daughters', 135).

41 Jeremy Hooker, *The Presence of the Past: Essays on Modern British and American Poetry* (Bridgend: Poetry Wales Press, 1987), p. 154.

42 Soper, *What is Nature?*, p 101.

43 Peach, "'Imagination's caverns'", p. 152.

44 According to the *Oxford English Dictionary*: 'blanco' is 'A white preparation for whitening accoutrements' from which 'blancoed' is derived; 'daps' is a colloquialism/dialect word for 'Rubber-soled shoes; *spec.* (*a*) slippers; (*b*) plimsolls'.

45 Gillian Clarke, *Snow on the Mountain* (Swansea and Llandybïe: Christopher Davies, 1971), p. 19.

46 M. Wynn Thomas, 'Staying to mind things: Gillian Clarke's early poetry', in Menna Elfyn (ed.), *Trying the Line: A Volume of Tribute to Gillian Clarke* (Llandysul: Gomer, 1997), pp. 59 and 55. For the original of the quotation from Clarke, see 'Beginning with Bendigeidfran', in Jane Aaron, Teresa Rees, Sandra Betts and Moira Vincentelli (eds), *Our Sisters' Land: The Changing Identities of Women in Wales* (Cardiff: University of Wales Press, 1994), p. 288.

47 Soper, *What is Nature?*, p. 99.

48 Clarke, *Letter from a Far Country*, p. 48.

49 Clarke, *Selected Poems*, pp. 108–9.

50 Gillian Clarke, *Letting in the Rumour* (Manchester: Carcanet, 1989), p. 38.

51 Gillian Clarke, *The King of Britain's Daughter* (Manchester: Carcanet, 1993), p. 5.

52 Gillian Clarke, *Five Fields* (Manchester: Carcanet, 1998), pp. 14–15.

53 Gillian Clarke, *Making the Beds for the Dead* (Manchester: Carcanet, 2004), pp. 72–3.

54 Poem 2 of the sequence recalls the drive to Fforest Farm, the speaker's face snugly in her father's coat. Talking of the beach 'A hundred yards from the door of the farm', Clarke has said: 'According to my father, the giant Bendigeidfran set off from the beach in such a terrible rage to wade the Irish Sea to rescue his sister Branwen from the Irish court, that his foot had printed a hollow into a black slab fallen from the cliffs' ('Beginning with Bendigeidfran', p. 287).

55 Clarke, *King of Britain's Daughter*, p. 5.

56 Clarke, *Making the Beds*, p. 72.

57 Peach, "'Imagination's caverns'", p. 150.

58 Clarke, *Making the Beds*, p. 70.

59 Clarke, *Letting in the Rumour*, pp. 46 and 47.

60 For Aberporth airfield, see Alan Phillips, *The Military Airfields of Wales* (Wrexham: Bridge Books, 2006), pp. 11–18. It is unclear whether Aberporth would actually have been the source for such jet flights. (I am grateful to Guy Jefferson, Albert Wright and John Wright for information about military airfields in Wales.)

61 Kirsti Bohata, *Postcolonialism Revisited* (Cardiff: University of Wales Press, 2004), p. 84. In identifying this tradition of Welsh-language political landscape work, Bohata points to writers such as 'Gwenallt, Waldo Williams, Islwyn Ffowc Elis and Tryfan'.

⁶² Clarke, *Sundial*, p. 12.
⁶³ 'Afforestation', in R. S. Thomas, *The Bread of Truth* (London: Rupert Hart-Davis, 1963), p. 17.
⁶⁴ Undertaken in the 1960s, the construction of Llyn Clywedog, near Llanidloes, meant that '615 acres of agricultural land [were] lost and three farms drowned'. As with the construction of Llyn Celyn (formed by the drowning of the Tryweryn valley), construction of the reservoir was opposed by 'the local people and many people in Wales', with the 'campaign against the drowning of the valley [being] led by members of Plaid Cymru'. Direct action – suspected to have been the work of 'MAC' (Mudiad Amddiffyn Cymru) – was also taken against the construction of the reservoir, when a bomb exploded on the site in 1966, causing £36,000 damage and the loss of six weeks' work: see 'Clywedog', *Ymgyrchu!*, National Library of Wales, 6 Dec. 2007 <*http://www.llgc.org.uk/ymgyrchu/Dwr/CLywedog/index-e.htm*>. Plaid Cymru's approach was to organize 'the purchase and sale of multiple plots of land which were to form part of the site of the ... reservoir' (Alan Butt Philip, *The Welsh Question: Nationalism in Welsh Politics 1945–1970* (Cardiff: University of Wales Press, 1975), p. 93). Indeed, it should be noted that Plaid Cymru's campaign against Llyn Clywedog inspired rather more response than the pursuit of the party's electoral fortunes (p. 88).
⁶⁵ Soper, *What is Nature?*, p. 155.
⁶⁶ Hooker, *Imagining Wales*, p. 147.

Notes to Chapter 5

¹ Ruth Bidgood, *The Given Time* (Swansea: Christopher Davies, 1972), inside front dust jacket.
² Bidgood herself identifies the house as Cluniau-fawr in the Camarch valley (personal communication to the author): see *Brecknockshire*, Sheet VII.10, 1:2,500 (Southampton: Ordnance Survey, 1888), parcel 10; NGR SN 887 557.
³ Bidgood's book of local history, *Parishes of the Buzzard* (Port Talbot: Gold Leaf, 2000), notes the 'conversion of huge tracts of North Breconshire into forest' since 1950 (p. 184).
⁴ Yi-Fu Tuan, *Space and Place: The Perspective of Experience* (Minneapolis, MN: University of Minnesota Press, 1977), p. 179; Pamela J. Stewart and Andrew Strathern (eds), *Landscape, Memory and History: Anthropological Perspectives* (London: Pluto, 2003), p. 229.
⁵ Tuan, *Space and Place*, p. 191.
⁶ Stewart and Strathern, *Landscape, Memory and History*, p. 4.
⁷ Bidgood, *Parishes of the Buzzard*, p. 184.
⁸ R. S. Thomas, *The Bread of Truth* (London: Rupert Hart-Davis, 1963), p. 17. For my discussion of this poem, see ch. 1 above.
⁹ Cluniau-fawr stands in Forestry Commission woodland.
¹⁰ As I have noted, the Forestry Commission became what Douglas Pringle calls

a 'direct Ministerial responsibility' in 1945 (see ch. 3, n. 50 above). Indeed, the 1960s saw a re-emphasis of the Commission's highly centralized nature with the abolition of its Directorates for England, Wales and Scotland: see George Ryle, *Forest Service: The First Forty-Five Years of the Forestry Commission of Great Britain* (Newton Abbot: David & Charles, 1969), p. 138, and Douglas Pringle, *The First 75 Years: A Brief Account of the History of the Forestry Commission 1919–1994* (Edinburgh: Forestry Commission, [1994]), p. 32.

[11]   The intertwining of imagination and memory is emphasized in Bonnie Thurston's assessment of Bidgood's work. Analysing the poem 'Chimneys' (*Given Time*, p. 15), Thurston observes that 'Like the speaker in the poem, we build the past again in our remembering, but perhaps the past we build is not the past that was' (Bonnie Thurston, '"A scatter of little sights and happenings": the poetic vision of Ruth Bidgood', *The Way*, 45, 1 (2006), 95). It is, of course, precisely the point that Bidgood's use of memories – the 'stories [which] are still told / Of men who lived there', as 'The Given Time' has it – always works to create a particular construct (a distinct discourse or vision) of the past.

[12]   Kirsti Bohata, *Postcolonialism Revisited* (Cardiff: University of Wales Press, 2004), p. 84.

[13]   Ruth Bidgood, *Kindred* (Bridgend: Poetry Wales Press, 1986), p. 32.

[14]   See Ruth Bidgood, 'Heartland', *Poetry Wales*, 26, 3 (1991), 8: 'At first I wrote a number of poems directly about this area, some of them tinged with the nostalgia I imbibed from the older people of Abergwesyn, who felt it acutely.'

[15]   As the 1889 Ordnance Survey map of the area indicates, Digiff ('Digyff' on the map) is close to the Afon Irfon, just upstream from Abergwesyn itself: see *Brecknockshire*, Sheet IX.4, 1:2,500 (Southampton: Ordnance Survey, 1889), parcel 129; NGR SN 845 531.

[16]   Bidgood, *Parishes of the Buzzard*, p. 226.

[17]   Merryn Williams, 'The poetry of Ruth Bidgood', *Poetry Wales*, 28, 3 (1993), 38.

[18]   It should be noted, however, that *Parishes of the Buzzard* also indicates some of the changes that have taken place as a result of a growing leisure industry in more recent years, when Bidgood observes that 'Some of the old farmhouses and cottages have become "second homes", some are let to holidaymakers in summertime' (p. 226).

[19]   For the problematic relationship between picturesque readings of places and their character as worked environments, see Stephen Copley, 'William Gilpin and the black-lead mine', in Stephen Copley and Peter Garside (eds), *The Politics of the Picturesque: Literature, Landscape and Aesthetics since 1770* (Cambridge: Cambridge University Press, 1994), pp. 42–61.

[20]   A. M. Allchin, 'The mystery that complements precision: reading Ruth Bidgood's poetry', *Logos: The Welsh Theological Review/Cylchgrawn Diwinyddol Cymru*, 4/5/6 ([1993]), 9. Wynn Thomas has also observed how 'ubiquitous [houses] seem in Welsh poets as signifiers of continuities' (personal communication to the author).

160 NOTES

²¹ Tuan, *Space and Place*, p. 179.
²² Ruth Bidgood, *The Print of Miracle* (Llandysul: Gomer, 1978), p. 12.
²³ Allchin, 'The mystery that complements precision', 9.
²⁴ Jason Walford Davies, 'History is now and Wales: Ruth Bidgood interviewed by Jason Walford Davies', *Planet*, 137 (1999), 50.
²⁵ Ruth Bidgood, *Lighting Candles: New and Selected Poems* (Bridgend: Poetry Wales Press, 1982), p. 64.
²⁶ Bidgood, *Print of Miracle*, p. 41. For a discussion of the burial cist to which this poem is apparently referring, see Bidgood, *Parishes of the Buzzard*, p. 17.
²⁷ The importance of lead mining to the Abergwesyn area is made clear by Bidgood in *Parishes of the Buzzard*: see, for example, the opening map, which locates two such mines to the west of the Irfon river and pp. 209–16 for her discussion of the area's lead-mining history. Bidgood identifies 'Image' as responding to the upper Culent valley to the south-west of Abergwesyn (personal communication to the author).
²⁸ Bidgood, *Kindred*, p. 34.
²⁹ Bidgood's sense of Welsh environment here might usefully be compared to that of Mary Lloyd Jones, whose use of vivid colours in her paintings suggests the effects of minerals on Welsh land and streams. See, for example, 'Ochre Pool, Cwm Rheidol' and Anne Price-Owen's commentary which, noting 'the toxins from ore mines that blot the [Welsh] landscape', observes the 'thickly-applied, unmixed oils' that 'echo the accumulative seeping ore': Mary Lloyd Jones, *First Language* (Llandysul: Gomer, with the National Library of Wales, 2006), pp. 50 and 49.
³⁰ Bidgood, *Given Time*, p. 40. Bidgood indicates that 'Stone' is variously inspired by 'the upper Gwesyn valley (leading up to [the hill called] Drygarn)' and the megaliths on 'another valley-side, Nant y Rhestr, near the upper Irfon' (personal communication to the author).
³¹ Bidgood, *Given Time*, p. 34.
³² Matthew Jarvis, 'Repositioning Wales: poetry after the Second Flowering', in Daniel Williams (ed.), *Slanderous Tongues: Welsh Poetry in English 1970–2005* (Bridgend: Seren, forthcoming).
³³ See Bidgood, *Given Time*, pp. 20, 23 and 29–30, and Ruth Bidgood, *Selected Poems* (Bridgend: Seren, 1992), pp. 45–54.
³⁴ Bidgood, *Selected Poems*, p. 45.
³⁵ R. S. Thomas, *Song at the Year's Turning: Poems 1942–1954* (London: Rupert Hart-Davis, 1955), p. 92. For my discussion of this poem, see ch. 3 above.
³⁶ Ruth Bidgood, *The Fluent Moment* (Bridgend: Seren, 1996), p. 49.
³⁷ For Dôlfach (or 'Dol-fâch' as it is given on the map), see *Brecknockshire*, Sheet XII.9, 1:2,500 (Southampton: Ordnance Survey, 1889), parcel 311; NGR SO 052 493. For the historical background to the events that Bidgood renders in 'Waterspout, 1853', see 'A tragedy at Dolfach', *Powys Digital History Project*, 27 May 2007 <http://history.powys.org.uk/school1/builth/flood2.shtml>.
³⁸ Kate Soper, *What is Nature? Culture, Politics and the Non-Human* (Oxford: Blackwell, 1995), pp. 155 and 156.

[39] Lawrence Buell, *Writing for an Endangered World: Literature, Culture, and Environment in the U.S. and Beyond* (Cambridge, MA: Belknap, 2001), p. 246.

[40] Bidgood, *Selected Poems*, p. 54.

[41] Ibid., pp. 16–19. Bidgood has explained that 'When you go up the Irfon valley towards Tregaron, if you keep on up the river and don't go up the Devil's Staircase you come to a very formidable and strange rock that sticks out across the valley, called The Rock of the Birds': Angela Morton, 'Interview: Ruth Bidgood', *New Welsh Review*, 10 (1990), 41. Carreg yr Adar is at NGR SN 83 57.

[42] Ruth Bidgood, *Not Without Homage* (Swansea: Christopher Davies, 1975), p. 36; *Print of Miracle*, p. 20; *Lighting Candles*, pp. 63 and 64; *Kindred*, pp. 52–3; *Fluent Moment*, p. 59.

[43] Bidgood, *Kindred*, p. 49.

[44] Bidgood, *Fluent Moment*, p. 55.

[45] The Acts of the Apostles 1: 9 and 10 (King James Version).

[46] See Allchin, 'The mystery that complements precision', 8, for a discussion of a related moment, in the poem 'Rainy Day' (Bidgood, *Given Time*, p. 77), in which, according to Allchin, 'There is a hint even of the divine fire itself glimpsed in the bush which burns but is not consumed.'

[47] Morton, 'Interview', p. 42. Bidgood goes on to concur with her interviewer's assessment that 'you see the darkness as crucial'. A. M. Allchin also suggests that 'it is clear that [Bidgood] has learned to speak starkly of the darkness and despair which sometimes assails our fancied security' ('The mystery that complements precision', 13).

[48] From the 'New Poems' section in Ruth Bidgood, *New & Selected Poems* (Bridgend: Seren, 2004), p. 252.

[49] In *Writing for an Endangered World*, Lawrence Buell discusses what he calls 'toxic discourse', which he defines as 'expressed anxiety arising from perceived threat of environmental hazard due to chemical modification by human agency' (pp. 30 and 31). What Bidgood describes here is not 'chemical'; but, manifestly, her sense of a landscape polluted through 'modification by human agency' – albeit in terms of vegetation – is very strong in this poem.

[50] W. Rhys Nicholas, *The Folk Poets*, Writers of Wales ([Cardiff]: University of Wales Press, 1978), p. 6.

[51] Jeremy Hooker, 'Ceridwen's daughters: Welsh women poets and the uses of tradition', *Welsh Writing in English: A Yearbook of Critical Essays*, 1 (1995), 133–4.

[52] Bidgood, 'Heartland', 8.

[53] Bidgood, *Print of Miracle*, pp. 12 and 21.

[54] Ruth Bidgood, *Singing to Wolves* (Bridgend: Seren, 2000), pp. 7–11.

[55] Jonathan Bate, *The Song of the Earth* (London: Picador, 2001; orig. 2000), p. 205.

[56] Bidgood, *Print of Miracle*, p. 21. The tale is given particulars in *Parishes of the Buzzard*, in which Bidgood explains that 'Mr C. Hope, who used to farm at [Pentwyn in Abergwesyn], remembered helping to lift a great recumbent stone

from this field [Dôlmaen], and finding under it black traces of burning. For a time this stone, he said, did duty as a gatepost, but it seems now to have disappeared. To it was attached the archetypal legend of the "drinking stone", which at midsummer dawn went down to the Gwesyn to drink' (p. 18).

57 Allchin, 'The mystery that complements precision', 11.

58 Nicholas, *Folk Poets*, p. 6.

59 Bidgood, *Parishes of the Buzzard*, p. 265.

60 Emphasis added; quoted from Nicholas, *Folk Poets*, p. 60.

61 Hooker, 'Ceridwen's daughters', p. 136.

62 Jeremy Hooker, *The Presence of the Past: Essays on Modern British and American Poetry* (Bridgend: Poetry Wales Press, 1987), p. 170. For 'Stone', see Bidgood, *Given Time*, p. 40.

63 Bidgood, *Given Time*, p. 45. For Hennant ('Hen-nant' on Ordnance Survey maps), see *Brecknockshire,* Sheet IX.4, parcel 133; NGR SN 846 529.

64 Buell, *Writing for an Endangered World*, p. 84.

65 Peter Berg and Ray Dasmann, 'Reinhabiting California', *The Ecologist*, 7 (1977), 399; quoted in Buell, *Writing for an Endangered World*, p. 297.

66 'Cenfaes': Bidgood, *Fluent Moment*, p. 40.

67 Brian Morris, *Harri Webb*, Writers of Wales (Cardiff: University of Wales Press, 1993), p. 62.

Notes to Chapter 6

1 Sam Adams, 'Robert Minhinnick in conversation with Sam Adams', *PN Review*, 24, 1 (1997), 21. For Cwrt Colman, see *Glamorgan*, Sheet XL.2, 1:2,500, Revision of 1940 (Southampton: Ordnance Survey, 1945), parcel 471; NGR SS 883 818.

2 Robert Minhinnick, *Native Ground* (Swansea: Triskele, 1979), p. 20. 'The Gamekeeper' is the third poem of the sequence 'Poems from Childhood' (pp. 18–23).

3 Sharon Zukin, *Landscapes of Power: From Detroit to Disney World* (Berkeley, CA: University of California Press, 1991), p. 19.

4 Martin Jones, Rhys Jones and Michael Woods, *An Introduction to Political Geography: Space, Place and Politics* (London: Routledge, 2004), p. 116.

5 As Eben Jones makes clear, the Llewellyn family has been 'traced back ... to a farmer of Ystradyfodwg (the former parish which included the Rhondda Valleys)': see Eben Jones, *Baglan and the Llewellyns of Baglan Hall* (Baglan, Port Talbot: Eben Jones, 1987), pp. 65–6. According to the family tree that Jones's volume offers, the farmer – Llewellyn Evan – died in 1757 (p. 142). Moreover, as Jones observes, 'The history of the Llewellyns typifies the emergence of the gentry from the lower ranks of the social scale. Llewellyn Evan was a yeoman farmer, a step above the rank of commoner, although the earlier pedigree of the family is claimed to have gone back through Morgan Vychan, Lord of Afan and Afan Wallia to Jestyn ap Gwrgan, Prince of Glamorgan'

(p. 69). The family's relationship with Cwrt Colman began in 1837, when the estate was bought by Llewellyn Evan's grandson, William Llewellyn (1773–1840): see Eben Jones, *The Llewellyns of Baglan and Cwrt Colman* (Baglan, Port Talbot: Eben Jones, 1989), explanatory text for plate 3.

6 Robert Minhinnick, *Life Sentences* (Bridgend: Poetry Wales Press, 1983), pp. 25–6. Eben Jones records that William Herbert Clydwyn [*sic*] Llewellyn (1883–1976) had inherited the Cwrt Colman estate in 1910 and that 'The Llewellyn connection with Cwrt Colman finally ended in 1961 when it was sold by auction, and some years later was converted into [a] residential hotel ... W H C Llewellyn spent the rest of his life (he died in 1976) at the house called Whitehall which he had built in the grounds of Cwrt Colman before he sold the estate': Jones, *Llewellyns of Baglan*, explanatory text for plate 3.

7 Robert Minhinnick, *Hey Fatman* (Bridgend: Seren, 1994), pp. 21–2.

8 Minhinnick, *Native Ground*, pp. 38–9.

9 Linden Peach, 'Wales and the cultural politics of identity: Gillian Clarke, Robert Minhinnick, and Jeremy Hooker', in James Acheson and Romana Huk (eds), *Contemporary British Poetry: Essays in Theory and Criticism* (Albany, NY: State University of New York Press, 1996), p. 384.

10 Edward W. Soja, *Postmodern Geographies: The Reassertion of Space in Critical Social Theory* (London: Verso, 1989), p. 6.

11 Ibid., p. 10.

12 Minhinnick, *Native Ground*, p. 43. Minhinnick has indicated that, in his mind, the poem takes place on the 'long private drive' between Cwrt Colman mansion and the church of All Saints, Pen-y-fai (personal communication to the author). The eponymous JP was William Herbert Clydwyn Llewellyn (for whom, see n. 6 above).

13 Peach, 'Wales and the cultural politics of identity', p. 384.

14 Peach's mistake is duplicated by Ian Gregson in the latter's recent book, *The New Poetry in Wales* (Cardiff: University of Wales Press, 2007), p. 37.

15 Kirsti Bohata, *Postcolonialism Revisited* (Cardiff: University of Wales Press, 2004), p. 5. On Welsh complicity with the imperial idea, Bohata observes, for example, 'Welsh involvement in imperial missionary work throughout the Empire (a role which was, indeed, visualized as something that only the uniquely moral Welsh might fulfil, a project closely followed in the Welsh-language press), as well as Welsh colonization of Patagonia, not to mention of North America, Australia, and so on.'

16 A contrary argument might be advanced on the grounds that William Herbert Clydwyn Llewellyn's mother was from English stock (see Jones, *Baglan and the Llewellyns*, p. 68) – but this is manifestly not enough to make him simply English. More importantly, however, in 'J.P.', the magistrate represents owner-ship of the Cwrt Colman estate, and thus the paternal family line of the Llewellyns.

17 Peach, 'Wales and the cultural politics of identity', p. 384.

18 Significantly, in an interview with David T. Lloyd, Minhinnick responds to the interviewer's comment about manor houses as 'present[ing] a class problem' by

saying 'Yes, that's what I like': David T. Lloyd (ed.), *Writing on the Edge: Interviews with Writers and Editors of Wales* (Amsterdam: Rodopi, 1997), p. 58.

[19] Minhinnick indicates that Cwrt-y-felin is 'based on a real house known to us as "Cuckoo Mill". On the map it's "Felin Gwcw"'; the 'Cwrt-y-' element of the name is Minhinnick's own addition (personal communication to the author). For Felingwcw, see *Glamorgan*, Sheet XL.2, parcel 401; NGR SS 885 816.

[20] Minhinnick, *Hey Fatman*, pp. 58–63.

[21] For the association between water and the sacred in ancient Celtic culture, see my discussion of Gillian Clarke's 'At Ystrad Fflur' in ch. 4 above and Miranda Green, *The Gods of the Celts* (Stroud: Sutton, 1997), p. 138, who says that 'Water held a fascination for the Celts: rivers, lakes, bogs, springs and of course the sea were sources of especial veneration.' Green goes on to observe the existence of 'abundant evidence for the veneration of unnamed prehistoric supernatural powers associated with water'.

[22] Ian Gregson, 'On the Street of Processions: Robert Minhinnick interviewed by Ian Gregson', *Planet*, 167 (2004), 47.

[23] Robert Minhinnick, *A Thread in the Maze* (Swansea: Christopher Davies, 1978), p. 15.

[24] Val Plumwood, *Environmental Culture: The Ecological Crisis of Reason* (London: Routledge, 2002), p. 4.

[25] In an interview with Jackie Aplin, Minhinnick objects to the interviewer's use of the phrase 'nature poems' to describe material in *A Thread in the Maze*, saying that 'it's a term which is too easy. I don't write about "nature" – there are poems about creatures, about eels, grasshoppers, but there are also poems about people. It's about what I saw around me at Pen-y-fai at the time': Jackie Aplin, 'Interview with Robert Minhinnick', *Poetry Wales*, 25, 2 (1989), 23.

[26] Plumwood, *Environmental Culture*, p. 98; Lloyd, *Writing on the Edge*, p. 57.

[27] Minhinnick, *Thread in the Maze*, p. 20.

[28] Minhinnick, *Native Ground*, p. 12.

[29] Robert Minhinnick, *The Dinosaur Park* (Bridgend: Poetry Wales Press, 1985), p. 29. For Kenfig Sands, see NGR SS 78 81.

[30] Robert Minhinnick, *The Looters* (Bridgend: Seren, 1989), p. 39.

[31] Minhinnick, *Hey Fatman*, p. 32.

[32] Robert Minhinnick, *After the Hurricane* (Manchester: Carcanet, 2002), p. 27.

[33] Minhinnick, *Dinosaur Park*, pp. 25 ('Surfers') and 26 ('Snaps').

[34] From the very beginning of *Environmental Culture*, Plumwood paints the contemporary situation as one of 'ecological crisis', with dominant global cultures having set 'in motion massive processes of biospheric degradation': 'In the ecological parallel to the *Titanic* story, we have reached the stage in the narrative where we have received the iceberg warning, and have made the remarkable decision to double the engine speed to Full Speed Ahead and go below to get a good night's rest ... Nothing, not even the ultimate risk of the death of nature, can be allowed to hold back the triumphant progress of the ship of rational fools' (p. 1).

[35] 'The Track', in Minhinnick, *Looters*, p. 50.

[36] Minhinnick, *After the Hurricane*, p. 85.

[37] Minhinnick, *Life Sentences*, p. 41. Cwm y Gaer is to be found on the edge of the dunes to the east of Porthcawl (NGR SS 85 77).

[38] By 'the category of the natural', I mean to suggest Kate Soper's 'metaphysical' concept of nature: see Kate Soper, *What is Nature? Culture, Politics and the Non-Human* (Oxford: Blackwell, 1995), p. 155.

[39] Minhinnick, *Thread in the Maze*, p. 11.

[40] See Gregson, *New Poetry in Wales*, p. 59.

[41] Minhinnick, *Hey Fatman*, pp. 32–8. Dunraven Bay (NGR SS 88 72) is near the village of Southerndown, to the south-east of Porthcawl.

[42] Minhinnick, *Hey Fatman*, p. 32.

[43] Peach, 'Wales and the cultural politics of identity', p. 389.

[44] Minhinnick, *Looters*, p. 42.

[45] For Baudrillard, the twentieth century manifests a cultural condition in which a 'saturated world' sees appearance (image) become dominant to such an extent that the reality behind the appearance (the meaning) is obliterated: 'There is no more hope for meaning. And without doubt this is a good thing: meaning is mortal. But that on which it has imposed its ephemeral reign, what it hoped to liquidate in order to impose the reign of the Enlightenment, that is, appearances, they, [*sic*] are immortal ...' See Jean Baudrillard, *Simulacra and Simulation*, trans. Sheila Faria Glaser (Ann Arbor, MI: University of Michigan Press, 1994), pp. 161 and 164. For his explicit connection between the twentieth century and the era of postmodernity, see pp. 160–1.

[46] Peach, 'Wales and the cultural politics of identity', p. 388. For 'Ghost Train', see Minhinnick, *Looters*, p. 45.

[47] Jonathan Bate, *The Song of the Earth* (London: Picador, 2001; orig. 2000), p. 282.

[48] Gregson, *New Poetry in Wales*, p. 42.

[49] Minhinnick, *After the Hurricane*, p. 14.

[50] Gregson, *New Poetry in Wales*, p. 58.

[51] Somewhat contrary to Gregson's desire to read 'much of [Minhinnick's] writing' as an exercise in environmentalist protest (*New Poetry in Wales*, p. 43), Minhinnick himself has – as I have already indicated – declared himself suspicious of producing a poetry that is straightforwardly 'green'. Drawing a comparison with the writing that he produced for Friends of the Earth Cymru, which he describes as 'polemical', Minhinnick observes that his 'poetry is compelled, I think, by individual people or places or experiences' rather than by any desire to be 'preacherly or evangelical' (Lloyd, *Writing on the Edge*, p. 57).

[52] Gregson, *New Poetry in Wales*, p. 53.

[53] Minhinnick, *After the Hurricane*, p. 12. Edwards Electrical is to be found on Well Street, Porthcawl.

[54] Gregson, *New Poetry in Wales*, p. 58.

[55] In 'Transnationalism, postcolonialism or transcolonialism? Reflections on Los

Angeles, geography, and the uses of theory', *Emergences: Journal for the Study of Media and Composite Cultures*, 10, 1 (2000), Françoise Lionnet deploys the terms 'transcultural' (30) and 'transcolonial' (27) as part of a 'relational approach' (31) to issues of identity which, concentrating on the complexities of 'circuits that traverse national identities' (30) and the networks that are constructed 'amongst sites marked differentially by the imperial project and the colonial will to power' (31), constitutes a movement away from the binaries of the discourse/counterdiscourse rhetoric implicit in much postcolonial theory (32–3).

Notes to Chapter 7

¹ Wayne Burrows, 'A dissident voice: Wayne Burrows interviews Mike Jenkins', *New Welsh Review*, 9 (1990), 56. For his poem 'An Escape', see Mike Jenkins, *A Dissident Voice* (Bridgend: Seren, 1990), p. 39.

² David T. Lloyd (ed.), *Writing on the Edge: Interviews with Writers and Editors of Wales* (Amsterdam: Rodopi, 1997), p. 135.

³ Jenkins has lived in Heolgerrig since the late 1970s (personal communication from Mike Jenkins to the author).

⁴ For Cwm Glo, see *Glamorgan*, Sheet XI.NE, 1:10,560, 2nd edn (Southampton: Ordnance Survey, 1905) and *Glamorgan*, Sheet XII.NW, 1:10,560, 2nd edn (Southampton: Ordnance Survey, 1905); NGR SO 03 05. The Glamorgan-Gwent Archaeological Trust's 'Historic Landscape Characterisation' project suggests the area's complexity, dividing it into 'Cwm Glo, north', 'Cwm Glo: tramroad, plateway and incline corridor', and (part of) 'Winch Fawr, Pen-yr-Heolgerrig, Cwm Du, and upper Cwm Glo workings'. The first of these divisions is characterized as 'An agricultural/settlement landscape', 'less affected by industrial incursion than surrounding area [*sic*]' (Glamorgan-Gwent Archaeological Trust, 'Historic landscape characterisation: Merthyr Tydfil: 069 Cwm Glo, north', 19 Apr. 2008 <*http://www.ggat.org.uk/cadw/historic_landscape/Merthyr%20Tydfil/English/Merthyr_069.htm*>); the second is a 'relict industrial and agricultural settlement' ('Historic landscape characterisation: Merthyr Tydfil: 070 Cwm Glo: tramroad, plateway and incline corridor', 19 Apr. 2008 <*http://www.ggat.org.uk/cadw/historic_landscape/Merthyr%20Tydfil/English/Merthyr_070.htm*>); the third is an 'extractive landscape dating to the 18th and 19th century [*sic*]' ('Historic landscape characterisation: Merthyr Tydfil: 064 Winch Fawr, Pen-yr-Heolgerrig, Cwm Du, and upper Cwm Glo workings', 19 Apr. 2008 <*http://www.ggat.org.uk/cadw/historic_landscape/Merthyr%20Tydfil/English/Merthyr_064.htm*>). As the photographs provided on these web pages illustrate, Jenkins's common land now variously has the appearance of rough grazing land, light woodland and open moor.

⁵ Mike Jenkins, 'Merthyr, my adopted home', *Poetry Wales*, 32, 4 (1997), 23–4.

⁶ Kate Soper, *What is Nature? Culture, Politics and the Non-Human* (Oxford: Blackwell, 1995), p. 156.

7 Jenkins, 'Merthyr, my adopted home', 24.

8 Jeremy Hooker has observed the importance of Jenkins's 'personal poems': see Jeremy Hooker, *The Presence of the Past: Essays on Modern British and American Poetry* (Bridgend: Poetry Wales Press, 1987), pp. 188–9.

9 Jenkins's first collection, *Rat City: Poems from Northern Ireland* (Barry: Edge, 1979), was a pamphlet of nineteen poems. Whilst acknowledging *Rat City*, the back cover notes of Mike Jenkins, *Empire of Smoke* (Bridgend: Poetry Wales Press, 1983) talk of *The Common Land* as 'his first book'.

10 Mike Jenkins, *The Common Land* (Bridgend: Poetry Wales Press, 1981), p. 21.

11 Lawrence Buell, *Writing for an Endangered World: Literature, Culture, and Environment in the U.S. and Beyond* (Cambridge, MA: Belknap, 2001), p. 297, n. 1.

12 Jenkins, 'Merthyr, my adopted home', 23.

13 See *Glamorgan*, Sheet XI.NE and *Glamorgan*, Sheet XII.NW on which are marked, variously, features such as 'Old Coal Level', 'Old Shaft', 'Old Coal Shaft', 'Coedcae Pit (Disused)', and 'Cwm-glo Pit (Disused)'.

14 Buell, *Writing for an Endangered World*, pp. 30, 31 and 33.

15 Hooker, *Presence of the Past*, p. 187.

16 Buell, *Writing for an Endangered World*, p. 35.

17 See Leo Marx, *The Machine in the Garden: Technology and the Pastoral Ideal in America* (Oxford: Oxford University Press, 1964), p. 25. See also Buell's useful summary in *Writing for an Endangered World*, p. 37.

18 Martin Jones, Rhys Jones and Michael Woods, *An Introduction to Political Geography: Space, Place and Politics* (London: Routledge, 2004), p. 115.

19 Dolores Hayden, *The Power of Place: Urban Landscapes as Public History* (Cambridge, MA: MIT Press, 1995), p. 20.

20 'The Last Coal': Jenkins, *Dissident Voice*, pp. 62–71; 'Sensing the Waun': Mike Jenkins, *This House, My Ghetto* (Bridgend: Seren, 1995), pp. 44–8.

21 Jenkins, *Common Land*, pp. 14 and 15.

22 For an extended discussion of the notorious China district of Merthyr, see Keith Strange, 'In search of the celestial empire', *Llafur: The Journal of the Society for the Study of Welsh Labour History*, 3, 1 (1980), 44–86. The name 'China' came from the region's association with organized crime which 'seized control of the district and constructed a primitive, yet successful system of institutions and organizations, which, in the wake of British expansion in the Far East, came to be sarcastically termed the "Empire", its inhabitants, the "Chinese", and its leaders, "Emperors", "Empresses", and "Mandarins"' (78). The formal name of the district was 'Pont-Storehouse' or 'Pontystorehouse', although China itself was really 'limited to a maze of hovels known as "Park's Cellars", or simply, "the Cellars"' (45).

23 Geraint H. Jenkins, *A Concise History of Wales* (Cambridge: Cambridge University Press, 2007), p. 199; for Merthyr's massive nineteenth-century growth, see p. 183.

24 John Davies gives the detail of cholera's depredations, explaining that 'Cholera was first recorded in Britain in 1832, when it killed 160 in Merthyr and 152 in

Swansea. The epidemic of 1848–9, when 1,682 died in Merthyr alone, was much more serious': see John Davies, *A History of Wales*, revised edn (London: Penguin, 2007), p. 385.

[25] Jenkins, *Concise History*, p. 179. For the growth and decline of the iron industry in Merthyr, see Davies, *History of Wales*, pp. 319–21 and 392–3.

[26] For the notion of 'contaminated communities', see Buell, *Writing for an Endangered World*, p. 36.

[27] For locations of principal ironworks, see the map 'The iron industry in the south Wales coalfield', in Davies, *History of Wales*, p. 341.

[28] Buell, *Writing for an Endangered World*, p. 34.

[29] Ibid., p. 36.

[30] Sharon Zukin, *Landscapes of Power: From Detroit to Disney World* (Berkeley, CA: University of California Press, 1991), pp. 19 and 16.

[31] Jones, Jones and Woods, *Introduction to Political Geography*, p. 116.

[32] Zukin, *Landscapes of Power*, p. 19.

[33] Davies, *History of Wales*, p. 321.

[34] Mike Jenkins, *Laughter Tangled in Thorn and Other Poems* (Llanrwst: Carreg Gwalch, 2002), p. 11.

[35] Zukin, *Landscapes of Power*, p. 19.

[36] For his discussion of slum areas in nineteenth-century Wales, see Ieuan Gwynedd Jones, 'Religion and society in nineteenth century Wales', in John Rowlands and Sheila Rowlands (eds), *Second Stages in Researching Welsh Ancestry* (Ramsbottom: Federation of Family History Societies; Aberystwyth: University of Wales, Aberystwyth, 1999), p. 5. For the despised status of nineteenth-century China, see Strange, 'In search of the celestial empire', pp. 44–5.

[37] Sir John Guest 'sat as a member of Parliament for Honiton from 1825 until 1831. It was largely through his influence that the new parliamentary constituency of the Merthyr borough … was created. He was returned unopposed in 1832 (as a Liberal and Free Trader) as the first M.P. for the Merthyr borough, and kept his seat until his death in 1852': see John Edward Lloyd and R. T. Jenkins (eds), *The Dictionary of Welsh Biography down to 1940* (London: The Honourable Society of Cymmrodorion, 1959), p. 321. John Davies suggests that, by 1847, Guest 'was the owner of the world's largest iron company' and observes – startlingly – that 'it is likely he had more people working for him than had any other employer on the face of the earth' (*History of Wales*, p. 372).

[38] Jenkins, *Common Land*, p. 15.

[39] For Idris Davies, see 'The Angry Summer', poem 37, in Dafydd Johnston (ed.), *The Complete Poems of Idris Davies* (Cardiff: University of Wales Press, 1994), p. 39; for Gwenallt see 'Colomennod', in D. Gwenallt Jones, *Eples* (Llandysul: Gomer, 1951), p. 15, and 'Sir Gaerfyrddin', in D. Gwenallt Jones, *Ysgubau'r Awen* (Llandysul: Gomer, [1939]), p. 83 – these latter two poems translated, respectively, as 'Pigeons' and 'Carmarthenshire', in Joseph P. Clancy (trans.), *Twentieth Century Welsh Poems* (Llandysul: Gomer, 1982), pp. 99 and 96.

[40] Jenkins's poetics reflect, in a striking way, the situation of cultural and polit-

ical controls outlined by John Davies: 'The ironmasters were not merely employers; frequently they were the owners of their employees' dwellings and through the truck system many workers were obliged to buy their goods in company shops; the masters sat on the magistrates' bench and they dominated the parish meeting, the only form of local government in the coalfield communities' (*History of Wales*, p. 339).

41 According to John A. Owen, 'In 1844 the Dowlais Iron Company to further add to the scanty amenities of the town, built a reading room and library': *The History of the Dowlais Iron Works, 1759–1970* (Newport: Starling, 1977), p. 34.

42 Jenkins's specific titular reference would seem to be to the new library which was built in Dowlais as a memorial to Sir John Guest. Under the heading of 'The Guest Memorial Hall', John A. Owen writes that 'in March 1854, at a public meeting of Dowlais workmen it was decided to erect a monument to the memory of Sir John Guest, and that it should consist of a library and reading room ... The trustees finished and opened the Memorial Library & Reading Rooms in 1863' (ibid., pp. 49 and 50). For the impact of monuments to the Guest family on the identity of Dowlais, see Glanmor Williams, *A Life* (Cardiff: University of Wales Press, 2002), p. 4.

43 Jenkins, *Common Land*, pp. 19–20.

44 Cyfarthfa Castle was commissioned by William Crawshay II (1788–1867). In his book *The Visual Culture of Wales: Industrial Society* (Cardiff: University of Wales Press, 1998), Peter Lord explains that the symbolism of the house has a fairly detailed context: 'Cyfarthfa Castle was a medieval fantasy designed by Robert Lugar and completed in the boom year of 1825. That Crawshay, a leader in the most technically advanced industry in the world, should choose to present himself in the guise of a feudal lord of the middle ages might seem eccentric were it not characteristic of a number of his peers' (p. 72). Thus, as Lord notes, 'The imagery [of the house] was addressed primarily to the owner's peer group' (p. 69). However, it is significant that he also observes the way in which 'historicist houses' such as Cyfarthfa Castle 'added a symbolic distance to the physical distance which their owners were placing between themselves and the source of their wealth' (p. 72). Finally, Cyfarthfa Castle, like Dowlais House, 'looked down on the works from an elevated position' (p. 74) – so, in 'Chartist Meeting', Jenkins is subverting the implicit power relationships of height by placing the working people in a position where *they look down on* the Castle.

45 Davies, *History of Wales*, p. 364.

46 Jenkins, *Dissident Voice*, pp. 40–1; Mike Jenkins, *Graffiti Narratives: Poems 'n' Stories* (Aberystwyth: Planet, 1994), pp. 17–18.

47 John Pikoulis suggests that, in his fully developed dialect work, Jenkins 'reproduc[es] every stray aitch, contraction and voiced fricative of Cwmtaffian [Merthyr] speech. He represents the "barbaric yawp" of south Wales in all its singularity': see John Pikoulis, '"Some kind o' beginnin'": Mike Jenkins and the voices of Cwmtaff', *Welsh Writing in English: A Yearbook of Critical Essays*, 10 (2005), 122.

48 Jenkins, *Common Land*, p. 26.
49 Jenkins, *Empire of Smoke*, p. 22.
50 Mike Jenkins, *Coulda Bin Summin* (Aberystwyth: Planet, 2001), p. 59.
51 For further information about the area's history as 'Reclaimed industrial landscape', see: Glamorgan-Gwent Archaeological Trust, 'Historic landscape characterisation: Merthyr Tydfil: 078 Dowlais Great Tip, Trecatti, Trehir and Twyn-y-Waun', 19 Apr. 2008 <*http://www.ggat.org.uk/cadw/historic_landscape/Merthyr%20Tydfil/English/Merthyr_078.htm*>.
52 Buell, *Writing for an Endangered World*, pp. 30, 37 and 36.
53 Ibid., p. 37.
54 Greg Garrard, *Ecocriticism* (London: Routledge, 2004), p. 12.
55 Zukin, *Landscapes of Power*, p. 19.
56 Jenkins, *Coulda Bin Summin*, p. 43.
57 Mike Jenkins, *Red Landscapes: New and Selected Poems* (Bridgend: Seren, 1999), p. 104; Mike Jenkins, *The Language of Flight* (Llanrwst: Carreg Gwalch, 2004), p. 34.
58 Hayden, *Power of Place*, p. 30.
59 Jenkins, *Language of Flight*, p. 31.
60 Jones, Jones and Woods, *Introduction to Political Geography*, p. 125.
61 Ibid.; emphasis added.
62 Jenkins lived in Northern Ireland for a short while in the 1970s, as John Pikoulis explains: 'Following graduation [from the then UCW Aberystwyth in 1974], [Jenkins and his wife-to-be] moved to Portglenone in Co. Derry and were married; after a year's teaching (this was the time of the Troubles) they decided to leave for West Germany' ('"Some kind o' beginnin"', 137).
63 M. Wynn Thomas, *Corresponding Cultures: The Two Literatures of Wales* (Cardiff: University of Wales Press, 1999), p. 55.
64 Ibid.
65 'Returning to the Nant', section v: Jenkins, *Dissident Voice*, p. 75. Nant Gwrtheyrn (NGR SH 349 448) is now home to the Welsh Language and Heritage Centre.
66 Roger Geary, 'The dragon and the flame: an analysis of the Welsh arson campaign', *Contemporary Review*, 1537 (1994), 82.
67 As Geary explains, it is 'unlikely that a single group has been entirely responsible for such a sustained campaign ... and focusing on such diverse targets'. Instead, he argues that it seems 'rather more likely that several independent groups, perhaps supplemented by individuals acting on their own discretion, have been willing to allow their various actions to contribute to the myth of "Meibion Glyndwr [*sic*]"' ('The dragon and the flame', 81).
68 Geary, 'The dragon and the flame', 82.
69 Zukin, *Landscapes of Power*, p. 19.
70 Jenkins, *This House*, pp. 34–5.

Notes to Chapter 8

¹ 'Enlli and the arts', *Ynys Enlli/Bardsey Island*, 6 Dec. 2007 <*http://www. bardsey.org/english/the_island/arts.htm*>. When not living on Bardsey, Evans's home is the Llŷn Peninsula. Bardsey itself is about two miles off the tip of the Llŷn Peninsula.

² Christine Evans, *Island of Dark Horses* (Bridgend: Seren, 1995).

³ Yi-Fu Tuan, *Space and Place: The Perspective of Experience* (Minneapolis, MN: University of Minnesota Press, 1977), p. 17; emphasis added.

⁴ Dorian Llywelyn, *Sacred Place: Chosen People; Land and National Identity in Welsh Spirituality* (Cardiff: University of Wales Press, 1999), p. 16.

⁵ Tuan, *Space and Place*, p. 86.

⁶ Llywelyn, *Sacred Place*, p. 16.

⁷ Evans, *Island of Dark Horses*, p. 62; subsequent references to this volume are given in the text.

⁸ Evans's use of 'myth' in this poem is close to Tuan's first sort of mythical space; in other words, it refers (at least in part) to a *world of fantasy* beyond the horizon. However, I shall substitute the word 'mystery' for Evans's 'myth' to avoid confusion with the more precisely defined notion of mythical space with which I am primarily dealing here.

⁹ In Arthurian legend, Avalon is the 'island to which Britain's legendary king Arthur was conveyed for the healing of his wounds after his final battle … It was ruled by the enchantress Morgan le Fay and her eight sisters, all of them skilled in the healing arts' ('Avalon', *Encyclopædia Britannica*, 2007, Encyclopædia Britannica Online, 6 Dec. 2007 <*http://search.eb.com/eb/article-9011399*>). In a specifically Welsh context, 'Ynys Afallon (The Isle of Avalon) is a later form' of the name 'Ynys Afallach', which appears in *Brut y Brenhinedd* as the rendition of Geoffrey of Monmouth's 'insula Avallonis' (*Brut y Brenhinedd* being the title generally given to the various Welsh versions of Geoffrey's *Historia Regum Britanniae*). The name 'Ynys Afallach' derives either from the sense that it 'contains the word "*afall*" ("apple-tree(s)")' – thus the 'supposed meaning "place of apples"' – or from the '*Aballac(h)* or Afallach who appears in several early Welsh genealogies as an ancestor-deity from whom a number of ruling dynasties in Wales and the Old North claimed descent'. See Meic Stephens (ed.), *The New Companion to the Literature of Wales* (Cardiff: University of Wales Press, 1998), entries for 'Afallach' (p. 7), '*Brut y Brenhinedd*' (pp. 70–1) and 'Ynys Afallon' (p. 821).

¹⁰ According to Geoffrey of Monmouth, 'The Fortunate Island' is so-called because 'it produces all manner of plants spontaneously': Geoffrey of Monmouth, *Life of Merlin*, ed. and trans. Basil Clarke (Cardiff: University of Wales Press, 1973), p. 101. As Clarke explains in his notes, 'Geoffrey's equivalent island in *HRB* [*Historia Regum Britanniae*] 11. 2 is *insula Avallonis*' (p. 182) – in other words, Avalon.

¹¹ Tuan, *Space and Place*, p. 98.

¹² Ibid., pp. 99–100; emphasis added.

¹³ Ibid., p. 149.

14 The currents around Bardsey are notoriously difficult, as Brenda Chamberlain observes in *Tide-race*. Shortly after having moved to the island (as opposed to being merely a seasonal visitor), Chamberlain notes that 'The currents in their amazing complexity baffled and sometimes frightened us': Brenda Chamberlain, *Tide-race* (Bridgend: Seren, 1987; orig. 1962), p. 139.

15 Interestingly, Chamberlain also refers to the sea as muscular, perhaps suggesting the sense amongst Bardsey islanders of the sea's sheer strength. Thus, she asks 'What am I? Whence did I come? Whither shall I go? Among rock-bones in the deeps of the muscular ocean?' (*Tide-race*, p. 46).

16 Tuan, *Space and Place*, p. 149.

17 Ibid.

18 Ibid., p. 100.

19 Chamberlain, *Tide-race*, pp. 28 and 61.

20 Tuan, *Space and Place*, p. 149.

21 Ibid., p. 98.

22 In their study *Celtic Heritage: Ancient Tradition in Ireland and Wales* (London: Thames & Hudson, 1961), Alwyn Rees and Brinley Rees note the 'belief that in the Other World everything is inverted', observing that 'with regard to ghosts of the dead and other spirits, ... our day is their night' (p. 145). It is within this context that Bardsey – existing within the world of the spirit as island of the saints – renders the locus of the cursed as the locus of the sacred. Of course, this process of inversion also suggests that what is here presented most emphatically as beyond the '*At last*' can exist simultaneously, in the alternate geography of the spiritual, as a centre-point – the place of pilgrimage, for example, to which Brenda Chamberlain refers at the very start of *Tide-race* (p. 16).

23 Doreen Massey, *Space, Place and Gender* (Cambridge: Polity, 1994), p. 264.

24 Tuan, *Space and Place*, p. 98.

25 Ibid., p. 86.

26 Ibid.

27 Brenda Chamberlain's Bardsey is also constructed in terms of female space: see, for example, *Tide-race*, p. 18, where Chamberlain talks of the island in terms of '*her* sides' and '*her* enchantments' (emphases added).

28 For the notion of 'pragmatic' space, see Tuan, *Space and Place*, p. 86.

29 Mircea Eliade, *The Sacred and the Profane: The Nature of Religion*, trans. Willard R. Trask (London: Harcourt Brace Jovanovich, 1987), pp. 26 and 27.

30 Belinda Humfrey, 'Prelude to the twentieth century', in M. Wynn Thomas (ed.), *Welsh Writing in English*, A Guide to Welsh Literature, 7 (Cardiff: University of Wales Press, 2003), p. 33.

31 Belinda Humfrey makes clear that the English Romantic response to Wales was based on 'travel in Wales' ('Prelude to the twentieth century', p. 33), and goes on to observe the extensive 'tourist literature' about Wales which 'sprang up in the late eighteenth century when Europe was closed by wars and young gentlemen needed a substitute for the Alps; these works flowed into the first half of the nineteenth century' (pp. 33–4).

32 Chamberlain, *Tide-race*, p. 220.

³³ For the way in which *Tide-race* presents the relationship between Chamberlain and other islanders see, for example, p. 141; for her involvement in island work, see the opening lines of part 4, section 33 (p. 195). Kate Holman, *Brenda Chamberlain*, Writers of Wales (Cardiff: University of Wales Press, 1997), pp. 27–8, points out that certain elements within *Tide-race* are recastings of events that did not happen on Bardsey. However, it is Chamberlain's *presentation* of a deep engagement with the island and its community which is important here – and her consequent implicit rejection of any notion that Bardsey's material life is merely some passing backdrop for revelation.

³⁴ See Peter Hope Jones and R. S. Thomas, *Between Sea and Sky: Images of Bardsey* (Llandysul: Gomer, 1998), p. 12.

³⁵ Matthew Jarvis, 'The politics of place in the poetry of Ian Davidson', *Welsh Writing in English: A Yearbook of Critical Essays*, 10 (2005), 154–6.

³⁶ Justin Wintle, *Furious Interiors: Wales, R. S. Thomas and God* (London: HarperCollins, 1996), p. 358; emphasis added.

³⁷ Jones and Thomas, *Between Sea and Sky*, pp. 14 and 15.

³⁸ Eliade, *The Sacred and the Profane*, p. 20.

Notes to Chapter 9

¹ Ian Davidson, *At a Stretch* (Exeter: Shearsman, 2004), p. 109. Davidson is probably the least well-known of the poets in my study, and his history of small-press publication can make some of his work – especially the earliest volumes – hard to find. However, to aid readers who may wish to pursue his work more extensively, Davidson's collections and pamphlets to date (early 2008) have been: with John Muckle, *It is Now as it was Then* (London: MICA in association with Actual Size, 1983); *No Passage Landward (Environmental Studies)* (Hebden Bridge: Open Township, 1989); *Human to Begin With*, Poetical Histories, 16 (Cambridge: Peter Riley, 1991); *The Patrick Poems* (London: Amra Imprint, 1991); *Wipe Out* (Cheltenham: Short Run, 1995); *Human Remains & Sudden Movements* (Nether Edge, Sheffield: West House, 2003); *Harsh* (Peterborough: Spectacular Diseases, 2003); *At a Stretch* (2004); *No Way Back* ([Nether Edge, Sheffield]: Gargoyle, 2005); *As if Only* (Exeter: Shearsman, 2007); with Zoë Skoulding, *Dark Wires* (Nether Edge, Sheffield: West House, 2007).

² Personal communication to the author. Davidson explains that 'The dig was right on the beach. From the top of the dune in the dig you could see the Inland Sea, the water that comes up through Four Mile Bridge and is hemmed in by the Stanley Embankment (now the A55) on the other side.' Trearddur Bay is at NGR SH 25 78.

³ Davidson, *No Passage Landward*, p. 8. The lighthouse referred to in the poem is off Trwyn Penmon, at the furthest eastward tip of Anglesey itself (NGR SH 641 814): personal communication from Ian Davidson to the author.

[4] See ch. 6 above and Linden Peach, 'Wales and the cultural politics of identity: Gillian Clarke, Robert Minhinnick, and Jeremy Hooker', in James Acheson and Romana Huk (eds), *Contemporary British Poetry: Essays in Theory and Criticism* (Albany, NY: State University of New York Press, 1996), p. 384.

[5] Personal communication to the author.

[6] Sharon Zukin, *Landscapes of Power: From Detroit to Disney World* (Berkeley, CA: University of California Press, 1991), p. 193.

[7] With thanks to Ian Davidson for access to his copy of *No Passage Landward*. For 'The Country's Up for Grabs', see Davidson, *No Passage Landward*, p. 3.

[8] Yi-Fu Tuan, *Space and Place: The Perspective of Experience* (Minneapolis, MN: University of Minnesota Press, 1977), pp. 17–18.

[9] Lawrence Buell, *Writing for an Endangered World: Literature, Culture, and Environment in the U.S. and Beyond* (Cambridge, MA: Belknap, 2001), p. 61.

[10] Although I am drawing here on Tuan's theory of spaces being formed through the conceptual interconnection of particular important points of reference (what he calls 'places'), I use the word 'place' in Buell's broader sense of defined space in general. Tuan himself moves towards just such a sense of place when he suggests that 'Enclosed and humanized space is place' (*Space and Place*, p. 54).

[11] The poems in *Human Remains & Sudden Movements* are numbered from one to seventeen. The collection does not have page numbering, so references throughout this discussion will be to poem numbers.

[12] Charles Olson, 'Projective verse', in Donald Allen (ed.), *The New American Poetry, 1945–1960* (Berkeley, CA: University of California Press, 1999), p. 392. For a useful brief summary of the significance of this essay, see Jon Cook (ed.), *Poetry in Theory: An Anthology 1900–2000* (Oxford: Blackwell, 2004), p. 288.

[13] Tuan, *Space and Place*, p. 17.

[14] For the notion of 'radical landscape poetry', see Harriet Tarlo, 'Radical landscapes: contemporary poetry in the Bunting tradition', in James McGonigal and Richard Price (eds), *The Star You Steer By: Basil Bunting and British Modernism* (Amsterdam: Rodopi, 2000), p. 149.

[15] According to Davidson, the lighthouses in question are 'probably South Stack and Penmon' (personal communication to the author) – respectively on the western edge of Holy Island (NGR SH 201 822) and on the eastern edge of Anglesey (NGR SH 641 814). The poem's 'heap of / rock' is thus arguably the entirety of the Anglesey area.

[16] Personal communication to the author.

[17] It is significant that, although the chapel to which these lines are referring is a particular place – Davidson identifies it as Capel Towyn, in Trearddur Bay (personal communication to the author) – the poem itself in no way seeks to offer such information.

[18] Matthew Jarvis, 'West House Books: recent poetry', *English*, 204 (2003), 271.

[19] For Buell's discussion of 'environmental unconscious', see *Writing for an Endangered World*, p. 22.

[20] Quoted in Cheryll Glotfelty, 'Introduction: literary studies in an age of en-

vironmental crisis', in Cheryll Glotfelty and Harold Fromm (eds), *The Ecocriticism Reader: Landmarks in Literary Ecology* (Athens, GA: University of Georgia Press, 1996), p. xix.

21 Buell, *Writing for an Endangered World*, p. 130.

22 In the rendition provided by the King James Version, Psalm 121:1 reads: 'I will lift up mine eyes unto the hills, from whence cometh my help.'

23 See James D. G. Dunn and John W. Rogerson (eds), *Eerdmans Commentary on the Bible* (Cambridge: Eerdmans, 2003), p. 424, which states that Psalm 121 'was not originally written as a pilgrim song. The hills spoken of in 121:1 are not the hills which the pilgrims had to cross on their journey to Jerusalem. In view of the polemic qualities that are evident in the rest of the psalm, hills should also be interpreted in a polemic sense, namely, as the dwelling place of the gods.'

24 Ian Gregson, *The New Poetry in Wales* (Cardiff: University of Wales Press, 2007), p. 13. I briefly question Gregson's analysis of Clarke in Matthew Jarvis, '[Review of Ian Gregson, *The New Poetry in Wales*]', *New Welsh Review*, 78 (2007), 87.

25 See Great Britain Historical GIS Project, 'The Isle of Anglesey Wales through time | historical statistics on social structure for the district/unitary authority | rate: percentage of working-age males in class 4 and 5', *A Vision of Britain Through Time*, 6 Dec. 2007 <*http://www.visionofbritain.org.uk/data_rate_ page. jsp?u_id=10056688&c_id=10001043&data_theme=T_SOC&id=2*> and 'Gwynedd Wales through time | historical statistics on social structure for the district/unitary authority | rate: percentage of working-age males in class 4 and 5', *A Vision of Britain Through Time*, 6 Dec. 2007 <*http://www.visionofbri- tain.org.uk/data_rate_page.jsp?u_id=10076766&c_id=10001043&data_theme= T_SOC&id=2*>. Gwynedd here refers to the area of the post-1996 unitary authority.

26 See Great Britain Historical GIS Project, 'Wales through time | historical statistics on social structure for the nation | rate: percentage of working-age males in class 4 and 5', *A Vision of Britain Through Time*, 6 Dec. 2007 <*http:// www.visionofbritain.org.uk/data_rate_page.jsp?u_id=10001055&c_id=10001043 &data_theme=T_SOC&id=2*>.

27 Given Davidson's identification of the archaeological dig to which the title of the collection refers as being 'at a place called Capel Towyn' (personal commu- nication to the author), his concern with human remains recalls the description of Capel Towyn in *Archæologia Cambrensis* as 'full of coffins and bodies, ... probably once surmounted by a chapel': [H. L. Jones], 'List of early British remains in Wales: no. III', *Archæologia Cambrensis: The Journal of the Cambrian Archæological Association*, 3, 1 (1855), 21.

28 See my discussions in chs 6 and 7 above.

29 'Plas Newydd belonged from about 1470 to the powerful Griffith family of Penrhyn, who built the original house here early in the following century, and from whom the estate descended by marriage respectively to the Bagenal and Bayly families': National Trust, *Plas Newydd: Isle of Anglesey*, revised edn

([London]: National Trust, 1983), p. 4. Davidson himself has had experience of living on the land of large estates in Wales, and 'the big house' was his family's phrase for the idea of the *plas* (personal communication to the author).

[30] John Davies, *A History of Wales*, revised edn (London: Penguin, 2007), pp. 399 and 432.

[31] S.R., as cited in Davies, *History of Wales*, p. 399.

[32] Davies, *History of Wales*, p. 432.

[33] Buell, *Writing for an Endangered World*, p. 16.

[34] With thanks to Ian Davidson for clarifying this point (personal communication to the author).

[35] Doreen Massey, *Space, Place and Gender* (Cambridge: Polity, 1994), p. 4.

Notes to Chapter 10

[1] Carolyn Davies and Lynne Bebb, *Kyffin Williams: Painting the Mountains* (Llandysul: Pont, 2005), pp. 15, 17 and 8.

[2] Kyffin Williams, *The Land & the Sea* (Llandysul: Gomer, 1998), pp. 16–17.

[3] For Wynn Thomas's remarks and for the quotation from R. S. Thomas, see M. Wynn Thomas, 'For Wales, see landscape: early R. S. Thomas and the English topographical tradition', *Welsh Writing in English: A Yearbook of Critical Essays*, 10 (2005), 14.

[4] Linden Peach, 'Wales and the cultural politics of identity: Gillian Clarke, Robert Minhinnick, and Jeremy Hooker', in James Acheson and Romana Huk (eds), *Contemporary British Poetry: Essays in Theory and Criticism* (Albany, NY: State University of New York Press, 1996), p. 375.

[5] M. Wynn Thomas, 'Prints of Wales: contemporary Welsh poetry in English', in Hans-Werner Ludwig and Lothar Fietz (eds), *Poetry in the British Isles: Non-Metropolitan Perspectives* (Cardiff: University of Wales Press, 1995), p. 103.

[6] Fiona Owen, 'Mystery at the heart of things: an interview with Jeremy Hooker', *Green Letters*, 8 (2007), 7 and 6.

[7] Matthew Jarvis, 'The politics of place in the poetry of Ian Davidson', *Welsh Writing in English: A Yearbook of Critical Essays*, 10 (2005), 154.

[8] Michael P. Cohen, 'Blues in the green: ecocriticism under critique', *Environmental History*, 9, 1 (2004), 12 Mar. 2004 <*http://www.historycoopera-tive.org/journals/eh/9.1/cohen.html* >, para. 64.

Bibliography

Maps

Brecknockshire, Sheet VII.10, 1:2,500 (Southampton: Ordnance Survey, 1888).
Brecknockshire, Sheet IX.4, 1:2,500 (Southampton: Ordnance Survey, 1889).
Brecknockshire, Sheet XII.9, 1:2,500 (Southampton: Ordnance Survey, 1889).
'Elan Valley and Builth Wells', Sheet 147, 1:50,000 (Southampton: Ordnance Survey, 1974, 1982, 1996).
Glamorgan, Sheet XI.NE, 1:10,560, 2nd edn (Southampton: Ordnance Survey, 1905).
Glamorgan, Sheet XII.NW, 1:10,560, 2nd edn (Southampton: Ordnance Survey, 1905).
Glamorgan, Sheet XL.2, 1:2,500, Revision of 1940 (Southampton: Ordnance Survey, 1945).

Books and Articles

Aaron, Jane, and M. Wynn Thomas, '"Pulling you through changes": Welsh writing in English before, between and after two referenda', in M. Wynn Thomas (ed.), *Welsh Writing in English*, A Guide to Welsh Literature, 7 (Cardiff: University of Wales Press, 2003), pp. 278–309.

Adams, Sam, 'Robert Minhinnick in conversation with Sam Adams', *PN Review*, 24, 1 (1997), 20–5.

'Administrative Wales', *The National Gazetteer of Wales*, 6 Dec. 2007 <*http://homepage.ntlworld.com/ geogdata/ngw/admin.htm*>.

Allchin, A. M., 'The mystery that complements precision: reading Ruth Bidgood's poetry', *Logos: The Welsh Theological Review/Cylchgrawn Diwinyddol Cymru*, 4/5/6 ([1993]), 7–15.

Aplin, Jackie, 'Interview with Robert Minhinnick', *Poetry Wales*, 25, 2 (1989), 23–8.

Ashby, A. W., and I. L. Evans, *The Agriculture of Wales and Monmouthshire* (Cardiff: University of Wales Press, 1944).

'Avalon', *Encyclopædia Britannica*, 2007, Encyclopædia Britannica Online, 6 Dec. 2007 <*http://search.eb.com/eb/article-9011399*>.

Barnie, John, 'Touch the snake', *New Welsh Review*, 74 (2006), 19–25.

Bate, Jonathan, *The Song of the Earth* (London: Picador, 2001; orig. 2000).

Baudrillard, Jean, *Simulacra and Simulation*, trans. Sheila Faria Glaser (Ann Arbor, MI: University of Michigan Press, 1994).

'Beet', *Encyclopædia Britannica*, 2007, Encyclopædia Britannica Online, 6 Dec. 2007 <*http://search.eb.com/eb/article-9014114*>.

Berg, Peter, and Ray Dasmann, 'Reinhabiting California', *The Ecologist*, 7, 10 (1977), 399–401.

Bidgood, Ruth, *The Given Time* (Swansea: Christopher Davies, 1972).

—— *Not Without Homage* (Swansea: Christopher Davies, 1975).

—— *The Print of Miracle* (Llandysul: Gomer, 1978).

—— *Lighting Candles: New and Selected Poems* (Bridgend: Poetry Wales Press, 1982).

—— *Kindred* (Bridgend: Poetry Wales Press, 1986).

—— 'Heartland', *Poetry Wales*, 26, 3 (1991), 7–9.

—— *Selected Poems* (Bridgend: Seren, 1992).

—— *The Fluent Moment* (Bridgend: Seren, 1996).

—— *Parishes of the Buzzard* (Port Talbot: Gold Leaf, 2000).

—— *Singing to Wolves* (Bridgend: Seren, 2000).

—— *New & Selected Poems* (Bridgend: Seren, 2004).

Bohata, Kirsti, *Postcolonialism Revisited* (Cardiff: University of Wales Press, 2004).

Bromwich, Rachel (trans. and ed.), *Dafydd ap Gwilym: A Selection of Poems* (Llandysul: Gomer, 1982).

Buell, Lawrence, *Writing for an Endangered World: Literature, Culture, and Environment in the U.S. and Beyond* (Cambridge, MA: Belknap, 2001).

Burrows, Wayne, 'A dissident voice: Wayne Burrows interviews Mike Jenkins', *New Welsh Review*, 9 (1990), 54–8.

Chamberlain, Brenda, *Tide-race* (Bridgend: Seren, 1987; orig. 1962).

Clancy, Joseph P. (trans.), *Twentieth Century Welsh Poems* (Llandysul: Gomer, 1982).

Clarke, Gillian, *Snow on the Mountain* (Swansea and Llandybïe: Christopher Davies, 1971).

—— *The Sundial* (Llandysul: Gomer, 1978).

—— *Letter from a Far Country* (Manchester: Carcanet, 1982).

—— *Selected Poems* (Manchester: Carcanet, 1985).

—— *Letting in the Rumour* (Manchester: Carcanet, 1989).

—— *The King of Britain's Daughter* (Manchester: Carcanet, 1993).

—— 'Beginning with Bendigeidfran', in Jane Aaron, Teresa Rees, Sandra Betts and Moira Vincentelli (eds), *Our Sisters' Land: The Changing Identities of Women in Wales* (Cardiff: University of Wales Press, 1994), pp. 287–93.

—— *Five Fields* (Manchester: Carcanet, 1998).

—— *Making the Beds for the Dead* (Manchester: Carcanet, 2004).

'Clywedog', *Ymgyrchu!*, National Library of Wales, 6 Dec. 2007 <*http://www.llgc.org.uk/ymgyrchu/Dwr/CLywedog/index-e.htm*>.

Cohen, Michael P., 'Blues in the green: ecocriticism under critique', *Environmental History*, 9, 1 (2004), 12 Mar. 2004 <*http://www.historycooperative.org/journals/eh/9.1/cohen.html*>.

'Conferences', *American Nature Writing Newsletter*, 4, 2 (1992), 7.

Conran, Tony, *Frontiers in Anglo-Welsh Poetry* (Cardiff: University of Wales Press, 1997).

—— '*Poetry Wales* and the Second Flowering', in M. Wynn Thomas (ed.), *Welsh Writing in English*, A Guide to Welsh Literature, 7 (Cardiff: University of Wales Press, 2003), pp. 222–54.

Cook, Jon (ed.), *Poetry in Theory: An Anthology 1900–2000* (Oxford: Blackwell, 2004).

Copley, Stephen, 'William Gilpin and the black-lead mine', in Stephen Copley and Peter Garside (eds), *The Politics of the Picturesque: Literature, Landscape and Aesthetics since 1770* (Cambridge: Cambridge University Press, 1994), pp. 42–61.

Davidson, Ian, *No Passage Landward (Environmental Studies)* (Hebden Bridge: Open Township, 1989).

—— *Human to Begin With*, Poetical Histories, 16 (Cambridge: Peter Riley, 1991).

—— *The Patrick Poems* (London: Amra Imprint, 1991).

—— *Wipe Out* (Cheltenham: Short Run, 1995).

—— *Harsh* (Peterborough: Spectacular Diseases, 2003).

—— *Human Remains & Sudden Movements* (Nether Edge, Sheffield: West House, 2003).

—— *At a Stretch* (Exeter: Shearsman, 2004).

—— *No Way Back* ([Nether Edge, Sheffield]: Gargoyle, 2005).

—— *As if Only* (Exeter: Shearsman, 2007).

—— and John Muckle, *It is Now as it was Then* (London: MICA in association with Actual Size, 1983).

—— and Zoë Skoulding, *Dark Wires* (Nether Edge, Sheffield: West House, 2007).

Davies, Carolyn, and Lynne Bebb, *Kyffin Williams: Painting the Mountains* (Llandysul: Pont, 2005).

Davies, John, *A History of Wales*, revised edn (London: Penguin, 2007).

Dunn, James D. G., and John W. Rogerson (eds), *Eerdmans Commentary on the Bible* (Cambridge: Eerdmans, 2003).

Eliade, Mircea, *The Sacred and the Profane: The Nature of Religion*, trans. Willard R. Trask (London: Harcourt Brace Jovanovich, 1987).

'Enlli and the arts', *Ynys Enlli/Bardsey Island*, 6 Dec. 2007 <*http://www.bardsey.org/english/the_island/arts.htm*>.

Evans, Christine, *Island of Dark Horses* (Bridgend: Seren, 1995).
Forestry Commission, *Britain's Forests: Coed y Brenin* (London: HMSO, 1950).
—— *Coed y Brenin* (n.pl.: Forestry Commission, n.d.). National Library of
     Wales: XSD46.C67.G78 (4to).
—— *National Inventory of Woodland and Trees: Wales* (Edinburgh: Forestry
     Commission, 2002), 19 Nov. 2007 <*http://www. forestry.gov.uk/PDF/
     niwales.pdf/$FILE/niwales.pdf*>.
Garrard, Greg, *Ecocriticism* (London: Routledge, 2004).
Geary, Roger, 'The dragon and the flame: an analysis of the Welsh arson
     campaign', *Contemporary Review*, 1537 (1994), 80–7.
Geoffrey of Monmouth, *Life of Merlin*, ed. and trans. Basil Clarke (Cardiff:
     University of Wales Press, 1973).
Gifford, Terry, *Green Voices: Understanding Contemporary Nature Poetry*
     (Manchester: Manchester University Press, 1995).
Glamorgan-Gwent Archaeological Trust, 'Historic landscape characterisa-
     tion: Merthyr Tydfil: 064 Winch Fawr, Pen-yr-Heolgerrig, Cwm Du, and
     upper Cwm Glo workings', 19 Apr. 2008 <*http://www.ggat.org.uk/
     cadw/historic_landscape/Merthyr%20Tydfil/English/Merthyr_064.htm*>.
—— 'Historic landscape characterisation: Merthyr Tydfil: 069 Cwm Glo,
     north', 19 Apr. 2008 <*http://www.ggat.org.uk/cadw/historic_landscape/
     Merthyr%20Tydfil/English/Merthyr_069.htm*>.
—— 'Historic landscape characterisation: Merthyr Tydfil: 070 Cwm Glo:
     tramroad, plateway and incline corridor', 19 Apr. 2008 <*http://www.
     ggat.org.uk/cadw/historic_landscape/Merthyr%20Tydfil/English/Merthyr_0
     70.htm*>.
—— 'Historic landscape characterisation: Merthyr Tydfil: 078 Dowlais Great
     Tip, Trecatti, Trehir and Twyn-y-Waun', 19 Apr. 2008 <*http://www.ggat. org.
     uk/cadw/historic_landscape/Merthyr%20Tydfil/English/Merthyr_078.htm*>.
Glotfelty, Cheryll, 'Letter to *ANWN* subscribers and ASLE members',
     American Nature Writing Newsletter, 5, 2 (1993), 1–2.
—— '[Letter]', *American Nature Writing Newsletter*, 7, 1 (1995), 1–2.
—— 'Introduction: literary studies in an age of environmental crisis', in
     Cheryll Glotfelty and Harold Fromm (eds), *The Ecocriticism Reader:
     Landmarks in Literary Ecology* (Athens, GA: University of Georgia Press,
     1996), pp. xv–xxxvii.
'Gold torc from the Llanwrthwl hoard', *Gathering the Jewels*, 6 Dec. 2007
     <*http:// www.gtj.org.uk/en/item1/ 25857*>.
Great Britain Historical GIS Project, 'Gwynedd Wales through time | histor-
     ical statistics on social structure for the district/unitary authority | rate:
     percentage of working-age males in class 4 and 5', *A Vision of Britain
     Through Time*, 6 Dec. 2007 <*http://www.visionofbritain.org.uk/data_rate_
     page.jsp?u_id=10076766&c_id=10001043&data_theme=T_SOC&id=2*>.

—— 'The Isle of Anglesey Wales through time | historical statistics on social structure for the district/unitary authority | rate: percentage of working-age males in class 4 and 5', *A Vision of Britain Through Time*, 6 Dec. 2007 <*http://www.visionofbritain.org.uk/data_rate_page.jsp?u_id=10056688&c_i d=10001043&data_theme=T_SOC&id=2*>.

—— 'Wales through time | historical statistics on social structure for the nation | rate: percentage of working-age males in class 4 and 5', *A Vision of Britain Through Time*, 6 Dec. 2007 <*http://www.visionofbritain.org.uk/ data_rate_page.jsp?u_id=10001055&c_id=10001043&data_theme=T_SO C&id=2*>.

Green, Miranda, *The Gods of the Celts* (Stroud: Sutton, 1997).

—— and Ray Howell, *Celtic Wales: A Pocket Guide* (Cardiff: University of Wales Press and The Western Mail, 2000).

Gregson, Ian, 'On the Street of Processions: Robert Minhinnick interviewed by Ian Gregson', *Planet*, 167 (2004), 43–50.

—— *The New Poetry in Wales* (Cardiff: University of Wales Press, 2007).

[Griffiths, Bryn] (ed.), 'London Anglo-Welsh: a brief anthology', *London Welshman*, 19, 7 (1964), 19–22.

—— 'A Note for R. S. Thomas', *Poetry Wales*, 1, 2 (1965), 23.

—— (ed.), *Welsh Voices: An Anthology of New Poetry from Wales* (London: Dent, 1967).

Hayden, Dolores, *The Power of Place: Urban Landscapes as Public History* (Cambridge, MA: MIT Press, 1995).

'The Heyope ribbon torcs (Bronze Age)', *Gathering the Jewels*, 6 Dec. 2007 <*http://www.gtj.org.uk/en/item1/25853*>.

Holman, Kate, *Brenda Chamberlain*, Writers of Wales (Cardiff: University of Wales Press, 1997).

Hooker, Jeremy, *The Presence of the Past: Essays on Modern British and American Poetry* (Bridgend: Poetry Wales Press, 1987).

—— 'Ceridwen's daughters: Welsh women poets and the uses of tradition', *Welsh Writing in English: A Yearbook of Critical Essays*, 1 (1995), 128–44.

—— *Imagining Wales: A View of Modern Welsh Writing in English* (Cardiff: University of Wales Press, 2001).

Humfrey, Belinda, 'Prelude to the twentieth century', in M. Wynn Thomas (ed.), *Welsh Writing in English*, A Guide to Welsh Literature, 7 (Cardiff: University of Wales Press, 2003), pp. 7–46.

Ingram, Annie, 'ASLE treasury is the healthiest it has ever been', *ASLE News*, 16, 1 (2004), 5.

Jarvis, Matthew, 'West House Books: recent poetry', *English*, 204 (2003), 269–78.

—— 'The politics of place in the poetry of Ian Davidson', *Welsh Writing in English: A Yearbook of Critical Essays*, 10 (2005), 144–59.

—— '[Review of Ian Gregson, *The New Poetry in Wales*]', *New Welsh Review*, 78 (2007), 85–7.

—— 'Repositioning Wales: poetry after the Second Flowering', in Daniel Williams (ed.), *Slanderous Tongues: Welsh Poetry in English 1970–2005* (Bridgend: Seren, forthcoming).

Jenkins, Geraint H., *A Concise History of Wales* (Cambridge: Cambridge University Press, 2007).

Jenkins, Mike, *Rat City: Poems from Northern Ireland* (Barry: Edge, 1979).

—— *The Common Land* (Bridgend: Poetry Wales Press, 1981).

—— *Empire of Smoke* (Bridgend: Poetry Wales Press, 1983).

—— *A Dissident Voice* (Bridgend: Seren, 1990).

—— *Graffiti Narratives: Poems 'n' Stories* (Aberystwyth: Planet, 1994).

—— *This House, My Ghetto* (Bridgend: Seren, 1995).

—— 'Merthyr, my adopted home', *Poetry Wales*, 32, 4 (1997), 23–6.

—— *Red Landscapes: New and Selected Poems* (Bridgend: Seren, 1999).

—— *Coulda Bin Summin* (Aberystwyth: Planet, 2001).

—— *Laughter Tangled in Thorn and Other Poems* (Llanrwst: Carreg Gwalch, 2002).

—— *The Language of Flight* (Llanrwst: Carreg Gwalch, 2004).

Johnston, Dafydd (ed.), *The Complete Poems of Idris Davies* (Cardiff: University of Wales Press, 1994).

Jones, D. Gwenallt, *Ysgubau'r Awen* (Llandysul: Gomer, [1939]).

—— *Eples* (Llandysul: Gomer, 1951).

Jones, Eben, *Baglan and the Llewellyns of Baglan Hall* (Baglan, Port Talbot: Eben Jones, 1987).

—— *The Llewellyns of Baglan and Cwrt Colman* (Baglan, Port Talbot: Eben Jones, 1989).

[Jones, H. L.], 'List of early British remains in Wales: no. III', *Archæologia Cambrensis: The Journal of the Cambrian Archæological Association*, 3, 1 (1855), 18–27.

Jones, Ieuan Gwynedd, 'Religion and society in nineteenth century Wales', in John Rowlands and Sheila Rowlands (eds), *Second Stages in Researching Welsh Ancestry* (Ramsbottom: Federation of Family History Societies; Aberystwyth: University of Wales, Aberystwyth, 1999), pp. 1–14.

Jones, Martin, Rhys Jones and Michael Woods, *An Introduction to Political Geography: Space, Place and Politics* (London: Routledge, 2004).

Jones, Peter Hope, and R. S. Thomas, *Between Sea and Sky: Images of Bardsey* (Llandysul: Gomer, 1998).

Jones, R. Merfyn, 'Beyond identity? The reconstruction of the Welsh', *Journal of British Studies*, 31, 4 (1992), 330–57.

Kennedy, J. N., 'Forests', in Herbert L. Edlin (ed.), *Cambrian Forests*, 2nd edn (London: HMSO, 1975), pp. 3–17.

Linnard, W., *Welsh Woods and Forests: A History* (Llandysul: Gomer, 2000).

Lionnet, Françoise, 'Transnationalism, postcolonialism or transcolonialism? Reflections on Los Angeles, geography, and the uses of theory', *Emergences: Journal for the Study of Media and Composite Cultures*, 10, 1 (2000), 25–35.

Lloyd, David T. (ed.), *The Urgency of Identity: Contemporary English-Language Poetry from Wales* (Evanston, IL: TriQuarterly, 1994).

—— (ed.), *Writing on the Edge: Interviews with Writers and Editors of Wales* (Amsterdam: Rodopi, 1997).

Lloyd, John Edward, and R. T. Jenkins (eds), *The Dictionary of Welsh Biography down to 1940* (London: The Honourable Society of Cymmrodorion, 1959).

Lloyd Jones, Mary, *First Language* (Llandysul: Gomer, with the National Library of Wales, 2006).

Llywelyn, Dorian, *Sacred Place: Chosen People; Land and National Identity in Welsh Spirituality* (Cardiff: University of Wales Press, 1999).

Lord, Peter, *The Visual Culture of Wales: Industrial Society* (Cardiff: University of Wales Press, 1998).

McIntyre, Amy, 'News from the managing director', *ASLE News*, 18, 1 (2006), 3.

Marx, Leo, *The Machine in the Garden: Technology and the Pastoral Ideal in America* (Oxford: Oxford University Press, 1964).

Massey, Doreen, *Space, Place and Gender* (Cambridge: Polity, 1994).

'The Milford Haven torc hoard', *Gathering the Jewels*, 6 Dec. 2007 <http://www.gtj.org.uk/en/item1/25848>.

Minhinnick, Robert, *A Thread in the Maze* (Swansea: Christopher Davies, 1978).

—— *Native Ground* (Swansea: Triskele, 1979).

—— *Life Sentences* (Bridgend: Poetry Wales Press, 1983).

—— *The Dinosaur Park* (Bridgend: Poetry Wales Press, 1985).

—— *The Looters* (Bridgend: Seren, 1989).

—— *Hey Fatman* (Bridgend: Seren, 1994).

—— *After the Hurricane* (Manchester: Carcanet, 2002).

Morgan, Christopher, *R. S. Thomas: Identity, Environment, and Deity* (Manchester: Manchester University Press, 2003).

Morris, Brian, *Harri Webb*, Writers of Wales (Cardiff: University of Wales Press, 1993).

Morton, Angela, 'Interview: Ruth Bidgood', *New Welsh Review*, 10 (1990), 38–42.

Murphy, Patrick D., 'Editor's note', *ISLE: Interdisciplinary Studies in Literature and Environment*, 2, 2 (1996), pp. iii–iv.

National Trust, *Plas Newydd: Isle of Anglesey*, revised edn ([London]: National Trust, 1983).

Nicholas, W. Rhys, *The Folk Poets*, Writers of Wales ([Cardiff]: University of Wales Press, 1978).

[Nitecki, Alicia, and Scott Slovic], 'From the editors', *American Nature Writing Newsletter*, 4, 2 (1992), 2.

Norris, Leslie, 'From Leslie Norris', *Poetry Wales*, 7, 4 (1972), 118–21.

Olson, Charles, 'Projective verse', in Donald Allen (ed.), *The New American Poetry, 1945–1960* (Berkeley, CA: University of California Press, 1999), pp. 386–97.

Owen, Fiona, 'Mystery at the heart of things: an interview with Jeremy Hooker', *Green Letters*, 8 (2007), 3–12.

Owen, John A., *The History of the Dowlais Iron Works, 1759–1970* (Newport: Starling, 1977).

Peach, Linden, *Ancestral Lines: Culture & Identity in the Work of Six Contemporary Poets* (Bridgend: Seren, [1993]).

—— '"The imagination's caverns": identity and symbolism in the work of Gillian Clarke and Christine Evans', in Belinda Humfrey (ed.), *'Fire Green as Grass': Studies of the Creative Impulse in Anglo-Welsh Poetry and Short Stories of the Twentieth Century* (Llandysul: Gomer, 1995), pp. 146–55.

—— 'Wales and the cultural politics of identity: Gillian Clarke, Robert Minhinnick, and Jeremy Hooker', in James Acheson and Romana Huk (eds), *Contemporary British Poetry: Essays in Theory and Criticism* (Albany, NY: State University of New York Press, 1996), pp. 373–96.

Perrin, Jim, 'Land & freedom', *New Welsh Review*, 74 (2006), 8–18.

Philip, Alan Butt, *The Welsh Question: Nationalism in Welsh Politics 1945–1970* (Cardiff: University of Wales Press, 1975).

Phillips, Alan, *The Military Airfields of Wales* (Wrexham: Bridge Books, 2006).

Phillips, Dana, *The Truth of Ecology: Nature, Culture, and Literature in America* (New York: Oxford University Press, 2003).

Pikoulis, John, '"Some kind o' beginnin'": Mike Jenkins and the voices of Cwmtaff', *Welsh Writing in English: A Yearbook of Critical Essays*, 10 (2005), 121–43.

Plumwood, Val, *Environmental Culture: The Ecological Crisis of Reason* (London: Routledge, 2002).

Pringle, Douglas, *The First 75 Years: A Brief Account of the History of the Forestry Commission 1919–1994* (Edinburgh: Forestry Commission, [1994]).

Rees, Alwyn D., and Brinley Rees, *Celtic Heritage: Ancient Tradition in Ireland and Wales* (London: Thames & Hudson, 1961).

Roberts, Lynette, *Collected Poems*, ed. Patrick McGuinness (Manchester: Carcanet, 2005).

Robinson, David M., and Colin Platt, *Strata Florida Abbey; Talley Abbey*, 2nd edn (Cardiff: Cadw, 1998).

Rosser, David G., 'MPs table censure on Brooke', *Western Mail* (2 Aug. 1957), 1.

Ryle, George, *Forest Service: The First Forty-Five Years of the Forestry Commission of Great Britain* (Newton Abbot: David & Charles, 1969).

Schama, Simon, *Landscape and Memory* (London: HarperCollins, 1995).

Smith, K. E., 'The poetry of Gillian Clarke', in Hans-Werner Ludwig and Lothar Fietz (eds), *Poetry in the British Isles: Non-Metropolitan Perspectives* (Cardiff: University of Wales Press, 1995), pp. 267–81.

Soja, Edward W., *Postmodern Geographies: The Reassertion of Space in Critical Social Theory* (London: Verso, 1989).

Soper, Kate, *What is Nature? Culture, Politics and the Non-Human* (Oxford: Blackwell, 1995).

Stephens, Meic, 'The Second Flowering', *Poetry Wales*, 3, 3 (1967–8), 2–9.

—— (ed.), *The New Companion to the Literature of Wales* (Cardiff: University of Wales Press, 1998).

Stewart, Pamela J., and Andrew Strathern (eds), *Landscape, Memory and History: Anthropological Perspectives* (London: Pluto, 2003).

Strange, Keith, 'In search of the celestial empire', *Llafur: The Journal of the Society for the Study of Welsh Labour History*, 3, 1 (1980), 44–86.

Tarlo, Harriet, 'Radical landscapes: contemporary poetry in the Bunting tradition', in James McGonigal and Richard Price (eds), *The Star You Steer By: Basil Bunting and British Modernism* (Amsterdam: Rodopi, 2000), pp. 149–80.

Thomas, Einion, *Capel Celyn: Deng Mlynedd o Chwalu: 1955–1965/Ten Years of Destruction: 1955–1965*, 1st bilingual edn, English text by Beryl Griffiths (n.pl.: Cyhoeddiadau Barddas and Gwynedd Council, 2007).

Thomas, M. Wynn, 'Prints of Wales: contemporary Welsh poetry in English', in Hans-Werner Ludwig and Lothar Fietz (eds), *Poetry in the British Isles: Non-Metropolitan Perspectives* (Cardiff: University of Wales Press, 1995), pp. 97–114.

—— 'R. S. Thomas: war poet', *Welsh Writing in English: A Yearbook of Critical Essays*, 2 (1996), 82–97.

—— 'Staying to mind things: Gillian Clarke's early poetry', in Menna Elfyn (ed.), *Trying the Line: A Volume of Tribute to Gillian Clarke* (Llandysul: Gomer, 1997), pp. 44–68.

—— 'Place, race and gender in the poetry of Gillian Clarke', in Katie Gramich and Andrew Hiscock (eds), *Dangerous Diversity: The Changing Faces of Wales; Essays in Honour of Tudor Bevan* (Cardiff: University of Wales Press, 1998), pp. 3–19.

—— *Corresponding Cultures: The Two Literatures of Wales* (Cardiff: University of Wales Press, 1999).

—— 'For Wales, see landscape: early R. S. Thomas and the English topographical tradition', *Welsh Writing in English: A Yearbook of Critical Essays*, 10 (2005), 1–31.

Thomas, R. S., *The Stones of the Field* (Carmarthen: Druid Press, 1946).

—— *Song at the Year's Turning: Poems 1942–1954* (London: Rupert Hart-Davis, 1955).

—— *The Bread of Truth* (London: Rupert Hart-Davis, 1963).

—— *Pietà* (London: Rupert Hart-Davis, 1966).

—— *Not That He Brought Flowers* (London: Rupert Hart-Davis, 1968).

—— *Autobiographies: 'Former Paths', 'The Creative Writer's Suicide', 'No-one', 'A Year in Llŷn'*, trans. and ed. Jason Walford Davies (London: Dent, 1997).

Thurston, Bonnie, "'A scatter of little sights and happenings": the poetic vision of Ruth Bidgood', *The Way*, 45, 1 (2006), 93–104

'A tragedy at Dolfach', *Powys Digital History Project*, 27 May 2007 <*http://history.powys.org.uk/school1/builth/flood2.shtml*>.

Tripp, John, *Diesel to Yesterday* (Cardiff: Triskel, 1966)

Tuan, Yi-Fu, *Space and Place: The Perspective of Experience* (Minneapolis, MN: University of Minnesota Press, 1977)

Walford Davies, Jason, "'Thick ambush of shadows": allusions to Welsh literature in the work of R. S. Thomas', *Welsh Writing in English: A Yearbook of Critical Essays*, 1 (1995), 75–127.

—— 'History is now and Wales: Ruth Bidgood interviewed by Jason Walford Davies', *Planet*, 137 (1999), 47–54.

[Webb, Harri], 'The breed of the sparrowhawk', *The Welsh Nation* (Oct. 1962), 3.

—— 'The Boomerang in the Parlour', *Poetry Wales*, 1, 1 (1965), 14.

—— *The Green Desert: Collected Poems 1950–1969* (Llandysul: Gomer, 1969).

—— 'From Harri Webb', *Poetry Wales*, 7, 4 (1972), 121–3.

—— *Collected Poems*, ed. Meic Stephens (Llandysul: Gomer, 1995).

Westling, Louise H., *The Green Breast of the New World: Landscape, Gender, and American Fiction* (Athens, GA: University of Georgia Press, 1996).

Williams, Glanmor, *A Life* (Cardiff: University of Wales Press, 2002).

Williams, John Stuart, and Meic Stephens (eds), *The Lilting House: An Anthology of Anglo-Welsh Poetry 1917–67* (London: Dent; Llandybïe: Christopher Davies, 1969).

Williams, Kyffin, *The Land & the Sea* (Llandysul: Gomer, 1998).

Williams, Merryn, 'The poetry of Ruth Bidgood', *Poetry Wales*, 28, 3 (1993), 36–41.

Williams, Raymond, *Keywords: A Vocabulary of Culture and Society*, revised edn (London: Fontana, 1988; orig. Flamingo, 1983).

Wintle, Justin, *Furious Interiors: Wales, R. S. Thomas and God* (London: HarperCollins, 1996).

Zukin, Sharon, *Landscapes of Power: From Detroit to Disney World* (Berkeley, CA: University of California Press, 1991).

Index